FOREWORD BY JACK CANFIELD

THE
BILLION DOLLAR
SECRET

20 Principles of Billionaire
Wealth and Success

BASED ON FACE-TO-FACE INTERVIEWS
WITH OVER 20 SELF-MADE BILLIONAIRES

RAFAEL BADZIAG

W0010188

The Billion Dollar Secret
20 Principles of Billionaire Wealth and Success

First published in 2019 by
Panoma Press Ltd
48 St Vincent Drive, St Albans, Herts, AL1 5SJ UK

info@panomapress.com
www.panomapress.com

Cover design by Neil Coe
Typeset by Westchester Publishing Services

ISBN 978-1-784521-63-9

PRAISE FOR THIS BOOK

This book can transform your financial life.

—Brian Tracy, author of numerous bestsellers on
success psychology, such as *Million Dollar
Habits, Eat That Frog!,* and *The Psychology of Achievement*

The Billion Dollar Secret *is a thorough and insightful masterpiece that puts on full display the dedication, ingenuity, and grit that are woven into the souls of Rafael Badziag and the 20+ billionaires he interviewed. Its strength as a worthwhile read for any entrepreneur is the almost scientific nature of Badziag's methods: meticulously researching data from a diverse set of individuals who have exponentially divergent backgrounds and paths and finding the common threads among each experience that can be attributed to shared traits of their financial and professional successes.*

This is not a piece written from the imagination and opinions of an armchair writer, but a labor of love written by a man who has literally traveled the world to learn from the best and share what he has learned with the people who have the same passion for success burning within.

—Jannelle So, TV host/producer at TFC and Lifestyle Network

I highly recommend this book. It is a very thoroughly researched book on successful philosophies of life.

—Tony Tan Caktiong, Filipino billionaire, the World Entrepreneur
of the Year 2004

Thank you, Rafael! A "must-read book" because every decade a book comes along that opens doors otherwise closed to most of us that changes the way we think about growth, financial success, and business. Excellent research, thought-provoking, and inspiring.

—Dr. Albert Allen, Lord of Crofton of Greater London, best-selling author, Emmy Award-winning film documentary co-producer, entrepreneur, commercial real estate investor, philanthropist

This is an unusually thoughtful book on the topic of success. It is also a product of extraordinary effort on the part of Rafael Badziag meeting with and extracting valuable lessons from the world's top entrepreneurs. I am confident that the lessons can improve the businesses and lives of many people around the world.

—David Choi, PhD, professor of entrepreneurship and director of the Fred Kiesner Center for Entrepreneurship, Loyola Marymount University

Since the current economy is under huge competition, I recommend all entrepreneurs to go and have a look at this sensational book.

—Cho Tak Wong (Cao Dewang), Chinese billionaire, the World Entrepreneur of the Year 2009

Rafael Badziag demonstrates that privilege, education, upbringing, and big inheritances are not the prerequisites to building wealth. The billionaires in this book made their own way through hard work, ingenuity, dedication, nonconformity, and unbridled passion for what they do. The book is an inspiration to entrepreneurs everywhere.

—Nikos Kalaitzidakis, general manager, Coca-Cola HBC Poland

Finally, a book that unlocks the window to the highly guarded world of the most prolific, enigmatic, and mega-successful business icons across the globe. Rafael Badziag was able to masterfully weave the unique life stories of each of the featured rags-to-riches billionaires into a tapestry of traits and principles commonly shared by the ultra-successful. I also applaud the amount of in-depth research conducted to bring this book to life. A must-read for entrepreneurs, executives, and practically anyone who wants to learn from the best of the best and are tired of the usual run-of-the-mill motivational books flooding the market today. At last, a modern-day Napoleon Hill.

—**Melody Avecilla, entrepreneur, founder, Runway Heels**

I recommend this book because it contains all the essentials of how you can make your business a big success.

—**Vincent Lo, Hong Kong billionaire, founder and chairman of Shui On Group**

Badziag gives a narrative journey of the private lives of billionaires with candid insight into their trials and tribulations and ultimate path to success. He identifies society's misconceptions of this very small percentage of the population and a deep insight into the distinct similarities amongst billionaires. Badziag's book brings out the entrepreneurial spirit in us all and the realization that anything is possible with hard work, passion, and a little bit of luck along the way.

—**Tatania Minguet, senior manager, National Accounts, Mattel**

Rafael's book gives a unique insight into the mindset of this rare breed of beings who have the power and financial resources to change our world—for better or for worse. Rafael's personal relationships have given him unrivaled behind-closed-doors access to this exclusive (and often reclusive) club of the wealthiest 0.0001%. His interviews and anecdotes both dispel and sometimes confirm the myths that surround this Ultra High Net Worth Magic Circle. Definitely a fascinating and riveting read!

—**Adam Jenkins, entrepreneur and CEO of Pekao TFI, preeminent investment fund manager in Poland**

I highly recommend this book. It gives real-life stories of not only 1 but over 20 successful billionaire entrepreneurs. It's not only a great pleasure to read this book, but I think it gives really exciting and valuable insights on how these entrepreneurs became so successful and how they built their fortune. And all of them did it from scratch. They did not inherit a family fortune. These are the stories of entrepreneurs who started with nothing and built a billion-dollar fortune. I think it's really useful, interesting and enjoyable to read.

—**Lars Windhorst, German billionaire, founder of Sapinda Group**

Rafael Badziag knows what he wants, and he approaches his goals with focus. In the same way, he selectively and with determination interviews 20+ extremely successful people. It is great cinema: take a seat and marvel at how billionaires think and act. It is a great privilege for the reader to learn many aspects of these extraordinary entrepreneurs and human beings.

—**Wolfgang Allgäuer, entrepreneur, author, and coach, awarded the Entrepreneurial Oscar by the Austrian Secretary of Commerce**

This book has great insights and a unique perspective about the successful billionaires who have earned that revered title. Their battle scars and war wounds come from breaking barriers and disregarding norms, without compromising their values or quelling their inner rebels. It has many inspirational tales and uplifting stories that can inspire many an entrepreneur or a disruptor to reach for the stars, instead of just stardust—that is the difference between being a millionaire or a billionaire.

—Sandy Bhargavi, CEO VR.org, entrepreneur

This book would have been the right book for me when I was young. It would have saved me reading more than 20 biographies that I bought and read at that time.

**—Lirio Albino Parisotto, Brazilian billionaire,
founder and president of Videolar**

I will never forget the first time Rafael told me about his book project. Back then I simply thought this would be impossible—but I soon realized that if anyone could pull this off, Rafael could. The book is more than a portrait of brilliant minds. It provides unprecedented insights on how the world's wealthiest people think. Instead of repeating the stories of celebrity billionaires, Rafael made the right choice to focus on "off-radar" personalities, billionaires with contrasting backgrounds and compelling stories you have never heard before. A must read!

**—Thomas Pamminger, serial entrepreneur, angel investor, and founder at
Wollzelle and WeAreDevelopers**

[This book contains] guiding success principles wrapped in compelling real-life stories of living self-made billionaires. Rafael delivers access and insights you have not read before, without Western world boundaries. A practical, inspiring read that is well worth your time . . . if you could use a billion.

—Paul Finck, State Farm executive

Most successful people I know have an innate curiosity and desire to find out what paths others took that led to their success. This book answers that challenge for everyone as it spells out the characteristics and steps that enabled many successful entrepreneurs to reach their goals.

A great road map that everyone can benefit from by learning from others.

—Jack Cowin, Australian billionaire, founder, chairman, and managing director of Competitive Foods Australia

Rafael Badziag's The Billion Dollar Secret *is both a motivational and informative read for any entrepreneur seeking to build a highly successful business enterprise. His research on the guiding principles and mindset of self-made billionaires provides insights and a useful framework for anyone determined to build wealth.*

—Richard Stafford, PhD, associate dean and director of Executive MBA program, Loyola Marymount University

I got to know the author at a 100 km run through the Namib desert. He was well prepared, following the advice of an accomplished ultra runner. With this book, he follows the same strategy: modeling excellence.

I believe that learning from the most successful people, like those interviewed for this book, will help me a great deal in my upcoming projects.

—**Martin Jansen, ultra runner, adventurer, and speaker**

I come from an era when everyone wanted to know how to be a millionaire. Rafael Badziag has compiled a new age book about what it is to be a billionaire in the world of digital and exponential growth. Over the decades I think the reader will find the foundations for being a leader are still the same, but with a twist. It is the twist that makes this book exceptional.

—**Chip Wilson, Canadian billionaire, founder of Lululemon Athletica**

I have always believed that if you dream big, you must go for it. This book proves that point. The billionaires in this book—who come from all around the world—are dreamers who think big but started small and never gave up. The 20 principles in The Billion Dollar Secret *light up all of the possibilities and guide you toward a life of abundance.*

—**Jacek Walkiewicz, psychologist, lecturer, top Polish TED speaker**

I first met Rafael at a personal development workshop. Among all of the speakers I heard, he was the only one who had extraordinary passion, credibility, and true commitment to his mission. He was so good I asked him to speak at one of my sports clubs. After that, he became one of my mentors. It is thanks to him that I started to believe I had to aim higher. I started my business following the rules I believe in, doing what I love, and doing it as good as I can. And it worked!

—**Miłosz Świć, owner and guide at the runners' club Wild Boar Commando**

It was a unique and inspiring experience to take part in this global book project. I would like to thank the author of the book for giving me this opportunity to pass my message to the audience of ambitious people and share my real-life experience with them. It would be my pleasure if my words could inspire these people and help them to achieve their goals in life.

I would also like to thank Rafael Badziag for conducting such an intriguing interview in a pleasurable, personal atmosphere. He took me for an enjoyable trip to the early days of my life during which I had the opportunity to touch my memories of how I built the success I have today. His questions let me think about every aspect of an entrepreneurial life. I had the chance to revisit the different stages of my career.

I've always valued the real stories of successful people from their very own tone of voice. Therefore, I would really be interested in learning about the success stories, mindsets, and motivations of the chosen business people around the world.

—Petter Stordalen, Norwegian billionaire and hotelier

I met Rafael in January 2015, and from the very beginning, I was impressed by his enthusiasm. He has an extraordinary ability to evoke positive emotions and fascination. Whatever he does, he does on a BIG scale and always with a smile: desert ultra marathons, relentless travels, Internet businesses, and, above all, this project. The fruit of his labor is this exceptional book, which I am sure will change the lives of millions of people around the world in the coming decades.

—Kamil Stasiak, ultra runner and entrepreneur

Rafael is truly inspiring.

—Y, magician, mentalist, and TV star, founder of Magic of Y

I was dubious about agreeing to be interviewed for this new book. I was, however, pleasantly surprised at how well you had researched both myself and my company and came fully prepared. Today there is a distinct lack of professionalism throughout all walks of life and industry. It was refreshing that you restored my faith.

I thoroughly enjoyed meeting you. I thought the questions you asked were relevant and sensible, and I look forward to not only reading what is said about me but also the many other successful people you hope to include in the book.

—**Peter Hargreaves, English billionaire, founder and chairman of Hargreaves Lansdown**

Rafael Badziag knows even more about how billionaires think than the billionaires themselves do. Unlike dime-a-dozen books that pitch overnight "get rich" schemes, Badziag's work gives you a front-row seat inside the brains of many of the world's wealthiest people and insights that can't be found anywhere else. The Billion Dollar Secret *is a road map to help entrepreneurs at any stage achieve even the most seemingly insurmountable financial goals.*

—**Rick Frishman, publisher, publicist, speaker, and author of numerous bestsellers, including *Guerrilla Publicity* and *Networking Magic***

For my family
I love you all

CONTENTS

FOREWORD

When Rafael Badziag approached me five years ago with his idea to interview over 20 billionaires from all around the globe and get them to share the secrets of their success, I wasn't at all convinced he could pull it off. Think about it. How do you convince over 20 billionaires to take serious time out of their incredibly busy schedules to work together on a book project? Millionaires, maybe. But billionaires who are running large multifaceted empires? I had been studying the principles and practices of successful people for more than 40 years, and I knew nobody had ever attempted that before.

As I continued to meet and correspond with Rafael several times over that five-year period, to my surprise I discovered how doggedly he was committed to the project, and by applying the same principles and disciplines he was learning from the billionaires he was interviewing, he actually pulled it off. And he did it on a global scale. And he not only managed to get access to 21 billionaires, he convinced some of the very best billionaire entrepreneurs in the world to work with him.

Since 2003, the most successful entrepreneurs from each country in the world have been coming together each year in Monaco to choose the World Entrepreneur of the Year, the person they believe to be the very best entrepreneur in the world that year. And since 2003, 8 of those 15 people named World Entrepreneur of the Year have been billionaires. And out of those 8, 5 chose to participate in this book and share their wisdom with Rafael and now you, the reader.

There is no other book available anywhere in the world that contains this much entrepreneurial experience, insight, and wisdom in it. From his countless hours of interviews with these highly accomplished billionaires, Rafael has managed to identify 20 powerful principles that led to their success . . . and that are now available to you to help you achieve your entrepreneurial and financial dreams.

You are now about to intimately get to know and learn from 21 no-nonsense business heroes who started with nothing and have gone on to build hugely successful companies, as well as contribute greatly to their local and global communities through their extensive philanthropic activities. They are now available as true role models for anyone with a compelling vision and who is willing to work hard and work smart to make that vision a reality.

As you will discover, Rafael has a unique gift in that he is able to get people who are mostly very private about their work and their wealth to open up their hearts and share their innermost thoughts and feelings about their journey to success. As you read this book, you are now the beneficiary of Rafael's gift as you gain true insider access to the beliefs and behaviors that are required to achieve greatness in the business world. And because of the way Rafael has organized the book, it feels like you are right in the same room with them. They share the challenges they faced, the lessons they learned, the disciplines they developed, the solutions they created and discovered, and the results they produced in everyday, easy-to-understand language.

The end result is this astonishing book that you hold in your hands. As you turn each page, you will find old ideas and misconceptions about billionaires being gently washed away. One of the most powerful things you'll discover is that these men did not start their careers by inheriting large sums of money that they were able to increase through a little bit of good luck. In fact, every one of the billionaires in this book is self-made. Some of them even came from extreme poverty and had seemingly hopeless beginnings, and you would have easily written them off if you had met them in their youth, but they never gave up and eventually achieved extraordinary things in business through their sheer, unbelievable tenacity.

As you get to know these remarkable men from their more human side, beyond what you would normally read about such people in *Forbes* or *Fortune* magazine, you'll discover that they are basically just the same as you and me, but what sets them apart is that they have mastered the art of self-belief, and they came to realize that the only limitations any of us have are the ones we place upon ourselves. As you read their stories and come to understand their billionaire mindsets, you'll see that when these psychological limitations are removed, the potential to achieve anything you desire is truly limitless.

You now have access to the inspiration, motivation, and information from 21 billionaires who will act as your mentors for the next 280 pages. And if you apply what they teach you with commitment, dedication, and perseverance, you'll find that your potential for greatness is as limitless as theirs.

I'd normally end this by saying "Good luck," but it is not luck that you need. It is simply the resolve and the courage to put into practice the life-changing principles and tools you are about to discover in this book. So instead I'll end by saying, "Enjoy the journey!"

—Jack Canfield
#1 *New York Times* best-selling author of *The Success Principles*, *How to Get from Where You Are to Where You Want to Be*, *Dare to Win*, *The Power of Focus*, and the *Chicken Soup for the Soul* series

How It Came About and What to Expect

If you can count your money,
you don't have a billion dollars.

–J. Paul Getty, the wealthiest man in the world in the 1950s

In 1908, when journalist Napoleon Hill was assigned an interview with Andrew Carnegie—the wealthiest man in the world at the time—he didn't imagine the journey that was awaiting him. Carnegie, himself an extremely successful entrepreneur, had the conviction that something resembling a success formula must exist—one that could be shaped into an infallible system that anybody could follow.

Impressed by Hill's wit, Carnegie asked him if he was up to the task of formulating such a system by interviewing the most successful people in America and analyzing the results. Hill jumped on the opportunity. Carnegie gave him a letter of introduction to automotive magnate Henry Ford. The latter then introduced him to Alexander Graham Bell (inventor of the telephone), Elmer R. Gates (inventor of the fire extinguisher), Thomas Edison (inventor of the light bulb), and Luther Burbank (agricultural pioneer).

Hill went on to interview these individuals and many others who were among the wealthiest and most successful people of his time. After 20 years of research, he published his Philosophy of Achievement as a formula for rags-to-riches success in his monumental work *The Law of Success*. He condensed this knowledge into his famous work *Think and Grow Rich*, which went on to become one of the best-selling books of all time—and continues to sell in multiple versions and formats.

Hill's publication was the seminal event in establishing a universal success philosophy. In the last 100 years, Hill's philosophy has come to dominate the Western—or shall we say, distinctly American—school of thought on this subject. All of the figures referenced in *Think and Grow Rich* were American, after all.

How It All Started

Five years ago, I was attending a success conference. Thousands of people were high-fiving each other and shouting enthusiastically, "You've got a millionaire mind!" I went there inspired by the success books I had read, books on millionaire thinking, including Hill's book. But I somehow felt awkward. Something didn't feel right, didn't let me cheer with others. There was something strange in the air, a feeling, a perception that I couldn't grasp. Then it struck me. Of course!

Of course, I've got a millionaire mind. Back in the 1990s, I was pioneering e-commerce in Europe. I created the first fully functional online shop selling bikes in the German-speaking market. Having built a multimillion-dollar company, I am a millionaire myself. So what? I don't feel like an overly successful entrepreneur with it. Others have developed their businesses faster, grew bigger with seemingly less effort. On top of that, my business felt like a continuous uphill battle. Being just a millionaire is rather a mediocre performance in the world of business. I'd rather have a billionaire mind. That would be something desirable for every entrepreneur. But this I apparently can't learn here, at this conference, from people struggling to reach their first million.

I left, disillusioned and determined to find a way to learn it.

Have you ever asked yourself why is it that despite all your hustle every day, you aren't where you want to be in life? How is it possible that some people during one life span manage to build organizations of hundreds of thousands of people and create the amount of value that an average person would need hundreds of thousands of years to create? What is their secret? Is it just a question of lucky circumstances? Is it their environment? Maybe it is their education? Or does the secret lie in their personalities? What are the keys to their phenomenal success? What do their belief systems consist of? How did they get where they are today, and how can you embark on the same journey to success? What are the mindsets and success rituals that these influential people have used to create such massive wealth? What drives them? What is the source of their exceptional motivation? What gives them the energy to relentlessly pursue such outrageous goals? What is it in the personalities of self-made billionaires that made them achieve so much more than an average entrepreneur and become so extremely successful in business?

This book in your hands, *The Billion Dollar Secret*, is the result of a five-year journey that took me several times around the globe to find the answers to these questions. It revives the 100-year-old idea of Napoleon Hill. However, I have taken the research one step further by interviewing some of today's most successful business personalities—all of them self-made billionaires. This time, in contrast to Napoleon Hill's work, I approached it globally, talking not only to American business giants but also to self-made billionaires from all parts of the world, representing different nations, cultures, and religions, as well as people from various industries, social backgrounds, and age groups. Today, we live in a globalized society. Asia now has a greater population of wealthy people than Europe and North America. Various cultures, religions, and mindsets around the world have developed their own paths to wealth.

The personalities of the self-made billionaires in this book are all quite different. They have their own areas of brilliance, their own unique personal interests, and their own individual quirks. In spite of these differences, however, there are specific common denominators, a set of personality principles shared by all of them that contributed to their successes and pushed them way over the top. It distinguishes them from everyone else. These principles aren't inborn. They can be learned, trained, and internalized.

I call this set of principles **the Billion Dollar Secret**.

It is one thing to analyze public appearances or to cull third-party materials and draw conclusions from them, as most authors have done in the past; it is an entirely different thing to ask the super achiever face-to-face about his or her methodology of success, motivation, and way of thinking, as I have done here. Firsthand data allows a genuine, inner view into the heads of these outstanding personalities; access to their true thoughts and emotions; and original insights into their understanding of business and the world.

This book is the first attempt to extract the success principles directly from the world's most successful self-made billionaire entrepreneurs themselves.

What Is a Billionaire?

The definition of a billionaire won't be a revelation to you: He or she is a person with a net worth of at least $1 billion. What you may not realize is that a billionaire is an extremely scarce creature. Statistically, only 1 out of every 5 million citizens in the world—or 1 in 10,000 millionaires—is a billionaire.

It is difficult for most people to imagine how much money $1 billion really is. You would need about 22,000 pounds of $100 bills to amass $1 billion.

All 21 individuals interviewed for this book created a multiple of that value in their lifetimes. They did not inherit their great wealth or "luck" into it through some other means; they earned their fortunes through painstaking work and had to overcome steep trials and tribulations to reach their current status.

I must clarify the most common misconception regarding billionaires. They don't sit on mountains of money. Nobody has a billion dollars in cash.

Seldom do these people have billions of dollars sitting in their personal bank accounts, either; when they do, this is only for a limited time between transactions. Rather, almost all of their money is invested in companies, stock, and/or real estate. It would be irresponsible to have so much cash lying around. The money would be eaten up by inflation, and there is also always the risk of a bank going bankrupt.

Artist Michael Marcovici created a work of art, *One Billion Dollar*, which physically depicted $1 billion in printed money. When the piece was exhibited in Vienna, Austria, Marcovici was asked why he didn't use real money. His answer? Nobody could afford the ticket. Even if he borrowed it at only 1% a year interest from a bank, it would cost around $200,000 to have that real money used in a one-week exposition.

An entrepreneur or investor usually wants to see profit from his money—say 5%. In this case, keeping $1 billion in cash around the house would mean $135,000 opportunity cost each and every day. This is more than most people earn in a year. Few people do this voluntarily.

Many people fail to see the difference between a millionaire and a billionaire. In reality, the differences are gargantuan. Consider the following examples from several interviewees in this book.

- An average millionaire may own a hotel. Norwegian billionaire Petter Stordalen owns a chain of almost 200 hotels.

- A wealthy multimillionaire may own a factory. Canadian billionaire Frank Stronach owns 400 of them.

- A millionaire may own a restaurant or possibly even several. Jack Cowin, an Australian billionaire, has interests in 3,000 restaurants.

- The run-of-the-mill millionaire may own a supermarket or two. Russian billionaire Sergey Galitskiy owns over 17,000 supermarkets and drugstores.

Maybe this anecdote will make the difference between a millionaire and a billionaire more tangible for you. Recently a friend told me he was making $500,000 profit a year, pretty impressive earnings for most people. He has been making this amount of money for several years already and investing it. His net worth is several million dollars. By all means, he is a millionaire. But what I realized is that in order for him to amass a billion dollars, he would have needed to be born before Jesus Christ and would have needed to save every penny, not pay taxes, and then only if there were no inflation. Compared to that, billionaires create a fortune of a billion dollars and more in just one life span.

The gap between millionaires and billionaires is colossal not only with respect to their wealth, but also in terms of the power and impact they have. Billionaires literally change the world.

The Billion Dollar Secret explains what distinguishes the billionaire thought process from everyone else's and answers these questions: Why do some successful people who become millionaires remain at this level, whereas others become billionaires and change the world? What makes the latter achieve so much more?

No matter what endeavor you are attempting, you should always learn from the world's best. Why? Because whether you learn from a third-league player or a world champion, the amount of time and effort you put in would be exactly the same. However, your results would be completely different.

If you desire is to be the world's best soccer player, for example, you won't get there by teaching yourself or by learning from a local hero—no matter how talented and experienced he or she might be. But if you were to get advice from past and present all-time greats, such as Lionel Messi, Cristiano Ronaldo, Pelé, and Mia Hamm, you would gain instant insights—both mental and physical—that would give you the best chance possible to achieve all-time greatness at the sport.

Likewise, if you seek to become successful in business, you need to learn from the world's best entrepreneurs. Yet how do you even determine who these individuals are?

There is one objective measure of business success: net worth. This is the universal score for business performance. Success might mean different things to different people, but in business it is relatively easy to determine the world's most successful entrepreneurs: These are the people who have created the most dollar value during their business careers, the highest net worth.

By definition, the world's best entrepreneurs are the wealthiest people in the world. Concretely, this means Billionaires—with emphasis on the capital B.

For the truly ambitious entrepreneur, it is senseless to consult with "average" millionaires or multimillionaires. In today's business world, these businesspeople are far removed from consideration as the best performers. In the United States, 1 in every 20 entrepreneurs is a millionaire. So don't learn from the millionaires. No, you need to learn from the best—from the billionaires.

Among other billionaires, the following top business personalities shared their wisdom for this book:

- Manny Stul, the World Entrepreneur of the Year 2016

- Mohed Altrad, the World Entrepreneur of the Year 2015

- Cho Tak Wong (Cao Dewang), the World Entrepreneur of the Year 2009

- Tony Tan Caktiong, the World Entrepreneur of the Year 2004

- N. R. Narayana Murthy, the World Entrepreneur of the Year 2003

As you read the book, you may be wondering how I managed to gain access to all these illustrious personalities and convince them to participate in this global book project. Well, that story would fill another book (which I may someday write). Suffice it to say, this project took me around the world several times and let me see behind walls that are normally inaccessible to outsiders.

Last but not least, it allowed me to meet the most extraordinary business personalities of our times—all for the purpose of sharing their innermost wisdom with you, dear reader. Yet this is not a book about them—the shining diamonds of our business world, the mavericks, the 1-in-5-million ones, the "black swans"—per se. It is about the secret of their phenomenal success, told directly by them, in their own words. It is about the Billion Dollar Secret.

This book provides you with a road map so you may embark on your journey toward achieving similar results in your life and business.

Let's begin.

CHAPTER 1

It's Inside You

Convictions are more dangerous
foes of truth than lies.

—Friedrich Nietzsche

It is astonishing to consider how deeply public opinion about billionaires is dominated by stereotypes. The average person knows little about their reality—a world that represents a mere 0.00002% of society.

This knowledge deficiency is distorted by the media, which focuses on flashy images and dramatic incidents to create and promulgate envious sentiments. The picture painted by the media and accepted as fact by the general public is heavily skewed and a far cry from reality—at least insofar as self-made billionaires are concerned.

Let's start by refuting some of the most common misconceptions. The following will give you a taste of the kind of people we are talking about and introduce you to their world.

Billionaire Misconception:
Billionaires are born in rich, developed countries.

If you think it is necessary for a person to be born in a rich, developed country in order to become a billionaire, you are mistaken. The story of Narayana Murthy provides a good example.

N. R. Narayana Murthy was born in 1946 in India, one of the poorest countries in the world. Narayana's family didn't have furniture; everybody sat and slept on the floor. His father advised him to choose his hobbies carefully and select ones that wouldn't drain his meager budget. Reading, listening to music, and talking to friends became his hobbies of choice. He couldn't afford to buy a newspaper, so he would go to the public library and read a copy there.

In the early 1980s, India not only was one of the poorest countries in the world. It was also one of the countries most hostile to free enterprise. India had a socialist government that had developed an array of restrictions and ridiculous regulations that made it almost impossible to conduct business. This led to extreme corruption; government officials had the power to decide which enterprises would succeed and which ones would fail. As a result, India's economy was strangled.

In 1981, when Narayana Murthy, together with several partners, founded the software company Infosys, the problems they encountered seemed insurmountable. The country's frequent power shortages were one of the lesser obstacles they eventually would face.

Consider this: Do you think it is possible to run a software company without a computer?

Well, Infosys didn't have one. Why?

Because a license was needed from the government in order to import a computer to India.

Narayana Murthy told me he had to endure three years and 50 visits to Delhi to obtain that license. The time frame barely hints at what was involved in this endeavor. Infosys was located in Bangalore, and Delhi was some 1,500 miles away. (To put this in perspective, it's 200 miles more than the distance from New York City to Miami, Florida.) Narayana couldn't afford to fly, so he needed to travel by train two days each way. As mentioned, the bureaucracy required 50 visits to Delhi; if you do the math, that is the equivalent of 200 days in total travel time in a three-year period!

Now, you are probably asking yourself: During the three years they didn't have a computer, how was it possible for them to run a software company? How did they program?

The team found a customer in America who was amenable to allowing them to program on his computer. Six of the cofounders traveled to the United States to work on this, while Narayana remained in India in order to clear up the formalities and obtain approval to import their own computer.

Communication was yet another problem. Narayana informed me that it took the average Indian company five to seven years to get a phone line. Aside from the technological backwardness, the reason for the long wait was that retired government officials were prioritized to get phone lines.

The obvious question here: How did he communicate with his cofounders and customers in the United States without a telephone (and in the days before email)?

Narayana made regular visits to the post office, where he used a public phone box to call them.

I asked Narayana what happened if they needed to contact him. He smiled at me and replied, "Well, they couldn't, they just couldn't."

After a year of struggling, they finally had a phone line installed. But having a phone line didn't necessarily mean they could also get connections—especially with the United States. Most of the time there was no signal on the line; when there was a signal, it was usually busy.

As previously mentioned, it took three years for them to obtain a license to import the computer. Yet having a license didn't mean they could afford a computer. Complicating matters further was the fact that the software they were creating required a minicomputer, which cost hundreds of thousands of dollars—money the founders just didn't have. Infosys was founded with

$250 saved up by seven founders. Narayana Murthy faced another problem and performed another miracle, which we will discuss later.

After the computer was imported and installed, the six cofounders returned to India to work on it. But that still wasn't the end of the bureaucratic obstacles they had to overcome. They now had to figure out how to get the code they produced to the customer in the United States. This occurred pre-internet, so it wasn't as if they could simply email the code to the customer. The only way to do it back then was to save the program on magnetic tape and send it via the traditional mail service. On the other side, the customer loaded it from the magnetic tape to his computer. Unfortunately, this solution didn't work between India and the United States.

Why not? Because any package being shipped from India to the United States needed to go through Indian customs. It took customs officials about two weeks to perform the customs procedure. This meant that it took three weeks for the code to be shipped from Infosys in India to the customer in the States. With every change Infosys made to the program, they needed to wait another three weeks before they could receive any feedback from their client. The consequence was that project durations extended to what seemed like an eternity. This process was unacceptable and akin to an entrepreneurial hara-kiri. They needed to shorten the shipment time considerably to speed up their production cycles.

How did they solve this? The team came up with the idea of printing out the code on paper and faxing it to the United States where, on the other side, another Infosys employee typed it manually from the fax into the customer's computer. Of course, this required additional manual work and wasn't error free. But it dramatically increased the speed of their software shipments.

That was not all when it came to challenges: Imagine the conditions they had to work in and the obstacles they needed to overcome while building their company in this poor developing country.

I had a firsthand taste of these conditions when conducting the interview with Narayana Murthy. At that time, it was 45 degrees Celsius (113 Fahrenheit) in Delhi. This kind of temperature isn't exactly conducive to performing physical or intellectual tasks. But people in India must perform their work in these conditions on a regular basis.

Today, Infosys is considered one of the wealthiest and most developed companies in India, offering the best working conditions available for their employees. And, of course, there was air-conditioning at the Infosys guest house in Delhi, where we conducted the interview.

Even so, there was a power outage during the meeting, and the air-conditioning system went out. Our own attempts to switch it back on failed, and the temperature rapidly became uncomfortable. Narayana called a maintenance team. After 10 minutes of fumbling, it finally clicked on. Five minutes later, there was another power outage, and the air-conditioning once again went out. We decided to leave it alone because we didn't want to lose any more time.

I had only a tiny glimpse of what working life is like in modern-day India. For those readers who have never had such an opportunity, can you imagine what it may have looked like to work in that environment 30 years ago—when India and Infosys were far less developed?

Today, Narayana Murthy is a billionaire. Infosys is the largest software company in the world, employing 200,000 programmers; this is more than Microsoft, Apple, and Google combined. In 2003, Narayana Murthy was named World Entrepreneur of the Year—the best entrepreneur in the world, if you will.

It is therefore a myth that only people born in rich, developed countries can become billionaires. In fact, not only has Narayana himself become a billionaire, but he also made six of his cofounders into billionaires and at least 4,000 of his employees into millionaires.

What most people fail to realize is that wealth in developing countries grows much faster than in industrialized countries. In 2016, the number of billionaires in Asia surpassed the total in all of North America.

In my research I stumbled upon the phenomenon of immigrant billionaires. Yes, a strikingly high percentage of self-made billionaires made it big outside their countries of origin. They came from poor or war-torn countries with nothing in their hands, yet found ways to build great wealth. We will discuss this in greater detail later in the book.

Billionaire Misconception:
Billionaires come from well-off, supportive families.

If you think a person must be born into a wealthy, supportive family to have a chance at becoming a billionaire, you are likely unaware of the story of Mohed Altrad.

Mohed Altrad was born a nomad in the Syrian Desert. His Bedouin tribe lived in tents. They set up camp where they found water for the animals and stayed there as long as the vegetation was enough to sustain their herds. Then they folded the tents and moved farther in search of better pastures.

When Mohed was born, his father disowned him. He expelled Mohed and his mother from their home and slaughtered his brother to death. Mohed was forced to live with his mother on the periphery of the tribe, his life so unimportant that nobody even noted the day or year of his birth. Even today he doesn't know when he was born. He told me that the dates he uses now were invented because his children wanted to celebrate his birthday with him.

That is far from being the end of this Dickensian tale. When Mohed was four, his mother died. His grandmother assumed responsibility for him and raised him with the belief that his destiny was to become a shepherd. She didn't want him to go to school because she thought it was for "do-nothings." Every day, Mohed escaped from home and walked barefoot through miles of desert to the nearby village, where he could attend school.

The teacher gave him a notebook and a pencil because he didn't have either of these things. He had gone to school empty-handed, as well as barefoot. The only thing Mohed owned was a torn *djellaba* (a type of robe), which he had outgrown years earlier.

On several occasions, Mohed tried to get basic support from his father to obtain the bare necessities, but was consistently rejected and humiliated by him—sometimes even beaten.

When Mohed was in third grade, however, a miracle occurred: He received a present from his father—an old bicycle. It was the first and only gift his father ever gave him.

With that bike, Mohed's entrepreneurial genius appeared for the first time. He rented the bike out to his schoolmates for a fee, earning him a bit of money. It wasn't much, but it allowed him to purchase some school materials.

Realizing that school was his only chance to get out of his lot in life, Mohed studied hard. Soon he became one of the best students in his region and was granted a scholarship to study abroad.

Many years later, after he completed his education, Mohed took over a bankrupt scaffolding company in France and developed it into a world leader in the industry. Over the next 30 years, he added over 200 companies to his business, the Altrad Group.

Today, Mohed Altrad is a billionaire. In 2015, he was named World Entrepreneur of the Year—the best entrepreneur in the world, if you will.

So, if you think one needs to be born in a well-off, supportive family in order to become a billionaire, you have been clinging to a misconception. Mohed Altrad was born a Bedouin on the margins of society in a poor country. He was disowned by his family, who wanted him to become a shepherd. But this didn't stop him on his way to achieving unbridled success, proving that it can be done.

My experiences with self-made billionaires reveal that a considerable percentage of them didn't have an untroubled, protected childhood. From early on they were forced by circumstances to take responsibility for their lives. We will talk about that in greater detail in later chapters.

Statistically, over 70% of the world's billionaires are self-made, meaning that they don't come from wealthy families. They created the mind-boggling value of at least $1 billion by their own means in less than a lifetime, which is astonishing in itself.

By contrast, this means that less than 30% of the billionaires inherited their wealth. Among this group there is a significant share of people who weren't born rich, but inherited their wealth from their spouses.

To summarize, the stereotype of the rich man born into a privileged family and enjoying affluence all his life may apply only to one-quarter of all billionaires.

Billionaire Misconception: They have studied at the best universities.

It would be fair for you to argue that, despite all the obstacles they faced, Narayana Murthy and Mohed Altrad did manage to receive good formal educations that were critical to their respective success. But what about those who didn't receive that education early on in life? Did all billionaires graduate from the best universities?

Cao Dewang (or, in official Mandarin pronunciation, Cho Tak Wong) grew up in war-torn China during the Cultural Revolution in a poor village in the Fujian Province. Before he was born, his father had abandoned the family and left for Shanghai without choosing a name for the expected child. This is especially important in Chinese tradition, where the father is supposed to give a name to the child.

As a result, the boy didn't have a real name and instead went by a nickname until the age of nine. He and his five siblings were raised in poverty by his mother.

It was required by law for children to go to school, but the family couldn't afford it for several years. Finally, he was able to go when he was nine, but still didn't have a name—an important detail for school attendance. His uncle gave the matter a great deal of careful thought and ultimately named him Dewang.

After Dewang's initial excitement, the school turned out to be a challenge for him. He felt restless and uncomfortable "as if there were nails sticking up through his seat." His defiant nature and taunts against the teachers behind their backs didn't earn him their sympathy. The boy's struggles weren't about his grades, but rather, his conduct. He was labeled a "bad kid" at an early age. Each time his teacher turned around to write on the blackboard, he would stand up and mimic him or her to make his classmates laugh.

When Cao was 12, his father finally returned home. Every evening, he sent his son to the liquor shop to buy booze for him. On his way home, Dewang started to take increasingly bigger sips from the bottles. Before long, he developed a drinking habit.

In the mornings, Dewang needed to wake up early to gather kindling for the home oven. This made him feel tired in the afternoons, and on one occasion, he fell asleep in class. The school director humiliated him in front of everyone, but Dewang refused to let him get away with it. "I caught him in the loo, climbed to the top of the wall, and merrily urinated on his head," he described to me.

Needless to say, this never happened again. Dewang was forced to leave school after finishing only five grades. His family actually felt relieved as they couldn't afford his education anyway.

It is important to note that dropping out of school in China after only five years of schooling essentially means that you are illiterate. Chinese scripture consists of 90,000 characters out of which 5,000 are used regularly. Chinese people spend their entire lives learning to write.

With limited education by the age of 14, Cao Dewang became a village doormat. He was assigned the task of taking care of only one communal cow. His salary was barely enough to survive. But nobody was willing to entrust an illiterate, rascally, alcoholic youth with greater responsibility. Dewang hit rock bottom simultaneously with the turning point in his life.

This was when Dewang refused to give up on himself and decided he would do anything needed to rise from poverty. He became determined to self-educate himself. He began by reading his older brother's schoolbooks, taking them with him as he watched the cow. Unfortunately, there were thousands of characters he couldn't understand. He tried asking his brother for help, but there were too many of them, and his brother grew impatient.

The solution: a dictionary. But a good one, like the *Xinhua Dictionary*, would cost 0.8 yuan—a huge sum of money for a cowhand at that time. Here his spirit started to show the first signs of genius and a relentless will.

He woke up early to trim grass at the river before going to work and sold it as hay to the horsekeepers in the village, saving them some hassle. They paid him pennies, but he saved them meticulously. After a full year of saving, he was finally able to buy the *Xinhua Dictionary* and at least understand the words. In order to accomplish this, he looked up each character in the dictionary until he could understand all of them.

Dewang remained unsatisfied with his body of knowledge. In order to gain a real understanding of the concepts in the books he wanted to read, he required an encyclopedia. It goes without saying that an encyclopedia cost even more than the dictionary: 3 yuan. It took him another three years of saving to be able to afford it.

As the years passed, he worked on improving himself step-by-step until his efforts paid off. Over the course of many years, he took on numerous jobs and positions, including greengrocer, tobacco trader, fungus grower, construction worker, engine repairer, cook, salesman, purchaser, and factory manager. Eventually, as an entrepreneur, he built Fuyao Glass—the world's largest auto glass manufacturer.

In 2009, nearly 50 years after hitting rock bottom, Cao Dewang was named the World Entrepreneur of the Year—the best entrepreneur in the world, if you will. He is now a billionaire.

Cao Dewang never graduated from any school. He never attended any university. He was born in a backward country, and his poor family couldn't even afford an elementary education for him. In spite of all that, he is now among the wealthiest people in China.

So, if you think that in order to become one of the world's wealthiest people one needs to be born in a rich, developed country, come from a well-off, supportive family, and graduate from a top university, then you are holding onto misconceptions and underestimating your capabilities. This way, you limit yourself and what you can achieve. Most of the self-made billionaires don't satisfy one or several of these conditions. Many, like Cao Dewang, don't satisfy any of them. They are myths unsupported by reality.

The first thing I learned from the billionaires is that external factors do not determine their success.

What is it, then, that enables some people to overcome seemingly hopeless beginnings and achieve unbelievable success, whereas others live regular lives and don't accomplish anything remarkable, despite having spent their lives surrounded by the best conditions?

It turns out that what determines extraordinary success is the right combination of internal factors that are all common among self-made billionaires. I call them the Billion Dollar Secret. The first one is the realization that you can overcome all unfavorable conditions and become extraordinarily successful in business despite or maybe because of them. It's your inner workings that make you excel in business, not the conditions outside you.

You will discover the other 19 principles on the following pages.

- Drifters believe you can only succeed when conditions are perfect, but whatever the conditions, there is always something stopping them.

- Millionaires are strong to take their lives into their hands but still believe their success depends on favorable conditions.

- Billionaires know they have it inside them, and they make it big in business independently of external factors.

For more stories on this topic, go to:
http://TheBillionDollarSecret.com/resources

CHAPTER 2

If You Want to Fly, First Leave the Nest

*It is not that we have a short life to live,
but that we waste a lot of it.*

—Seneca

In the previous chapter, you could see that the difference in results of an average entrepreneur and the outrageous success of self-made billionaires is not based on any outside factors. What, then, makes the difference?

In any given industry, all players have more or less the same business model. They use the same methods and tricks, so why are most defeated while some achieve so much more than everybody else?

Asked about that, Mohed Altrad, the refugee Bedouin turned World Entrepreneur of the Year, gave me this analogy:

It's a difference in the dimension of the person. It is as if I ask you what's the difference between a Porsche, high-class car, and a Ford. With a Ford maybe you could drive at a certain speed, and then you could go up to another speed. But if you go, for instance, to 200km/h, then the car is not stable. It's not going correctly. Whereas a Porsche doesn't have this limitation. Why is a Porsche like this? Because people designed it in such a way to have no limit.

For a car, the limit is given by its construction; for you as an entrepreneur, it's given by your inner setup: your mindset, your belief system, your attitudes, your worldview, your motivations, your skills, your habits, your knowledge, and your personality.

What about you? What is your limit that you can reliably operate on in business? Would you like to raise this limit dramatically in order to allow you to do really BIG things in business, things you never dared to dream about?

This book is the instruction to do exactly this.

Realize that the company you build is a reflection of who you are. It carries all your characteristics, including your limitations.

"As you change, you will see your business style, your strategy of the company, everything changes. . . . If you want to create a $10 billion company, you have to solve a $100 billion problem. That means you got to help a billion people."—said Naveen Jain, an American software billionaire and space entrepreneur.

In order to be able to achieve extraordinary success in business, you need to have the mental setup of people who are extraordinary in business, the best entrepreneurs in the world. In other words, you need to think like a billionaire.

This book will show you how self-made billionaires think and act, and they will teach you in their own words to do it as well.

Do you want to be a Porsche or a Ford?

This book is for those who want to be a Porsche in business, who are tired of mediocrity and want more out of their lives.

Stand on Your Own Two Feet

In order to achieve anything in life, you first need to become an independent human being.

All the billionaires I interviewed had to stand on their own two feet early.

Some, like Tim Draper, the legendary Silicon Valley investor, or Hüsnü Özyegin, the wealthiest self-made man in Turkey, left home for school at age 14 or even 10, respectively. But many self-made billionaires were born poor. This forced them to grow up earlier.

You may change your view on child work if you read the account of Ron Sim, the Singaporean billionaire who built the OSIM empire:

I always say I was lucky to be born poor, because it fuels the hunger. It fuels the despair, and it fuels the desire to make things right and good.

We all lived together, seven kids, parents, grandparents on mom's side, one uncle, one auntie. So 13 people living in the one-room flat. We all slept on the floor.

I started working at the age of nine.

Because at our home we didn't have enough to eat, I got a job in the afternoon in a store selling noodles. The owner told me, "Okay, you can take these two bamboo boxes and go and knock on the houses and get orders."

Ron was getting three to eight cents commission a bowl depending on the size.

So in the afternoon, between the school and 6:00 p.m., I could make up to 80 cents a day at the age of nine. It's a lot of money. Compared to today, it would be easily . . . five to ten dollars. Those days, our pocket money was only five cents.

Starting with Primary 4, I was always working. I survived on my own pocket money.

The earlier you start to work, the better. You learn the value of hard work and money and develop ideas on where wealth comes from.

In his childhood, Sergey Galitskiy, the internationally most respected Russian billionaire, spent a lot of time during the weekends doing physical work in his parents' garden, being forced to it by his father. "Of course, being a boy I didn't like it, but I am sure that hardworking spirit is what I received from him. I am sure that there are some things that you gain, and to be hardworking is something that I learned to become."

All the self-made billionaires I have interviewed started to work before the age of 18.

Some worked during school vacations, like the Canadian billionaire and Lululemon founder Chip Wilson, saving up for his university. At 14 he was tearing down barn farmhouses for five dollars a day, then trimming trees for the Parks Department or parking and washing cars.

Also Jack Cowin, the Australian billionaire and founder of Hungry Jack's, worked during vacations from the age of 12, in summer cutting lawns, in winter shoveling snow. He also bought a paper route. "Every day you have to deliver papers, you have to collect the money from the customers every week. So you had that responsibility; you knew how much revenue you were going to bring in. I'm like 12 years old at this stage of the game. I remember on the paper route, I had a wealthy section. I remember seeing the doctors and the lawyers always had the nicest cars and the nicest house and things like this. So I think the penny starts to drop in your head that affluence has something to do with education and something to do with the ability to save money, get into your own business, and things like this." With the money he saved up, he was able to buy a car when he was 16. "It's probably the independence thing. Being able to have enough money that you don't have to go to your parents."

But many now billionaires were working even before the age of 10:

Tim Draper got jobs around the house from his mother. "We just went out and we were paid a penny for every minute we worked. I did weeding in the garden, I shoveled dirt, I painted a trailer, I cut down a tree, I mowed the lawn. Did a lot of work just around the house for my penny a minute." That's how he was able to get some money and to start his career as an investor. "My dad got me investing when I was nine years old. When I was nine years old, I was able to buy one share of a stock."

Tony Tan Caktiong, the founder of Jollibee, started at age eight selling newspapers.

But the earliest starters were Hungarian-born, now Canadian billionaire and Linamar founder Frank Hasenfratz, as well as the Brazilian industrialist Lirio Parisotto, who were taking responsibility at the age of six.

Frank remembers: "We lived on a farm, and you had to feed the chickens when you were six years old, and it had to be done on time. You want to play? Yes, you can play, but at 6:00 p.m. you've got to feed the chickens again. All the way through, the older you got, the more responsibility—and not just responsibility, but also privileges—you got. Later on, you had to feed the pigs. Later on, you had to be 10 or 11 before you were allowed to feed the horses. No question, you had to work. That's the way it was."

Take Responsibility for Yourself and Others around You

Lirio Parisotto was born in the south of Brazil in a small farmer village populated by descendants of Italian immigrants. There was no electricity, no radio, no running water or paved road in the town. "It was basically subsistence. I didn't realize what I want for the future life. But one thing I knew: I didn't like to work in the fields. It was too hard, too hot, too many mosquitoes. We were poor. We had money for the basic things like food, clothing, but not more than that. We didn't have money to have a car, a jeep, or anything. And there was also a lot of disease because of the sanitary conditions. They didn't take care of the water, the food. We didn't have a refrigerator. We didn't have electricity. For lighting we used a kerosene lamp. Can you imagine?" He started earning money at age six: "We needed to take corn and extract the straw from the cob. It was used for wrapping tobacco and making what we called 'straw cigars.' I took it out, wrapped 25 together. We did it in the night after the dinner, two hours a day. Once a month someone came to the house and bought this." As the oldest child, Lirio had to take responsibility for his siblings: "I was the first of 11 children. I had to take care of the second, and third and fourth and the fifth because I was the oldest and we didn't have anyone to help my mother. She did all the food preparation, made clothes for all, took care of the animals, milked the cows to do the cheese. If my siblings did something wrong, the responsibility was mine, so I would put them under kind of a drill to make sure nothing would happen. [Laughs]"

Also Dilip Shanghvi, the world's wealthiest man in the pharmaceutical industry, and Kim Beom-Su, the Korean tech mogul, were made responsible for their siblings at an early age and were treated as adults.

Kim Beom-Su lived as a child in a one-room apartment with five siblings, grandma, and parents. As the oldest son, he was destined to take responsibility for the entire family, and following the Korean tradition, the family took special care of him in order to develop his ability and his sense of responsibility. His family wasn't well-off and had to make sacrifices so he could attend a university. He was the only one in the family to do that, a privilege he was aware of that he was grateful for and knew he would have to pay back in the future. "Because of these experiences, I was naturally able to give more after my success." But his parents' business went broke, and the family became homeless. "From then on, I worked like mad on part-time jobs. I worked so hard that the amount I earned then was several times more than what I earned working full-time after college. It was during that time that I came to jump straight into the world, instead of focusing on school and study."

Many billionaires supported their families even as kids either by giving the money they earned to their parents or by working in family businesses.

Narayana Murthy, the founder of Infosys, billionaire, and the World Entrepreneur of the Year 2003, was one of the top four students in the State of Karnataka and in grade 11 was awarded a National Scholarship. "I gave the money to my mother because we were eight children and we were brought up with the philosophy that we had to share whatever we had. Therefore, the natural thing to do was to give the money to the mother, who ensured that everyone benefited from it."

Sergey Galitskiy was 14 when he started working at the vegetable warehouse at his mom's job. "I was doing hard physical work. I was loading the Pepsi Cola trucks. We didn't have much of a choice at the time. We gave the money to our parents, but if we still wanted to leave some part for ourselves then they didn't mind, but we saw that the life is hard. Of course, it was not that we made the decision, but we felt that we had to give the money to our parents. And unfortunately after that, every year I was a hard lifter."

Some billionaires I have interviewed grew up with just one parent, some were even orphans. They needed to take full responsibility for themselves and others around them.

Start Your Own Business as soon as You Can

You can't become a billionaire as an employee. If you want to be financially ultra-successful, you have to get into your own business.

Jack Cowin, the fast-food mogul, had a reputation for making lots of money on the side as a small-business guy when he was graduating from university. He was looking for a good paid job. The head of the residence where he was staying advised him to go and see Bill Pollock, a seasoned entrepreneur in personnel help, temporary help, office overloads. Jack went and Bill gave him a piece of advice that changed Jack's future. He said, "I'm prepared to offer you a job, but you should really get into your own business if you want to be successful." Jack and Bill maintained a relationship. Bill became Jack's mentor and a shareholder in his future business.

Jack shares this advice about wealth building: "Don't get a job. Build a business. Get out of the personal exertion business. There is no eighth day, there is no 25th hour of the day. It's not dependent on how hard you can work. It's getting into a business that you can capitalize. That's where wealth creation comes from."

I asked Lirio Parisotto, the Brazilian billionaire who is also a doctor of medicine, how it was possible for a doctor to become so rich. His answer will surprise you: "If you want to become really rich being a doctor, first of all, stop working as a doctor." Instead, structure a medical business and form a working team out of top professionals.

So take full responsibility for your economic future. Take your fate in your hands. The sooner you start your business, the better. You will have a longer runway and more time for trial and error.

Ron Sim considers himself lucky he got into business early.

Peter Hargreaves, the founder of Hargreaves Lansdown, the largest financial services company in the United Kingdom, when asked what he would do differently if he could start again, answers: "Well, probably start sooner."

This is also the answer I got from Naveen Jain, who started his first company when he was in his late thirties. "I wish I had done it when I was early twenties; I would have 20 years more experience to be doing things. My first company may not have been as successful, but the point is you learn a lot more by doing it than by learning from someone else. So if I had done it for 20 years, maybe my first company wouldn't have been successful, second wouldn't have been successful, but a third company would have been. By that time I would be early thirties, not late thirties when I founded the first company."

Many billionaires founded their businesses because they couldn't be employees anymore. They saved up to start their business.

When Hüsnü Özyegin returned from the States to Turkey, he stumbled upon his old school friend Mehmet Emin Karamehmet, the owner of Yapi Kredi Bank. Karamehmet appointed the 29-year-old Hüsnü to the board of his bank and made him a president of the bank at the age of 32. "I managed Yapi Kredi for three-and-a-half years. It was a loss-making bank when I took over and within three-and-a-half years became profitable." He asked Karamehmet for 1% of the bank. "I wanted to be a shareholder of the bank with this 1%. I wanted to feel like the owner." But Karamehmet said, "I have three banks. If I give you 1%, the other guys will ask for it as well. I don't have a system like this. I'll give you a good bonus." And it was that day when he refused to give Hüsnü the 1% that Hüsnü decided to found his own bank. "It's interesting, I was upset when Mr. Karamehmet didn't grant the 1%, but obviously in retrospect he did me a huge favor, and today I am grateful to him."

In order to found a bank, capital is necessary. Hüsnü earned good money as a bank president in the years prior to this move. "I sold my two houses, for one-and-a-half million dollars, and moved into a leased apartment with my wife and two children, and then I borrowed another $1.5 million from three businessmen. I was able to own 65% of the bank with a capital of $8 million to start with, because I sold 35% of the bank with 50% premium to the first shareholders."

Nineteen years later, he sold the bank to the National Bank of Greece for $5.5 billion. This was the highest company sale in the history of Turkey, and it made him a billionaire. It was also a great deal for the other shareholders. "From the original 21 shareholders that bought 1% of Finansbank, only one kept the shares for 19 years, until the National Bank of Greece bought the bank. I saw him at a wedding. With his black-tie suit, and I had my black tie, in front of everybody he tried to kiss my hand, because he just had received $50 million on the tender offer from the National Bank of Greece against $120,000 that his father had bought for him."

Tony Tan Caktiong failed the job interview he was invited to by Pepsi Cola, because when asked what he wanted to do, he answered he wanted to have his own business. He may have been influenced by his father, who started as an employee, as a chef at the temple, but then he went on to open his own Chinese restaurant. "So maybe there's this model that I too wanted to have my own business."

Also Michał Sołowow, the wealthiest person in Poland, knew he didn't want to be an employee. After his graduation, he was working in car workshops in Germany in order to earn some money. He managed to save up $10,000, and this was his starting capital.

I asked Tim Draper about wealth building advice he would give to people around the world. His answer was just two words: **Start now!**

Control Your Environment and Your Destiny

It is important to face reality. Naveen Jain confessed to me: "It may come as crazy, I don't watch movies. And it's really the reasoning is so odd. Movies take you into a different world. And I love my world. I don't want to leave the world I live in so I don't want to go to a different world and live the fictional world and leave my beautiful world that I love every minute of it."

You need to be responsible in the sense of Chip Wilson—meaning, instead of complaining about something, do something about it. Take responsibility for your environment. Realize that your environment shapes you. How you grow up, how the people around you think, it all influences your end result. Don't let it be accidental.

As Jack Cowin says, "Most satisfied people I know have control over their own lives and affairs. We are probably all seeking the independence to do what we want to, when and where we want to do it. How many unhappy people are there? Ninety percent of the population are in jobs, activities, or relationships out of economic necessity? They stay in a job they hate because they've got a mortgage, got school payments, and they become prisoners. So how do you control it? How do you maintain your ability to control that?"

He told me about a talk to an MBA class he gave, where he said, "You guys have a big disadvantage over what I had. When I finished university, I got a job offer of $6,000 a year, and you're going to get a job offer of $150,000. You're going to develop a lifestyle. You're going to join the golf club; you're going to have private school for your kids. You're going to buy a big mortgage. You are going to become a prisoner of that lifestyle. When I made the decision I was going to go into business, I had everything to gain, not much to lose."

When Jack Cowin graduated from the university in Canada, he got a job with an insurance company. He did well and was making good money. He got married, had a child, bought a house, had a small mortgage. He was 25 years old.

And the only thing I knew for sure was I didn't want to work for a big company. I wanted to get into my own business, to have the freedom to do what I wanted to do. That's the only thing I knew for sure.

How do I get into a role in which I can control my own environment?

After five years on the job, he went with a friend to see a senior executive.

We wanted to set up our own agency and become an independent agent. Here's a big bureaucracy, big insurance company, one of the biggest insurance companies in Canada. We wanted to revolutionize this. And I could see his eyes glaze over. Here are 25-year-old kids coming in, and he could almost say, "Stop wasting my time." He had no interest in what we had told him.

So I left, came to Australia to get into my own business, and the other guy, he became a very successful franchisee of Canadian Tire and built a business. So we both did very well.

In fairness, I had a house and a mortgage. I was able to sell the house, and boom, we moved on. But I hadn't got into the stage whereby I said, "Do I really want to give all this up?" That was never an issue. I'm much more interested in the adventure.

If you want to read in full detail how Jack started in Australia, go to: http://TheBillionDollarSecret.com/resources.

Frank Stronach grew up in poor, war-destroyed Austria. When he was 21, he decided to take his destiny in his hands and change his environment. His account is a true dishwasher-to-billionaire story:

I wanted to see the world. So I applied for many visas—South Africa, Australia, the United States, Canada. Canada came first with the visa. So I wound up in Canada; I went with a ship. The cheapest fare. I had $200 in my pocket. And there were times when I was hungry, because I had no money to buy food.

My first job was in a hospital washing dishes. And the second job I got was in a very small factory. After half a year, I practically ran the company, so the owner said, "Look, I want you to be a partner of mine." But in reality I couldn't become a partner. He was a nice man, but he never wrote the offer down.

Apparently, the owner wasn't serious about it.

So I left there, worked for another company where I made more money, and lived very cheap. Just a small room. Saved every dime.

And then after two years, I bought some used machinery equipment, rented a small garage, and out I went, hustling. I said, "If a factory has a problem, I would like to look at it. And if I can't fix the problem, they don't have to pay me." Simple.

Today, Frank Stronach is a billionaire. He is the founder of Magna, one of the largest auto parts manufacturers in the world with revenue approaching $40 billion.

Billionaires are people who set the rules of the game themselves. Brian Kim Beom-Su liked to play soccer. He usually took the role of the team captain and spiced up the game by putting in additional fun rules or making up an entire new game for friends. He smiled, when I remarked: "So don't play a game when you don't set the rules yourself, right?"

Becoming self-dependent can have a cleansing effect on your psyche as it had on Brian, who for a long time during his life had difficulty with expressing his feelings, with getting angry, with crying: "It was during the time I had just begun my start-up and I was running the business during the day and coding and programming during the night, and there was the weight of doing something new and difficult, or scary, and I had to pay the staff as well. But there was also a strange sense of being in control, knowing that the company was under my lead and that I was independent, quit working for a company and having freedom. This fear and freedom met and formed a sort of catharsis when one day I was taking a shower, and I started crying. After that, taking a shower became a habit. Now I can cry even watching TV shows."

So, dear reader. If you want to fly, you have to leave the nest. Your destiny is in your hands. Get up and stand on your own two feet. Take responsibility for yourself and others around you. Start your own business as soon as you can. And take control of your environment and your life. Only this way can you embark on the journey to outrageous business success.

- Drifters never leave the nest and never fly.

- Millionaires leave the nest and try to fly.

- Billionaires jump off the nest and fly high.

For more stories on this topic, go to:
http://TheBillionDollarSecret.com/resources

CHAPTER 3

Hungry Eagles Soar Highest

Big results require big ambitions.

—Heraclitus

The scale of your thinking determines the size of your achievements, so you better be ambitious and dream big. In order to become BIG, you need to think BIG and have an insatiable desire for growth.

Manny Stul, the World Entrepreneur of the Year 2016, has built two companies in his career. With the first, a gift distributor, he became a millionaire, with the second, a toy manufacturer—a billionaire. "I think desire is very, very important. If you desire to be a million dollars or you desire to be a billion dollars, very big difference. There's a different scale and different scope about which you operate. I certainly had no desire to be a billionaire; I just wanted to be extremely successful. I'd say the difference is desire, scale, and vision. Thinking on a larger scale, thinking on a bigger scale. When I started my gift company, I could've just wanted to be successful in Perth, but I always wanted to be successful in Australia. With Moose, my second company, I didn't want to be successful in Australia, I wanted to be successful worldwide. They're just different scales of thinking."

Cai Dongqing, called the Chinese Walt Disney, stresses that you need to dare to dream and fight for it. Asked about the difference between millionaires and billionaires, he says: "They have different goals which will decide whether they will get going or feel satisfied with the status quo after they have reached the first level of success."

That's also what Frank Stronach, the Canadian billionaire and founder of Magna, confirms: "Once you stop dreaming, you're a dead person. There's no limits in dreaming. It's unlimited. Knowledge is limited. You must always have dreams. Once you have a dream, then you daydream, and then you say what you have to do to maybe fulfill those dreams."

I asked Lirio Parisotto, called the Brazilian Warren Buffett, what drove him in his enterprises. He told me how he stumbled upon his big dream when he had just one small retail store: "One night in the house of my girlfriend I saw a magazine that listed the 500 best and biggest Brazilian companies. Listed as number 221 I saw 'Parisotto,' just 'Parisotto.' So, who is this Parisotto? I did some research. In fact, Parisotto was the surname of the owner of a company involved in gross distribution. So I came up with the idea to put my company in the top 500 companies in Brazil as well. If you see one Parisotto here, why can't I put my company here also? If he could do that, why can't I do that?" In the year 2001, Lirio's company, Videolar, got into the top 500 biggest Brazilian companies and got listed in this exact magazine.

Dreaming big is one thing. Doing big things is another. Michał Sołowow, the wealthiest person in Poland, shares an interesting perspective on this: "I went into construction, because I have always believed that by making things big and expensive, I will obtain much greater margins than by doing small and cheap things. Therefore, instead of producing a hand-cleaning paste for a dollar, I preferred to build a building for $10 million. Assuming that by producing a hand-cleaning paste the margin will be none or minimal. In my construction industry the money was big, and in consequence I had more of it at my disposal and managed to use it."

So break up the limits that hold you back and do a bigger thing!

Your dreams will keep you on track so you won't lose your passion and motivation.

As Cai Dongqing puts it: "You need to have goals. When you have a goal, you will have a dream. So when faced with difficulties and challenges, you still have the motivation and passion to overcome them and keep moving ahead."

Your dreams will also inspire and attract top employees.

Don't Limit Your Thinking. Don't Live a Limited Life

Realize that the greatest obstacles are inside you. You should do everything to identify and overcome them.

Naveen Jain, an American space entrepreneur, explained to me his view on this topic:

I'm sure your parents and every parent will tell you, you are a bright son. You can do anything you want. Sky is your limit.

And then you realize the sky is nothing but a figment of your imagination. There is no such thing as sky. Sky is what we imagine because we can't see anything beyond. But when you go from here to the moon or Mars, you never pass the sky.

We create our own sky, we create our own limits. If you believe something is impossible, it becomes impossible for you, not for anyone else. So your belief and your mindset of what is possible is what allows you to do what is possible.

What is the next big industry? I believe it is space, because every resource that we think is limited on earth is in abundance in space. So, what if we can make space accessible? Why can't you go out and get the resources that you need on the moon?

That's how my company Moon Express was born. To me, Moon Express actually became to a large extent my dream about showing people about what a moon shot is, and this was literally a moon shot. So I'm thinking about what will inspire the next generation of people to show that everything is possible.

To me, going to the moon is the four-minute-mile problem. Nobody did it because people did not believe you can run a mile under four minutes until Mr. Bannister ran. And guess what? Within years, many more people did. So to me, going to the moon is that symbolic.

If I can land on the moon, what will you do? What is your moon shot? And every one of us can have a different moon shot. Your moon shot can be "I can cure cancer." My moon shot can be "I can cure poverty." My moon shot can be "I can build world peace." There is nothing that's impossible.

And I'm also building an unmanned space shuttle that's already manifested to go to the moon.

Naveen once got into trouble when he told an immigration officer at the airport his company was about to mine the moon, when answering the standard questions.

He looked at me and he said, "You are a crazy person, we don't allow crazy people in this country. I'm going to deny your visa unless you tell me what your company does." And I said, "My company is still going to mine the moon, but I'm really a software guy." He said, "That's what I want to hear. You're a software guy, you're in."

The immigration man couldn't fathom a human being who has the audacity to think he can mine the moon. And to him that was such a crazy idea. He thought I was mentally disturbed. And that tells you that people have lost the power to dream big. And society only progresses when you allow people to dream big and you take away the fear of failure.

To me, going to the moon is simply symbolic of doing things which people think are impossible.

Naveen likes to tell people: "Don't tell me the sky is the limit; I'm gonna mine the moon." He wants to be remembered as "the man who knew no limits." If it works out, Moon Express will be, after the USA, Russia, and China, the fourth superpower that has ever landed on the moon. So dare to dream and do the impossible!

Don't sell yourself short. Be like Michał Sołowow, who didn't accept living paycheck to paycheck. "That was how the majority lived back then. And perhaps I wanted to do something more and earn more. . . ."

Manny Stul was born the son of Polish Jews in a refugee camp in Germany. At nine months, he came to Australia. His father used to say: "If you're going to take a bite, take a really big bite. A really big bite, so your mouth is full, and there's blood running down the side of your mouth and on your chin and onto your chest. That's what you should be doing. Do something big and worthwhile. If you're going to bother taking a bite, take a big bite." So, Manny applied that attitude from when he got involved with Moose Toys. "If we take on a product, how big could it be? And is it worth the time and the energy and the effort?" Result: Within 15 years, Moose Toys became the fifth-largest toy manufacturer in the world, and Manny was awarded the World Entrepreneur of the Year 2016, the best entrepreneur in the world if you will. This transition from refugee to the World Entrepreneur of the Year shows the power of big ambitions.

> ## If you're going to take a bite, take a really big bite. A really big bite, so your mouth is full, and there's blood running down the side of your mouth and on your chin and onto your chest.
>
> **— Manny Stul #BillionDollarGoldNuggets**

You don't want to regret playing too small. Even some billionaires regret they haven't played a bigger game from the beginning.

I asked Ron Sim, the Singaporean creator of the OSIM empire, "What do you wish you knew when you were 20?" and he gave me this surprising answer: "I think I would have played a far bigger game. If I had what I had, I would play a far bigger game. I took a long road. It makes me very all-rounded, even more durable and stronger, but it shouldn't have taken me so long."

You may realize you have outgrown your environment. It became smaller than your ambitions and it limits your further development. Walk away to try something bigger!

Petter Stordalen, the later Norwegian hotel mogul, spent his childhood in the small town of Porsgrunn. He was supposed to take over his father's two grocery stores.

But then I went to a school where they teach people to be a leader of that kind of supermarkets in Oslo. I went there for one year and another year and went back to work with my father, but when I was coming back, I felt that the shop was smaller and smaller. I couldn't work with my father, because I can't spend all my life walking in his footsteps. I wanted to build something of my own. I don't know why; I just had this thing inside. I told my father, "I'll give this shop to my younger brother, because I can't do it." I think my father was very disappointed by my decision, but at the same time, he was very proud. He felt "Petter really has some ambitions." I didn't know what I should do with my life. I only wanted something different.

Sometimes you need to leave school like Cai Dongqing, the Chinese entertainment mogul. Sometimes you need to go as far as to change the country you live in, because your country doesn't offer enough to satisfy your ambitions. This is what many self-made billionaires in this book actually did.

Be Hungry, Keep the Fire Burning

Hunger, despair, and desire are the three emotions that fuel motivation. Your desire to achieve your goals creates a high level of energy in you.

So how badly do you want it? How ambitious are you? Do you have the desire to build an empire?

Ron Sim, the Singaporean billionaire I interviewed, sees life very simply:

We say it in the Chinese way: "You do, you die. You don't do, you also die," right? You've got one bloody life. Do your best and die. So if that's the case, then you should challenge yourself and maximize yourself. Leave a legacy as much as you can. There's a sense of achievement. What do I live for? Sorry, I don't live for God. I'm living for glory, the sense of achievement and what you can achieve before your run-out date comes. You create something and leave something behind.

This hunger for success doesn't seem to get satiated.

So what's the difference between a millionaire and a billionaire?

Jack Cowin, the Australian billionaire with shares in over 3,000 Hungry Jack's and Domino's Pizza restaurants, told me: "A millionaire is thinking: 'I had a very good idea, I'm successful, I built this business, I'm happy, and I'm prepared to accept the status quo of what the Good Lord has given me.' The billionaire is thinking, 'How high is high? Where's the limit? What is possible?'"

Billionaires don't ask the question "Why?", they ask "Why not?".

"Why?" is just trying to understand; "Why not?" is "Let's try and achieve it."

For Ron Sim, the difference boils down to: "How big is your heart? How big is the dream? That's the key difference. How big your heart is determines how big is your vision." And this, as we know, determines how big will be your results.

So, one of the main differences between the mindset of a millionaire and a billionaire is how ambitious they are and how much they want to achieve in their lives. They rise to higher and higher levels as long as their hunger isn't satiated.

But there is a danger lurking behind the corner that stops most millionaires on their way up. And its name is complacency. Don't get complacent! It will make you lazy! Complacency kills businesses.

Frank Hasenfratz was an outstanding toolmaker. He had to leave Hungary after the uprising in 1958. When he got to Canada, he wanted to get a job in his trade. He applied to W. C. Wood, who had an impressive tool room, but was rejected. He was too cocky, and the general manager, Mr. Zotter, didn't believe his claims. The first job offer he got was from the Canadian railroad. It paid very well. But his uncle advised him against it: "Don't take the job. You cannot take that job." "Why not?" "It pays too good, and you'll never quit. You'll never get anywhere. You'd have a good-paying job, better than anybody else, and it's too comfortable." So Frank turned down the job offer. Everybody was shocked. His cousins said, "You're kidding! You didn't take the job?" "No. Your father told me not to." Frank went back to Mr. Zotter in humility pretending not to have the abilities he was claiming he had the first time. Mr. Zotter got angry: "Now you are lying again." But Frank went: "Mr. Zotter, give me the job. Don't pay me. My uncle will pay. He'll bring me to work and I'll stay with him." Mr. Zotter agreed: "OK. One week and we don't pay you." At the end it turned out Frank was a very good toolmaker, and the owner even paid him for the first week. Frank had the job he wanted and could grow on the path he has chosen. Later, Frank built Linamar, one of the most profitable enterprises in the auto parts industry. The advice his uncle gave him made him a billionaire.

So don't get stuck in complacency. Avoid the golden cage.

Lirio Parisotto, the Brazilian billionaire industrialist, had a similar experience. The two most respected people in his village were the priest and the doctor. He associated these two professions from early age on with success and wealth, and it became his dream to pursue one of these careers. After being excluded from the seminary for misbehavior, he now wanted to become a doctor.

When preparing for the entry exam for the medical school, he tried his abilities in a public competition for a job at Banco de Brazil. It still is the biggest bank in Brazil today, an institution, and it was a dream of everybody to work for this great company. "At that time, the salary was the best in the market. And also, you have the lifetime job. You cannot be fired. The bank has a full pension fund, so you have the retirement guarantee." The competition at the exam was fierce because everybody tried his luck.

Lirio was one of the winners to get a job. He was sent to work in a branch in a small town in the south of Brazil. "I wanted to study. But they send me to a place where there was no university." He asked: "But don't you have other cities with university?" "No, we have just this one."

So Lirio took the job in hopes he would be transferred later on. He was just an "auxiliary of an auxiliary." It was the first level of the career ladder, "but the salary was already three, maybe even five times as much as in my previous job. And you had a lifetime guarantee because if you don't rob the bank, if you do nothing wrong, you will stay in the bank."

But after two weeks there, Lirio realized it was a dead end. "I realized out of the 23 employees of this little branch, all 23 asked to move from this place, including the guard. It dawned upon me that if I stay here I'll die here."

He quit. He didn't receive any money. He took his car and went back home to prepare for the medical school's competitive entry exam. People in his home town, including his parents, couldn't believe what he did. "You are crazy" was the common comment.

This was probably the most difficult decision of my life, because if you get such a good offer of salary and security, 99.9% of people accept.

I asked Lirio what made him take this decision.

I thought it was not enough for me. But remember, I abandoned this job not because I received a better offer or I had a business to take care of. No, I lost this job for nothing. I became unemployed. It was just confidence in myself. This was a big risk because it was possible that everything would go wrong. I exchanged a secure job, good salary for a goal. I needed to do more than that. I thought I needed to work more to have more. Of course, doctor was better. [laughs] At that time.

And then Lirio gave me this gold nugget: "I think if you want to achieve something in business, the worst thing is a good salary. Because you don't become rich with that, but also you have the guarantee. Most people give everything away for the safety. Safety meaning: to have a lifetime job. This is a dream of 99.9% of people."

So don't trade your future for safety, it's a bad trade. Lirio didn't do it and you shouldn't either. Also, don't become a prisoner of your lifestyle.

It's one thing to become successful; it's another thing to stay successful. For this you need sustainable hunger, sustainable desire.

Chip Wilson, a Canadian billionaire and founder of Lululemon, advises using the deathbed perspective:

At the end of the day, does anything matter other than laying on your deathbed and either you lived the life you wanted or the life you didn't? I think as human beings, we do so many things in the world to look good in front of other people. But I think on our deathbeds, looking good in front of other people means absolutely nothing. And I think about how many things that would've been incredible in my life that I didn't do because I didn't want to get turned down by that girl or I didn't want that guy to think that I wasn't smart or I didn't want something in that kind of realm.

We only have 35,000 days on this earth and then you're gone, and no one gives a shit after that. You're a little speck of germ in the whole universe. So it really doesn't matter what anyone else thinks; it's a matter of, did I completely fulfill every second of my life? It helps me stop doing a lot of things that aren't really, really, really important. Sometimes I think, if I only had three months to live, how would I change my calendar? What projects would I do, what wouldn't I do? It really helps me prioritize. Because I find myself taking on things that I should do or things that are really important.

I can't stand going to my deathbed and having an idea untried. I need to find out whether it's viable or not.

If you take these lines to heart, your fire will burn eternally, your hunger will never be satiated, and you will be able to achieve humongous success in business just like Ron Sim: "I'm still very hungry. I don't feel like a billionaire."

Don't Rest on Your Laurels

It's not enough to never stop. You should climb higher and higher. The day you think you have made it is the day you're going downhill. Frank Hasenfratz advises: "If you have a target to come to the top of the hill, before you get there, you'd better find out if there's a higher hill. If there isn't, there's only one way to go. You're not going to go to the top of the hill and stay there forever. Then you go downhill."

Don't settle for the bird in the hand.

Mohed Altrad, the Syrian Bedouin refugee to France and later World Entrepreneur of the Year 2015, upon graduating from the university, started to work for telecommunication companies, but soon left "because the suit was too short for me." He wanted more and found a job opportunity in Abu Dhabi. He became one of a handful of key people responsible for building the Abu Dhabi Oil Company. At that time, Abu Dhabi was merely a small village; now it's one of the wealthiest cities in the world with a population of 5 million people. He was a highly paid managing engineer. During his four years there, he made a fortune of the equivalent of $600,000 today for himself, and he created for Abu Dhabi wealth going into hundreds of billions of dollars. But he didn't have any shares in it.

Mohed left and went back to France to build something on his own. He invested all his savings in a computer company he created with his partner, Richard Alcock. They built one of the first portable computers in Europe. It was a suitcase format. With 30kg of weight it was featherlight for that time. Mohed sold the company within 18 months for double the amount of his investment and was ready for the next step.

Back to Lirio Parisotto. After quitting his lifetime job at the Bank of Brazil, Lirio committed himself to the study of medicine. Being a doctor became his dream after the failed priest career. During that time, he started a small business and hired a manager so he could focus on his studies. When Lirio started to practice at a hospital toward the end of his studies, he realized two things. First, "I realized a doctor is a slave. They work 24 hours a day. It's difficult to take a vacation or travel because they have their patients. And also, there is a lot of unhealthy competition between the doctors." So he decided to go into business. Second, he realized that although the medical profession itself was highly honorable, it didn't feel right to make a business out of it and make money with people in trouble. Upon graduation, instead of working as a doctor, he went to work in his store. "Not an easy step. Some people thought I was crazy. My company was very small at that time." He again decided in favor of an unsure future in his business that he had a greater vision for. Lirio turned this business step-by-step into a multibillion-dollar industrial company.

So don't settle for the bird in the hand. Do it like Lirio: never compromise your future for safety. Never settle, never get comfortable.

If you reach a dream, set another, bigger dream. Billionaires are never finished.

Naveen Jain, after having built several multibillion-dollar companies, still claims to be at the beginning: "Well, I am very early into this book; only a few chapters have been written. The majority of the chapters are yet to be written. I'm going after every one of the major industries. I started with space and I'm going into health care. Next thing I'll probably attack will be education. I'll probably attack the food, and I'm going to continue to attack these biggest problems because I know the biggest problems are the biggest opportunity for an entrepreneur. As an entrepreneur, I really think if I can solve any of these big problems, there is a massive business to be created."

If you reach a dream, set another, bigger dream.

— Rafael Badziag @BillionairePal #BillionDollarGoldNuggets

Billionaires never stop growing.

Hüsnü Özyegin, the Turkish billionaire I have interviewed, still founds new companies at the age of 70-plus. "We just started a pension company, for instance. We invest in a new wind farm every six months. We have five wind farms under construction as we speak. There are so many opportunities."

Let's end this chapter with the words of Peter Hargreaves, who perfectly summed it all up:

I think not many people want to go above a certain level. Once people have achieved the amount of success that will support more than their lifestyle for the rest of their lives, people get disincentivized from that, and there aren't many who want to go on and on and on and on. I think to go way beyond where you need to, you've got to want to make it bigger and better all the time, no matter how big. You've got to want to rule the world. I spend only a tiny percentage of my income.

And you? How high do you want to go, dear reader? What are your ambitions and dreams? How hungry are you to reach them? Is your desire strong enough to propel you throughout your career and not let you rest on your laurels?

- Drifters are defeated by life and have lost their dreams.

- Millionaires are complacent and have small dreams.

- Billionaires are ambitious with dreams larger than life, insatiable hunger, and a desire to soar higher than the skies.

For more stories on this topic, go to:
http://TheBillionDollarSecret.com/resources

CHAPTER 4

Build Your B.O.A.T.

They can because they think they can.

—Virgil

Like Noah's Ark, your B.O.A.T. will safely navigate you through the endless seas and the whirlwinds of your career. Your B.O.A.T. consists of Belief, Optimism, Assertiveness, and Trust in yourself. You need to be optimistic, confident, and assertive toward skeptics, and for all that you need belief! Together with enthusiasm these are some of the most important qualities of a successful entrepreneur and elements of the Billion Dollar Secret.

Optimism and Positive Mindset

Be an optimist. Tim Draper, the legendary Silicon Valley VC investor, told me: "You have a choice. You can be an optimist or you can be a pessimist. Optimists are the ones who accomplish everything. Pessimists don't accomplish anything. Pessimists just give you all the reasons why it's not going to work. The optimists show pessimists that 'Hey, every once in a while, guys, you're wrong. This might work.' So, be an optimist."

> **Optimists are the ones who accomplish everything. Pessimists don't accomplish anything. Pessimists just give you all the reasons why it's not going to work.**
>
> **— Tim Draper #BillionDollarGoldNuggets**

Billionaires don't spend time on negativity. Tony Tan Caktiong, the World Entrepreneur of the Year 2004, is quite extreme about it. He can't really remember sad or painful things. "Maybe the reason why I don't remember is that I have a very positive mindset. I always look at the positive side of things"

All the self-made billionaires I interviewed describe themselves as enthusiastic optimists, as positive-thinking people and they see it as their strength. They believe that hard times never last forever. They feel positive not only about themselves, but also about other people.

Have Faith

Mohed Altrad has always had unbounded faith in his future. It was the case when he rejected his destiny as a shepherd. It was the case when he moved to France. And it was the case when his seemingly blind optimism helped him to get into the right business. After selling his portable computer company as described in the previous chapter, he stumbled upon a bankrupted scaffolding company in his wife's village:

I was on vacation there and somebody came and said, "Do you want to buy a scaffolding company?" And believe me, this was the first time I'd heard the word scaffolding. Maybe you could say it's irrational the way I did it, but I believed in it. So I invested all the money I had in this business.

I just went to see the company, and although it was bankrupted, I saw in it a huge development potential because scaffolding is needed all over the world. If you want to paint your ceiling, you need a scaffold. If you want to renovate the outside of your house, it's a scaffold. If you want to work at refineries, nuclear centers, airports, you need this.

I saw an opportunity and I saw a way of being close to my wife, to her village. You ask yourself, am I in the right place and doing the right thing? This is the sort of feeling.

In the next 30 years, Mohed Altrad not only turned this company around but added over 200 other scaffolding companies to his Altrad Group, making it world's number one scaffolding company. This earned him the title World Entrepreneur of the Year 2015. He told me the most valuable advice in his life was: "Believe. You should have some faith in what you are doing."

And believe me, this was the first time I'd heard the word scaffolding.

— Mohed Altrad #BillionDollarGoldNuggets

This youthful enthusiasm and sometimes even ignorance help you in achieving great things, because you don't know that it can't work or you don't realize how hard it's going to be, and you make it happen.

This was the attitude the business pioneers of the Polish transition to the free market in the 1990s like Michał Sołowow had: "The opportunities that emerged were used by many people back then. Eventually those were the same people who often took the greatest risk because—paradoxically—they had no experience. They didn't have historical knowledge, didn't know the difficulty of conditions, were not limited by knowledge. They didn't know 'there is no way.'"

Jack Cowin has similar thoughts when he looks back on his career:

One of the interesting things about youth is you don't know what you don't know. It's youthful enthusiasm of we're climbing the mountain and we don't know how high it is. Heads up in the clouds, but it's an adventure.

You don't know what the limitations are. If I knew then all the things I know now, we wouldn't have done half the things. Because we made a lot of mistakes. Expanded geographically way too soon. But we survived. We were at the front end. Today you'd have competitors who'd put you out of business. We didn't know anything. But you survive, you make it work.

Jack, being a Canadian, came to Australia with the desire to bring fast, affordable food to this country. His first business was a KFC store, and then he built Hungry Jack's and Domino's Pizza there and became a billionaire during that process.

If I knew then all the things I know now, we wouldn't have done half the things.

– Jack Cowin #BillionDollarGoldNuggets

This faith and unbounded optimism are visible in billionaires' biographies and attitude. You can see it when Frank Stronach came to America with $200 in his pocket and the faith to make it big here, or you can see it in billionaires' statements, like Ron Sim's. When I asked him what had been his greatest success, he answered: "I would say the next 10, 15 years, we will see our real winners. I will candidly say that I am far from my goal. The greatest things are yet to come."

Anything Is Possible

It's almost hackneyed to say, "Limits are only inside you." Everybody considers himself as having no limits. But in reality, most of us deal with huge mental limitations on a daily basis without being aware of it.

Dilip Shanghvi, the world's wealthiest man in pharmaceuticals, told me, "All of us are capable of far more than what we think we are. We have so much inherent potential. So believe in yourself."

Tim Draper has a similar perspective: "Anything that can be imagined can actually happen. I watched *Star Trek* when I was younger, and there's a communicator now—it's the smartphone—there's a holodeck—it's the VR—the tricorder reading, that's happening. We have pretty much done everything except space travel to all the different planets." One of his life mottoes is "Anything is possible."

But how to do the "anything"? Sergey Galitskiy founded Magnit, the largest supermarket chain in Europe with now over 17,000 supermarkets and drugstores. When I was interviewing him, they were opening five new stores every day. Can you imagine it? Imagine what is needed to open a supermarket. First you need to find land, then to negotiate and buy it, then you need to get all the permissions, then build the store, then install all the systems, hire and train people, organize supply and logistics, then actually supply it and market it to the customers, then you can open it. And they do it five times each and every day? How is it possible?

"The successful entrepreneurial life is in fact the denial that this or another thing is impossible. Each of partners would say that it is impossible to open five stores per day and I would say the same, but when you are in this mode, every day why not more, why not more. The fact that a company like this was set up in impossibly hard conditions and became successful is already the denial of everybody's thoughts at that time, and some people did think that it was not impossible."

Belief and Confidence

If you don't believe in yourself, success in business will be difficult. So believe in yourself! This is the advice Frank Hasenfratz would give his 20-year-old self.

Ron Sim is quite pragmatic: "I always say that you can have nothing, but when you believe in yourself, you can build something. You've got to have that. Don't listen too much. Focus on what you believe and what you want to do."

When I asked Petter Stordalen what piece of advice had been the most valuable for him, he answered: "Believe in your dreams."

Cho Tak Wong, founder of the world's largest auto glass manufacturer, Fuyao Glass, and the World Entrepreneur of the Year 2009, bases his success on belief: "Believe in yourself, believe in your vision, believe you can get the resources to make it happen and then give it a try." But it's not blind belief. "If you want to do a project, you have to do a feasibility study and use all related materials." Then you build your belief on the results of the study. For him, the way to success consists of three steps: belief, vision, and execution. Base your goals on what you believe and go for it.

Confidence is needed for business success. It means also believing in your skills.

Peter Hargreaves believed in his business skills more than in those of his employer. That's how he went into business. "I think I probably had enough of working for other people who were good people trying to do their best, but I could see that I could do it better." One day he went to the office of his boss and said: "Bill, you're a great salesman, and you're a great ideas man, but you're not a great businessman. You run the sales and let me run the business, and we'll be very successful." But Bill wouldn't believe that. And so Peter thought, "Well, I'll do it on my own." He left together with his colleague Stephen Lansdown to found their own company, Hargreaves Lansdown.

Result: They are both billionaires and the only people in the world who created an FTSE 100 company without borrowing or acquisitions. At the time of writing, Hargreaves Lansdown has around $120 billion under management.

You need to believe you are good at what you do. Peter, like many billionaires, isn't modest about his business skills: "I have to be honest. I didn't think there were very many good businessmen about. I actually didn't think there was much competition. And that was the joy of being in business. But whenever things didn't go too well, I used to look at other businesses and think, 'Well, we're better than all those businesses. We have nothing to worry about.'"

You should definitely believe in your choices and fight for them. Tim Draper, the legendary Silicon Valley venture capital investor, learned it the hard way:

I brought Google into the partnership and my partners said, "We have all of these other competitors that we've invested in; why do we need another search engine?" I said, "But it's a good group of people and all that." They said, "Yeah, but we have a competitor that has better technology, so why would we do this?" That was a big mistake that I let them talk me out of that one.

I should have pushed super hard and I should have said "we need this one too."

As we all know, Google won that race, bringing gigantic profits to early investors, and all Google competitors lost.

Because of their positive mindset, billionaires have a "can-do attitude," billionaires believe they can do it. Tony Tan Caktiong, the World Entrepreneur of the Year 2004, told me that a lot of times people would keep on saying, "Oh, it cannot be done, it cannot be done," but he being a positive person, never entertained such thoughts.

Billionaires have boundless trust in themselves. If they find something they like, they believe they are the best man for the given task. It doesn't mean billionaires are objectively best in everything. There are always people better in some aspects.

Don't diminish yourself. You can still believe from the bottom of your heart you are the right person, the most suitable person for the given challenge. Hüsnü Özyegin told me: "There were always guys in my classes who were smarter than I was. Even now I never think of myself as the smartest guy in the room. . . . I try to instill in the students confidence and courage. I tell them that if they believe and they work hard—I worked very hard—they can be successful like me. I also tell them you have to have it in the bottom of your heart."

This attitude allowed him to run for the office of student body president in an American university of 14,000 students, although he was a foreign student, and not a really good one. Of course, he succeeded.

You will be stunned by what 24-year-old Petter Stordalen experienced at the time he went to the Norwegian School of Marketing in Oslo:

In Kapital, a Norwegian equivalent of Forbes, he finds an ad for a job. A head-hunting company is looking for a CEO for a soon to-be-built shopping center in Trondheim. It will be the largest and most up-to-date shopping center in Norway. They are looking for a seasoned 40- to 45-year-old manager with at least 20 years of experience, and asking for a vita, references, and diplomas. It is quite a challenge for a student with no managerial experience whatsoever, who hasn't even finished his schooling yet. He receives discouragement from his fellow students: "You think you can have that job? Can't you read? 40 to 45! You are 24, Petter." His answer is, "I can do it, and this job is actually a perfect fit for me." His sense of pride is challenged; his ambitions awaken. After all, it is the hottest job offered in Norway, the dream job of every business school student.

So I did send an application, but I only had one thing: a paper from my father saying, "Petter's a good boy. He's a good worker." I didn't even have papers from the school. And of course, what happened? Nothing. I didn't hear anything.

Petter doesn't give up on his ambition. He comes day after day to the address he has sent the application to until he sees a light glowing on the fourth floor. He rings the bell and they let him in. "Hello, I am Petter Stordalen." He explains he hasn't been invited for an interview and wants to know what has happened. "But you are totally out of the question!"

"Me? I'm perfect for the job." Petter sits there for 90 minutes, as long as it is necessary. And although the head hunter has two candidates matching the criteria, which Petter doesn't fulfill, he gives in and agrees that Petter go to Trondheim to appear before the board as the third candidate.

So with all his juvenile naivete he goes to Trondheim full of faith in his abilities. Surprisingly, he convinces the board he is the right man for the job. They like this cheeky youngster. They are fascinated by his passion, his courage and grit. and they think they can better influence an inexperienced greenhorn than a sly old dog. He gets hired as the youngest shopping center manager ever and is responsible for the biggest retail project in Norway. It's called City Syd, the first huge suburban mall in Norway.

This was how Petter started his shopping center career. Later, he made his first million from a bonus he got in a project whose doability nobody but he believed in. It was a development project, and they said, "It's not possible to get those three shopping centers together and put a roof over it." But he did it. You make the most money on projects others consider impossible and thus don't do it.

Reading this story, you will understand why Mohed Altrad says you should have a mindset of "I can do whatever I want," but you also should be able to translate it into reality.

Learn to Deal with Skeptics

Only if you believe in your ideas, your convictions, can you get anything done and not get bogged down by skeptics. Don't let anyone tell you that what you are dreaming is not possible. Don't let them steal your dreams. Don't listen to the countless naysayers and grouches trying to keep you from taking bold steps. Don't let people discourage you.

Lirio Parisotto was dreaming of becoming a doctor. In Brazil, a competitive exam is needed to be admitted to medical school.

Sometimes you have 50 openings but you have 5,000 people applying for this. It's highly competitive.

Lirio's boss, whose son studied there, didn't have the best opinion of him and wanted to talk him out of this idea. "You are crazy! My son studies a lot, it's difficult! It's impossible for you."

Lirio spent one year preparing for the exam.

I studied in the morning, in the afternoon, in the nights. Because in the priest seminary, we didn't have mathematics, physics, chemistry . . . so I needed to improve on these special skills.

I took second place among all the contestants. When I saw my name in the newspaper that published the results, I put it under my arm and went to the director. "Read my name here. I am going to be a doctor." And then it's the same thing. . . . He was like, "It's impossible. You will never manage."

But Lirio managed. Several years later he successfully graduated from the university as doctor of medicine.

So go for the things you believe in. This is how several years later, Lirio got involved in the best opportunity of his career:

In 1986, I was invited by Sony to an annual meeting in Tokyo. I was at that time the best retailer for Sony tapes and equipment in my region. And in Japan, I discovered they had a laboratory where they recorded videocassettes.

I noticed they didn't have finished videocassettes. They had big rolls of magnetic tape and cassettes without video. When they received an order, they reloaded just the time they needed for the recording. You record 70 minutes, they load 71, one minute for the margin. So, they didn't lose tape.

Easy, but no one did that in Brazil at that time. Of course, the video business had just started. I realized that the most expensive part of the videocassette was the magnetic tape. In Brazil, at that time, you had just three lengths of tapes, T-60, T-120, and T-160. If you had a 10-minute documentary, you would need to use the 60-minute tape. There was a lot of waste.

And also, in Sony they produce the complete thing. They do all the service. They do the recording, subtitles, they reload the cassettes, and also they put the box and the label. They do the packaging and the distribution. They do everything. Vertical integration, if you will.

This was the best idea to make money in this business. Because in Brazil we had six factories for videotapes. You had many companies who did the recording. Many companies did the subtitles. One produced boxes, the other produced labels, so no one had an integrated operation. And when the laboratory did the recordings, they sent it back to the studios. They had the copyright to put in the boxes, put the labels, and also do the invoicing and the distribution.

I realized maybe it's time to change my business, because in retail, you have strong competition. It's difficult to make good money because you don't have your own product. You just resell the products which the other stores also carry.

I decided to sell the retail business and invest in buying professional machines for all the operations.

Lirio wanted to sell the business to Lojas Arno, his biggest competitor.

The first time I told him the idea, he didn't believe. "No, you want to leave this business? No. What are you going to do?" "I want to record videotapes." "Record tapes? I record tapes at home." he told me. You see something on TV or camera you record it. "No, it's a professional system. . . ."

He didn't realize how important this kind of business was. But I did. I had the Video Club and the Rental Video. I knew the market grew very fast. A lot of people were interested in this. They didn't need to go to the movies. They could watch movies at home.

At first he didn't believe I wanted to sell. After that he realized maybe it's important because this is the most aggressive competitor leaving the market. So it was very easy to sell.

I received $2 million for this sale. And then I had some money from the profits during this time. This was the money I invested to start in another industry and become a manufacturer.

Videolar became very profitable because I offered this full-service package.

In the end, I had all six major companies like Sony Pictures, Fox, Warner, Paramount, Universal, and Disney. All the six companies were manufacturing inside of our factory for the Brazilian market. This is the only place in the world where this happened. Usually they don't want this. But I was very competitive, big capacity. And it became possible basically due to service and quality.

Lirio managed to hold 90% of the entire market in his hand. Videolar made him a billionaire.

Many times, people will underestimate you. Don't let it discourage you.

Frank Stronach remembers the time when he became a major supplier for General Motors.

I had 100 factories already. I was giving a lecture at General Motors, and there were their key managers there. One of the key managers said mockingly, "Look, if you grow that fast, you're going to be larger than General Motors." "Yeah," I said, "it's just a question of time before I take over General Motors."

They were laughing, and clapping. The idea seemed ridiculous to them.

But then, several years later, Frank actually had the opportunity and ability to really take a big chunk of General Motors.

We were bidding for Adam Opel AG, so to speak the European part of the corporation, and if politics didn't get into play, we would have taken it over.

Today, Frank is called the Magna man. He built one of the largest auto parts manufacturers in the world with close to $40 billion in sales and over 160,000 employees. Frank is one of the most powerful people in the industry.

So never get discouraged if people are trying to belittle you.

Don't let ridicule put you down. Tim Draper offers the right perspective on it:

If you're trying to do something extraordinary, you will be ridiculed.

Take Elon Musk. He was saying we're going to Mars. I'm sure he would get ridiculed by people who'd say, "You're never going to get to Mars. Are you crazy?" But there would be a few people, maybe 5%, who'd say, "Hey, how would we get to Mars?"

He has to put up with that ridicule for a long time, but each day he goes back and life still goes on. It doesn't affect his life. He still has a place to sleep and something to eat, and everything's fine.

If you're trying to do something extraordinary, you will be ridiculed.

— Tim Draper #BillionDollarGoldNuggets

Don't Get Overconfident

But there is also a flip side of your B.O.A.T. It's called overconfidence. In Germany, we say, "Arrogance comes before you fall." Overconfidence can slow you down or even destroy you. It is a dangerous pitfall especially if you have been successful in the past. If you get overconfident or too optimistic, your B.O.A.T. may flip over and you may drown. Don't let it happen!

Don't think you are invincible. Graveyards are full of invincible people. Don't let your success get in your way. Hüsnü Özyegin told me: "I think one of the most difficult things in life is for success not to lead to overconfidence. That's when you start to make mistakes. You maybe ask less questions, don't assess risks as diligently as you would, and begin to think you are invincible."

When I asked Petter Stordalen what had been the most dangerous idea he had had in his life, he surprised me with his answer: "The idea that I have succeeded. That I am immortal. That I am invulnerable. The next thing you know you are fired. It happened to me in Steen & Strøm. I thought they thought that I was irreplaceable. That was a part of my downfall."

Let me tell you the story of Cai Dongqing and his first ventures to illustrate to you what I mean by not letting your confidence become overconfidence.

Cai Dongqing wanted to start a business when he was 15. His father didn't believe in him and wanted him to find a job and work for others. However, it didn't lower Cai's desire to go on his own. This desire was supported by his mother, who borrowed RMB800 (around $100) for him to start up a business. He and his two brothers set up a workshop. His first product was a little plastic trumpet. They didn't have electricity at that time. They used diesel as the power to drive and heat. When manufacturing the trumpet, they needed to manually handle the machine to press the plastic into the form. This project was a success, and it encouraged Cai to do a bigger thing.

Because we did well in the first project, one of my relatives wanted to cooperate with me to do a bigger business. Our product was some fobs, small decorations of the key rings which had a plastic plate with a popular star's photo in it. Led by him, we began to expand and focus on sales volume.

However, they got overconfident and expanded too aggressively, buying too much equipment. It ended up a failure. Cai Dongqing not only lost all the earnings from his first project, he also ran into debt.

It's time to float your B.O.A.T., my dear reader! Do you believe in yourself and are optimistic about what you can achieve? Do you get discouraged by the naysayers, or are you assertive with them? Do you trust in your skills enough to make it big in business?

- Drifters don't believe in themselves and get easily discouraged by skeptics.

- Millionaires have limiting beliefs and thus pursue small dreams.

- Billionaires believe anything is possible and that they can achieve it.

For more stories on this topic, go to:
http://TheBillionDollarSecret.com/resources

CHAPTER 5

The Gold Digger's Trap

I was worth over a million dollars when I was 23,
and over 10 million dollars when I was 24,
and over 100 million dollars when I was 25.
And it wasn't that important,
because I never did it for the money.

—Steve Jobs

Money plays an important role in business. But it is a fallacy to think business is about money. Money is just the universal benchmark that you can use to measure performance in business. If you compare business to sports, money plays the role of the score. Better scores mean better performance and help you play the game at higher and higher levels, compete with better and better players.

Of course, you feel a sense of achievement when you are a winner in the business game. Michał Sołowow, the wealthiest person in Poland, likens it to the Olympics, where you get the gold medal as a symbol of your victory. But it's not the gold in the medal that you crave:

In business, things are as in every sports discipline: the runner at the Olympics runs for a medal. That medal will hang only on his own chest. From this medal he will have lucrative advertising contracts and appearance fees for participation in meetings later on. But when he stands on a podium and they play him the national anthem of his country, then he is moved, happy that he did something for people, that he fulfilled those people's craving for emotion and pride.

Money is not the primary factor in business.

Naveen Jain, the American space entrepreneur, told me: "Making money is a by-product of doing things."

Mohed Altrad, the World Entrepreneur of the Year 2015, cautions not to equate success with money:

Don't consider money as an objective, but as a sign of success. It's one of the signs of success. The success of the organization is to be sustainable, in which people are happy, in which humanity finds its foundation. That's the success. Tell me, what's the difference if you have 1 billion Euros in your pocket or 2 billion Euros? It doesn't really make a difference.

> **Don't consider money as an objective, but as a sign of success. It's one of the signs of success.**
>
> **– Mohed Altrad #BillionDollarGoldNuggets**

If Your Only Objective Is Money or Personal Luxury, You Will Fail

Mohed made it quite clear with this story he told me when I visited him:

I met a lot of people who started business more or less at the same time as me. Their objective was to create an organization they could sell at a high price at a given moment. Some of them failed immediately. Some of them reached some level of success, and somebody offered them, say, 1 million Euros for their business. They said, "That's not enough. I'll carry on. I want to grow it further." And then maybe a few years after, they were offered 100 million Euros. They said, "Not enough. I want 1 billion Euros." Then they worked hard to reach 1 billion Euros. Unfortunately, they failed. They went bankrupt. They got zero.

That's to say, if your company's only objective is money, this is a failure.

Making money is a by-product of doing things.

— Naveen Jain #BillionDollarGoldNuggets

Motivation is the main difference between the billionaires and the millionaires. If you do it for money, to live in luxury, you will lose your motivation as soon as you have reached that level, and you stay a millionaire or even lose it all, when your business suffers. But if you are motivated by competition, by winning, when the business game itself excites you, then you will keep on growing your company, and only then do you have a chance to reach billions.

If your company's only objective is money, this is a failure.

— Mohed Altrad #BillionDollarGoldNuggets

I asked Petter Stordalen, called the Hotel King in Scandinavia, about wealth-building advice. His answer:

Billionaires don't do it for the money. It's not the money that drives them, but the fun of the game.

It is about never settling, never getting comfortable, never longing for retirement. If you just try to get rich, you'll never get there. If you find and do what you love, you might stand a chance. If you are prepared to work very hard for it.

Do you think money can be a motivation? The game, the competition. That's the thing. And that's why I say, if you start with a calculator in your hand, you will go nowhere. I think a lot of people will have the same motivation like I have. Some do it in academia. Not much money. In science, not much money. But they still have the same thing. They get the Nobel Peace Prize in Stockholm or Nobel Prize in Stockholm in medicine or in physics or in chemistry.

If you do it for money, to live in luxury, you will lose your motivation as soon as you have reached that level, and you stay a millionaire or even lose it all, when your business suffers.

— Rafael Badziag @BillionairePal #BillionDollarGoldNuggets

Peter Hargreaves built Hargreaves Lansdown, the go-to financial services company in the United Kingdom with over $120 billion under management. Considering the industry he is in, Peter gave me surprising reasons for his success:

I think there are two reasons for my success. One is I love it, and the other one is I never did it for what money brought me, even though money keeps the score; I did it purely for the success.

I know another guy who's worked in this industry, and he always thought he was more successful than me, and of course, the last few years have proved otherwise, but he did it for the money, whereas I did it because I enjoyed it, and that was the most important thing. I loved every minute of it. I'd go back and do it again.

Billionaires don't do it for the money. It's not the money that drives them, but the fun of the game.

— Petter Stordalen #BillionDollarGoldNuggets

No amount of money will make it for you. This is something that Naveen Jain realized in America. He suffered poverty in India and also in the first year in the United States, which he spent in New Jersey. Craving money, he moved to California, where an Indian friend of his had just sold his business for $100,000.

And I said, God, what if I ever had $100,000 just like him? I would never have to work for a living in my life. My dreams would be true. Everything I ever wanted in my life. I would have made it. I would have just arrived.

Time went by and I left Silicon Valley and joined Microsoft, very early when Microsoft was a tiny company, had just gone public. And right after I joined, they came out with Windows 3.0, and the stock just exploded. Within six months, my stock options are now worth over $100,000.

Now, I should be happy. It suddenly occurred to me I forgot I have to pay tax. So $100,000 really doesn't mean anything unless you have $100,000 after tax. A month goes by, and now I have $150,000. After tax, I have $100,000.

My mind said, what I really meant was not having $100,000, you have to have a house. We really need to be able to have a house and $100,000. That's what really was going to make me happy.

Great. So we now have enough money to be able to buy a small house and $100,000. And it occurred to me, the house has to be comfortable enough for us to have a big family. After all, you can't just have a small house. So it has to be a decent-sized house and $100,000.

So now, you have money to have a decent house and $100,000. My mind said, times have really changed, and $100,000 really can't buy you anything. You have to have at least a million dollars if you're going to be comfortable living.

Guess what happens? You have a million dollars now. Point of the story was there was never a time you got tired and said my God, I just have enough money. It didn't matter how much you had, there would always be the next goal that you wanted. So point was that happiness didn't come to a guy who came from India. At the beginning, all he wanted was $100,000. And it didn't matter. It was never enough until your mind changed. And that to me is the story of how life changes.

If you just try to get rich, you'll never get there.

— Petter Stordalen #BillionDollarGoldNuggets

Ten Billionaire Motivations

Don't do it for the money. Billionaires have different motivations that allowed them to get that far. They like to create. It makes them get up in the morning. They love building businesses, improving them, optimizing their business models or processes, and most of all they love to see them grow.

If you start with a calculator in your hand, you will go nowhere.

— Petter Stordalen #BillionDollarGoldNuggets

1. Getting Out of Poverty

For many self-made billionaires, their first motivation was just to get out of poverty. Naveen Jain was born in rural India. I asked him who he wanted to become in his youth. "Oh God, I just wanted to get out of the poverty and do something useful in my life." He remembers vividly:

My mother was completely illiterate. And my only memory that I have is of my mother making sure that I got an education and her sitting down and asking me to solve a problem without me realizing she can't read.

And mom would say, "Give me your homework. Point to me and tell me the answer to this problem." And I would diligently write down and say, "Mom, the answer is this." And my mom would be stern and say, "Don't make me do it again." And I would do it again, and then mom would say, "Now, go to the next one."

And it was just her serious love wanting to make sure that we got out of the cycle of poverty. And she knew the only way you would do it would be through education.

> ## I never did it for what money brought me, even though money keeps the score; I did it purely for the success.
>
> **— Peter Hargreaves #BillionDollarGoldNuggets**

Lirio Parisotto, who was born on a Brazilian farm with no running water, didn't have a specific dream at the beginning; he just wanted to leave the farm, to get out of poverty. "The service in the farm was hard. Plowing was the most difficult. We did it with the bull, not the tractor. I hated that because it was hard and hot. For most of the services at the farm, it's easy when you got mechanical support. But we didn't have electricity, we didn't have a tractor, nothing. And in fact, I didn't know what I wanted. But one thing I didn't want was to stay there. So basically, my drive was to change my life."

> ## No amount of money will make it for you.
>
> **— Naveen Jain #BillionDollarGoldNuggets**

2. Freedom

Freedom is another major billionaire motivation. Some of my interviewees recognized early in their lives that escaping poverty would make them free. Frank Stronach grew up in postwar Austria and experienced hunger in his youth. He confessed to me:

I just wanted to work so I won't be hungry. And I wanted to work to be free, so I don't have to crawl and say "yes sir." My motivation was never to be hungry anymore. Be a free man.

This notion changed later to economic freedom:

If you're not economically free, you're not a free person. I wanted to be a free person. So I can say anything I want to say and can do the things I want to do.

And then to making other people free by saving them from poverty:

In the beginning, it was a question of not being hungry anymore. I'm also fighting for others, because I don't want to see anybody being hungry.

Freedom has a lot to do with having control over your life. That's also the case with Jack Cowin:

My main drive from the beginning was to have something that I could have some influence and control over and be a free person to do what I wanted.

3. Survival

But before you can become free, you and your business first need to survive:

When you start a business, the number one factor is survival. Will I survive? That is the number one drive. Survival. Not everybody admits it, but fear of failure, for most entrepreneurs I know, is a real-life factor.

So from the beginning, all you wanted to do is survive with the hope that this may turn into something that you're proud of having been part of, that people don't hate you for having ruined their lives because the thing went broke.

Of course, as your business grows, your motivations also develop.

4. Solving Problems

Billionaires focus on solving problems, not on making money. "If you want to be really successful in business, first find a problem to solve," advises Dilip Shanghvi. "If you can solve a problem that is currently unsolved, you can create an interesting business opportunity. Don't start a business to make money as an objective, money is just an outcome."

Michał Sołowow has a similar perspective: "I am motivated by problems. Every day I want things to work better. Those problems that I encounter in everyday life lead me to solving them. In other words, it's a self-propelling mechanism. I don't find motivation in being a billionaire or becoming a billionaire. It really doesn't turn me on."

5. Doing Things Well and Improving

What turns him on is to do things well: "I think that I am driven by a desire to do things well, not perfectly, but well. I say this consciously. If things are carried out well and they are better and better, then I definitely draw satisfaction from that. If I understand something and it happens as I have expected and I have certain effects—well, also those measurable in money after all—then that certainly gives me a lot of fun."

Petter Stordalen wants "to do things better today than yesterday, but not as good as tomorrow."

Tony Tan Caktiong's motivation is high quality as well: "I am happy when in business we achieve really good products. We have really good food and we really enjoy that." That's how the World Entrepreneur of the Year 2004 thinks.

I am driven by a desire to do things well, not perfectly, but well.

— Michał Sołowow #BillionDollarGoldNuggets

6. Doing Something New

For many billionaires, the venture itself is their motivation. Trying new things, breaking new ground, acquiring new knowledge. That's what drives them.

For Dilip Shanghvi, opportunity is the greatest source of motivation.

Petter Stordalen describes it as follows: "It's the willingness to leave behind, to seek new ventures, to take a leap, to take a step out, but you don't know how deep, how long. Just to go. Also to see opportunities where others don't see them."

For Manny Stul, the Australian toy maker and the World Entrepreneur of the Year 2016, the motivation is "breaking new ground, doing stuff that's different, acquiring new knowledge. Not standing still, that's the important thing. I find the new directions we're going to as a company and the new avenues we're going into extremely exciting. It's new and it's different. If we kept doing the same thing over and over, I'd be bored."

Tim Draper expresses it in clear words: "The world is discoverable. We should all discover it."

Don't start a business to make money as an objective, money is just an outcome.

– Dilip Shanghvi #BillionDollarGoldNuggets

7. Playing the Game of Business

A common denominator for all the billionaires is that they are passionate about business itself. They consider it to be great fun. If there is something like a natural-born businessman, it is Peter Hargreaves: "I love it. Do you know, I have no other great passion outside this business. I do a bit of fishing, I do a bit of golf—I'm crap at golf. I keep fit, I go to the gym. I love travel. But I'm passionate about the business. Completely passionate about it. It's my life's work. Of course, you're more passionate because it's so damn successful."

8. Competition and Winning

And here we come to the next billionaire motivation: winning. In order to win, you need to become the best, and for that you need to compete.

Peter Hargreaves remembers how he set up the goal for the company he created with Stephen Lansdown: "I just knew I wanted to be the biggest. And Stephen always said he wanted to be the best, and of course, you can't be the biggest unless you are the best. Did I envisage this success? Well, yes. The only thing I could not have envisaged was the size of the numbers. I could not have envisioned this business could be worth 7 billion pounds. I could not have imagined that we would hold 40-odd billion pounds of the clients' money (meanwhile it's over $120 billion). I couldn't have envisaged that my personal wealth would be this big, but I did envisage that we could be the biggest retailer in investments in the United Kingdom. I just didn't realize how big the numbers would be to be in that situation."

For Sergey Galitskiy, the first motivation was survival because he needed to feed his family. But then it changed to competition and winning: "My first meeting with my competition was a game changer. I didn't see any intellectual superiority on their part, and those were the strongest of competitors. And when you feel somebody's intellectual superiority, it wears you down, it pushes you down, and then you have to position yourself differently. But when you don't feel it, then you start realizing that you can become number one. And when you consider the scale size of this country, it inspires you. And the feeling and understanding that intellectually they were not stronger, it became an obsession for me."

The main motivation for Manny Stul is to succeed, to win. Ron Sim is motivated by achievements, Cho Tak Wong by success: "Everything I plan becomes a success."

9. Building and Creating

Billionaires are creators, they take pleasure in making their visions become reality, they play with their power to bring things to life.

Tony Tan Caktiong is clear about his motivation: "I just want to do things. I just want to build bigger things, bigger dreams."

Frank Hasenfratz is a creator as well: "I've got all the money in the world, but I'm at work every day." For him, it is about building a sustainable business: "Why do you want business? Is it money? Because money, of course, is a motivator. But to me, to build something that lasts is most gratifying. You know, we are over 50 years old, and we have second and third generation working here. It is really satisfying."

For others, like Chip Wilson, it's about leaving a dent in the world: "You get to where anything material in life that I want, I can have. So then I think the dream is to be able to leave the world with a mark on it that lasts for generations. I think of some of the major parks in the world, and cities, that people can enjoy for ever and ever. Something like that."

10. Social Impact

Another thing that Chip is excited about is social impact: "Money doesn't necessarily get me up in the morning. What gets me up in the morning is changing people's lives and focusing in first on people, their development. And because I'm very selfish, I want to be with people that I like to be with every day, and I find if the people I'm with are incredible, then my life is fun and it's incredible, and then great businesses occur out of that."

"You have an opportunity to make an impact, and you have about 80 years to do it. GO!" This is Tim Draper's life philosophy in a nutshell. That's why he is committed to spread entrepreneurship and venture capital around the world.

You have an opportunity to make an impact, and you have about 80 years to do it. GO!

— Tim Draper #BillionDollarGoldNuggets

Social impact is exactly the reason why the earlier leftist Narayana Murthy got convinced that business was the way to go:

As a child who grew up under the larger-than-life presence of Nehru, a socialist, it was very easy for me to be a sympathizer with socialism and communism leaders who rode the bandwagon of anticolonialism.

But I realized that the only way societies could solve the problem of poverty is through creation of jobs with good income and that entrepreneurship was the best instrument for such a solution.

You can't create wealth by sharing poverty. There is no way you can do that miracle. Not even by the magicians of communism.

This became Narayana's main motivation in business.

I am driven every day to go to office at 6 a.m. by my belief that the only way we can solve the problem of poverty in this world is through the creation of more and more, better and better income jobs. The fact that God has given this opportunity is my main motivation.

You can't create wealth by sharing poverty.

— Narayana Murthy #BillionDollarGoldNuggets

All of my interviewees have significant positive impact on our world. They touch the lives of millions through their products, their employees, or their philanthropic activities.

Motivation Changes

Of course, your motivation changes as you grow as a person.

Cai Dongqing's motivation changed from taking care of his family to doing something of value for society through his company:

The initial motivation was my desire to change the destiny of my family and the strong sense of responsibility to take care of my family and little brothers. Later on, in view of several successful strategic transformations of the company, Alpha is gradually forging ahead in China's pan-entertainment industry. Looking forward, I hope the company will be able to have a far-reaching influence on people's lives as we consistently bring dreams, joy, and wisdom to the world, which I think is the source of motivation along the way.

Kim Beom-Su dominates the modern communication channels in Korean society with his mobile messenger Kakao. His motivation shifted from success oriented to impact oriented:

There are two main stages. The first stage, when I started Hangame, I was interested in success, making a lot of money, achieving success, growing the company, etc.

Today, Kakao is doing what's called social impact, where we use our influence to bring about meaningful change in society, and this is the main motivation. What's so unique about Kakao is that it can influence the whole nation, even more than a government can. It gives me a sense of responsibility.

Mohed Altrad is humble also when talking about his motivation:

Very often it's personal. You are a foreigner, you are not from this country. And although you have a French passport, you're still a foreigner. I feel very strongly you have to prove, maybe 10 times more than a normal French person, I might say, that you earn your place in this country. And also prove it to your family and friends.

If everybody would only prove that they deserve their place in society, how much better would the world be?

What Is Your Why?

"Live life for a very good purpose" was the most valuable advice that Ron Sim has gotten in his life.

You are here for a purpose. Find it and do your best out of your life.

That's how Naveen Jain looks at life:

I'm not a religious guy, so I kind of see life as: "You must be here for a purpose." So if you are here for a purpose, you've got to maximize and be as useful as you can be, and make something out of nothing for yourself, for your family, for your friends, for your people. And leave something behind that probably people can learn from.

Sometimes, a purpose comes naturally to your life, especially for migrants like Jack Cowin, who came from Canada to build his life in Australia. "When you arrive in a new country, you just have to be successful. You just don't relax and go to the beach. You're there for a purpose, and you have to get established, and you don't have all the friends and family and things like this that you do when you grow up, wherever you grow up. I often think if I'd stayed in Canada, what would have happened to me? As to whether or not I would've gone."

Finding a purpose is as simple as finding out what you want and following it.

Manny Stul, the later World Entrepreneur of the Year 2016, at some point in his life knew he wanted to go into business.

From my experience at the bank, from my experience at auditing, from my experience at pulling beer, etc., I knew I didn't want to work for somebody else. I'm not talking about other people, but for me, I wasn't going to be successful working for somebody else.

To start a business, he needed some capital.

So I got a job on a construction site in the northwest of Australia for nine months. I wanted to raise some money, and that was the quickest way of raising money because it was high wages and nothing to spend your money on, except alcohol.

You live in these dongas, which is basically a tin shed. It's very hot up there. Everything was red dust. If there was any sort of wind, you'd go into the shower, and by the time you got back to your donga you had red dust on you.

We were building a ship loader for Dampier Salt. I was an office manager there.

Saved up about ten, twelve thousand dollars, then came back to Perth to start up this gift company.

Is there a method to find out what you want to do in business?

Chip Wilson says, yes. It's called the Hedgehog Principle.

You draw three overlapping circles. In the first one, you put all the things you are passionate about. In the second one, all the things you are or can be very good at, if possible the best in the world. And in the third one, all the things that can be profitable. In the intersection of these three circles, you will find the things that in your case are viable for a sustainable business venture. Choose one as the one you want to do and go for it!

And what's your motivation, my dear reader? Are you out for money or is it something else that drives you? Find your purpose, follow it, and avoid the gold digger's trap if you want to stand a chance of reaching billions.

- Drifters want to have income and never achieve personal wealth.

- Millionaires want to have personal wealth and lose their motivation when they achieve it.

- Billionaires are motivated by other things than personal wealth, they have a strong sense of purpose, and they never lose their motivation to grow.

For more stories on this topic, go to:
http://TheBillionDollarSecret.com/resources

CHAPTER 6

The Six Skills
of Business Mastery

Force has no place where there is need of skill.

—Herodotus

Billionaires are by no means ideals. They have their weaknesses and vices just like you and me. They just have the right set of skills, the right habits, and the right mindset that make them so extremely successful in business.

Take Lirio Parisotto. He's always had a problem with keeping a diet and losing weight. Don't get me wrong; he isn't obese or fat, but he has more weight that he would like to. He told me jokingly: "It's not difficult to make a lot of money. What is difficult is to make a lot of money and not put on weight."

As Cai Dongqing, the Walt Disney of China, said, "whether millionaires are able to continue their success into the next stage has a lot to do with their mindset, knowledge, personality, and skills."

So, if you want to step up your game, make sure you develop the following six universal skills of business mastery that you will need independently of the industry.

Skill 1: Logical Thinking

It's quite obvious that in order to do business you need common sense, but this skill can't be missing in this list. You absolutely need to think logically. Realize that your brain is your most valuable asset. And the better you can use it, the further you will get.

When I asked billionaires about their strong points, they almost unanimously gave common sense or logical thinking or the combination of these two in their answers.

Logical thinking is the first of the four qualities of a successful businessperson that Sergey Galitskiy provides (the other three being dreaming, taking risks, and diligence). And of course the faster you can think, the better. Playing chess in his youth helped Sergey to develop proficiency in thinking logically quickly.

And Manny Stul, the World Entrepreneur of the Year 2016, when asked the same question, told me: "I think common sense is a huge factor. Again, it's not about formal education. You can't be taught common sense." You need to develop it yourself.

In business, you deal with numbers, so you better be good at counting.

"Scientific mind definitely helps; counting is one of the basic and universal skills that are useful in many areas," says Michał Sołowow, the wealthiest person in Poland. "This world is based on numbers. A success in business is about numbers. You know, mathematics is also—on a humanistic level—in major part, a formal logic. If you know mathematical functions, then you also have ability in logical reasoning, arriving at conclusions. . . ."

Jack Cowin told me, "You have to be able to count, so that you don't run out of money."

Skill 2: Understanding People

You do business with people. You can't be successful in business unless you understand people. You need to understand what drives them and what triggers their emotions. Other people can be your greatest obstacle or your vehicle to success. Learn to cope with them.

You can't be successful in business unless you understand people.

— Rafael Badziag @BillionairePal #BillionDollarGoldNuggets

When I asked Jack Cowin what determined his success, he answered:

Probably the ability to understand people, what they want, how you enable them to achieve their goals while at the same time helping me achieve mine. So how do I get you to say, "Okay, I'm prepared to spend 5 or 10 years of my life trying to take on this project and make this work," which helps me get to where I want to go, and understand how I'm going to frame that and how I'm going to reward you, where you're going to live, what you're going to do. If I had one element of success, that's probably what it is.

Other people can be your greatest obstacle or your vehicle to success. Learn to cope with them.

— Rafael Badziag @BillionairePal #BillionDollarGoldNuggets

For Michał Sołowow, "the ideal combination for a businessperson is someone who can count and has light humanistic or psychological-sociological cravings. A person who naturally interacts with people must recognize their behavior, signals that they respond to, and with time indeed becomes a psychologist."

The ideal combination for a businessperson is someone who can count and has light humanistic or psychological-sociological cravings.

– Michał Sołowow #BillionDollarGoldNuggets

Some billionaires even went so far as to study the human mind in-depth at the university, like Lirio Parisotto:

I don't think you're successful in business unless you understand people. One of my favorite subjects during medical school was psychiatry. People say, "Oh, did you do accounting? Did you do finance?" And my answer is, "No, I didn't. You can hire accountants, you can hire lawyers, you can hire professional people." Business is all about people. How do you get them to do what you want them to do? How do you reward them? How do you make them feel good about themselves? How do you get them to accept the direction?

Business is all about people.

– Lirio Parisotto #BillionDollarGoldNuggets

But only understanding people is not enough. You should be able to see things from other people's perspective, empathize with them.

According to Sergey Galitskiy's business partner, Vladimir Gordeychuk, "Sergey can put himself in the shoes of another person, and he feels and sees and gets people very well. And that allows him to use the energy of other people in a correct way and guide them correctly."

Manny Stul learned to read people before he went into business by playing cards. He gambled a lot. Five-card stud was the game.

I made a lot of money. No, it wasn't through counting cards. If you sit there long enough, you understand the way people behave.

There's a joke about a dog playing cards with his owner. The guy watching can't believe it. The dog gets five cards, and he throws in three and he asks for another three, and he's sitting there and he's gambling with the owner. The guy sees this happen two or three times. He says to the owner, "That has got to be the smartest dog I've ever met." The owner calls him over and whispers in his ear, "He's not that smart. Every time he's got a good hand, he wags his tail."

Most people, nearly all people, when they've got a good hand or they're unbeatable or if they're bluffing, they'll wag their tail.

If you watch them long enough—it takes a long time—they'll have certain things. They'll play with the money in front of them, they won't play with the money in front of them. They'll pick up a lighted cigarette, they won't pick up a lighted cigarette. They'll look you in the eye, they can't look you in the eye. They'll start talking, they talk a lot, or they become very silent. It's a study in behavior. If you study it for long enough, people do certain things when they are unbeatable, and people do certain things when they're bluffing. I'm talking about the regular guys.

The professional guys wear glasses and a hat and they just sit there and do nothing. You can't read. There's nothing to read.

I certainly understand people in terms of dealing with them. You don't always get it right, of course, but most of the time I can understand the situation. I can understand what's going on. I can understand intuitively whether somebody's telling the truth or not. Very important. Very important to be able to read people. And I try these days not to do business with people I don't like or I don't trust. I sure as hell won't invest with them.

Skill 3: Relationships

Doing business means building relationships with people. This has always been among the skills that the interviewed billionaires named as essential for a businessperson or that had made them successful.

Naveen Jain, who built several billion-dollar companies, explains it in simple terms:

To me, everything is done by people. If I want to do business with IBM, I never look at IBM as a company because there is a person who you're talking to. And you need to understand and build trust with that person. And that person represents the company.

Most entrepreneurs go wrong because they say, "I want to do business with IBM." And they don't realize these companies are entities that are hollow. It's the person behind it that you really need to know and build trust with. And sometimes trust takes long time, sometimes it takes less time, but there's just no easy way out.

Look at Sean Rad of Tinder that you just met. I have met Sean maybe three or four times, but we have built this amazingly trusting relationship where we are able to share each other's secrets and vulnerabilities.

Relationships are the foundation of a sustainable business.

Jack Cowin, who as a foreigner started with zero and made billions by bringing convenient, affordable food to Australia, is considered a people person.

His relationship skills are astounding, his friendliness legendary. I asked him about the importance of relationships in business. Here is his answer:

Relationships for me are what it's all about. Business is about people and relationships. How do you get them to cooperate, do it together rather than against each other. So to me, if there's one thing that's important, that's it: relationships.

How to Learn Human Relations Skills

Human relations skills need to be developed relatively early in life. They don't change that much during your career.

Hüsnü Özyegin developed them in high school, where he was in a dorm and took advantage of numerous extracurricular activities, like basketball, volleyball, drama club. That allowed him later to become the president of the student body.

But the most important thing he learned at the university: "When I attended Harvard Business School, there were courses like accounting, marketing, financial management, investment management, management in lending, which I found relatively easy to follow, but I could not understand the course about human behavior in organizations, because I had no experience in organizations. But then during my business life, I thought that was the most important class that I attended. Because that's a skill which is very difficult to teach, and as people climb up the ladders of management, they learn about technical things more, but believe me, their human relations skills do not change that much."

Surround Yourself with the Right People

It is important to surround yourself with the right people.

Hüsnü Özyegin stresses the importance of this:

My father always said, "I know you have good grades, but make sure you have good friends." Who you make friends with, that's also very important in business. There are certain people you should not associate with.

The people you have around you determine your future. You need to choose them carefully.

Good Relationships

It's not the size of your network that matters, it's the depth of the relationships. Invest time and effort in maintaining them.

Dilip Shanghvi doesn't have a huge network of relationships, "but with whomever I have a relationship, I have a really deep relationship. It's clearly not about the quantity. But then I will go out of my way to help them, and they will also go out of their way to help me. It's not possible to do it for a large number of people. Life is too short to fight with people. So build and nurture relationships that you have."

Naveen Jain learned about building good relationships from Eastern philosophy.

Real relationships are built when you are able to be vulnerable. And because you are vulnerable and you are at the emotional level with people, it releases oxytocin, which is actually a true sign of bonding. And bonding only happens when you are able to make an emotional connection with someone rather than just an intellectual connection. When you have close bonding, it also creates the trust. And then you are able to have deep conversations. And when you build the trust, the business gets done. So what I realized is being honest and true to yourself and being vulnerable even though every business book will tell you, "Don't let them see you sweat. Man, don't get emotional." I don't have a problem talking about my life. And I find more business gets done with more people because I'm able to build real deep relationships.

Build relationships based on trust. This is something Naveen can't stress enough:

To me, the most important way of doing business is through building trust. That means getting to know the person. Trust takes time. I am a person who is willing to spend time with someone to get to know him as a human being before I do business with them.

The thing I am going to tell you is the secret to success. People do business with people. It is me doing business with you. It is not my company doing business with your company.

Here is what I have realized. If you go against your gut feeling of trust, those businesses never last. If I don't like someone or I don't trust someone, sooner or later I will find a reason not to trust you and get out of the business.

If you trust someone even though they're a hiccup, you say, "You know, I trust you but this thing that happened, can you fix it for me?" And they will do it. They'll go out of their way to fix it if you trust them.

Life is too short to fight with people. So build and nurture relationships that you have.

— Dilip Shanghvi #BillionDollarGoldNuggets

Skill 4: Communication

Communication skills are built on your people skills and allow you to be more effective in your business endeavors. Communication and storytelling are indispensable in public relations, marketing, and also sales.

Build relationships based on trust.

– Naveen Jain #BillionDollarGoldNuggets

Great communication skills will help you in every stage of your business.

Probably the best communicator I have met during this project is Petter Stordalen. I asked him what he would do if he had to start from zero again with no money. "I would find the best hotel manager ever in Norway and convince him that we should start a company together." It sounds so easy when you can use your words properly.

Petter is also an excellent storyteller, a quality most self-made billionaires possess. A good example of the power of storytelling is the hotel the Thief.

When we made the Thief, everybody said, "Just to name the hotel the Thief, people will think they are robbed. Because you say it will be the most expensive hotel in Oslo. You have the highest room rate. People will say, 'I stayed at the Thief, I was robbed.'"

And I turned out to be the other way around. Storytelling is everything. This used to be the island of the thieves, the robbers, the prostitutes. The last criminal that was executed in Norway was hanged here. So we have the story. This is the island of the thieves, and we made this hotel with The Horse Thief, *the original artwork by Richard Prince, one of the world's most famous photographers, in the reception.*

One guy told me, "Petter, why don't you have security in front of that picture? What will you do if somebody steals it?"

Just imagine, The Horse Thief *stolen at the Thief Hotel in Oslo. It will be on CNN, Wall Street, everybody will talk about it. It's perfect marketing. The only people who will cry will be the insurance company.*

We were sitting in the restaurant, on the wall was an interesting painting. I asked Petter how much it was.

This painting? It's $2 million. Andy Warhol, original. Where is the security? Nothing.

Condé Nast is the most famous traveling magazine. We have been featured there among 50 Top New Hotels in the World, we have been in the Wall Street

Journal, *the* Guardian. *Because we started the storytelling before we started the hotel. We had Sir Peter Blake to the hotel. We had a book about all the people who haven't had a great life but finally succeeded, and we said, "This was our beginning, and this is the biggest move ever from the island of the thief to the only new five-star hotel opening in Oslo in the last hundred years."*

And now, all the stars want to stay here. We made magic before we opened.

This is the power of storytelling.

People do business with people.

– Naveen Jain #BillionDollarGoldNuggets

You may say, and what if somebody isn't born an extrovert? Is it possible then to learn to communicate effectively?

Some billionaires among my interviewees are born introverts. Nevertheless, they managed to hone their communication skills during their career. Kim Beom-Su had a technical background, but he did a lot of projects when he worked for Samsung and did street marketing around universities, "so doing these things, I think I've overcome a lot of that."

Skill 5: Selling

Without sales there is no business! If you want to be successful in business, become a good salesperson. All the billionaires I interviewed are excellent salespeople.

Jack Cowin considers selling a significant skill that determined his success. He learned to sell in his childhood enterprises. "I remember as a kid, in the middle of summer, selling personalized Christmas cards with your name on it that you're going to send out." When he was going to university, he perfected his selling skills.

I got involved in a business selling nursery stock—trees, shrubs, plants—door to door, farm to farm. One of my professors said that one of the things he found very unfair was the fact that I was making as much money during the summer as a salesman as he was making a year as a university professor.

Even in a communist country like China, selling skills are key.

Interestingly, Cho Tak Wong, the World Entrepreneur of the Year 2009, learned to sell during his first job in the very same industry, namely selling saplings.

Chip Wilson learned to sell from his entrepreneurial grandma.

She was telling me about when you do a sale, if you go to make an appointment with someone, you always ask for two times. Because if you only give them one time, they can always say, "No, I'm busy," but no one can ever say no if you give them two times.

These early lessons paid off quickly in his childhood.

Money was tight. If I wanted money, I really had to go out and work for it, and I was very creative around that. I would set up a circus or I'd set up the basic lemonade stand or I'd sell things and have the rest of the kids in the neighborhood pay to come in and participate. I remember selling Boy Scout tickets, or selling something for the swimming club, selling soap dishes and this and that. I was always the number one salesman.

I asked Chip why he was so talented in sales.

I was excited by the sale and by perfecting my pitch. It's interesting. I think I had a personality that loved people, and maybe I had a little bit of my grandma in me.

Good selling skills help you in every business. Even if you don't have anything, you can still make money if you can sell. When I asked Peter Hargreaves what would he do if he had to start from zero with no money, he answered: "I'd design a website to sell something. Yeah, absolutely. Absolutely."

I asked Peter what made him so successful in selling. "You've got to make it easy for people to buy. People find it very easy to leave their money on deposit in the bank. That is very easy. They make some money; it's very easy to leave it there. So you've got to make it just as easy to move it into the investments we provide."

Manny Stul, the World Entrepreneur of the Year 2016, learned a very important lesson about selling early in his first business.

Going right back to Day 1 when I was trying to sell to all these people on the phone. There were so many people I was contacting, I couldn't remember everything that I said. So I developed a card system.

These days you'd have a computerized system for that, but in those days I would document on that card—say I was ringing you, Rafael, and I'd put the date that I rang you and the time that I rang you on the card, and I would write down everything relevant to our conversation. It was a kind of a CRM system. I'd write down about your marathon running, the last date that you went on a marathon run, whether you'd had any injuries, etc. I had hundreds, thousands of these. It's impossible to remember everyone unless you've got a photographic memory, which I don't. I wrote down both business and personal data, everything relevant. What I tried to sell you, what I didn't try to sell you, your intake and what had sold, what hadn't sold, etc.

So the next time I rang you, I had all this data in front of me. I'd just started the business and had been going for a couple of months, two or three months, and within that framework that's when I learned immediately never to lie. Because next time I talked to you, I didn't want to get caught lying. Otherwise, I wouldn't be able to sell you anything. So that was a pretty big lesson for me, and I've maintained that lesson ever since. It makes life so much easier and less complicated.

Skill 6: Leadership

It is not possible to create billions in value without help from others. Billion-dollar companies have thousands, sometimes even hundreds of thousands of employees. You need to be able to attract people and focus their actions in the right direction. You need to be able to lead them.

Leadership means getting things done through others. It is the business master class. It encapsulates all the elements from attracting people, inspiring them, and motivating them to take action to managing and leading them. It is the most advanced of the universal business skills, a skill that billionaires excel at.

It is no secret that business is a team sport. And in team sports the best team wins. Trying to win in business playing alone on your team is like trying to win a Soccer World Cup playing alone against the best teams in the world.

Leadership is about building and developing a winning team.

Jack Cowin explained to me when I talked to him in Sydney:

Business is a team effort. It's not just money; it's the involvement of other people in the process. Some people are very successful because they're strong individual performers. A 100-meter-run guy can run very fast. Team sports are different than that. If the coach says "you run that way" and you run the other way, you're getting yanked off the team. You're not going to be on the field too long.

Luckily, Jack realized he needed people on his team at the very beginning of his business career, when he burned his fingers during the KFC franchisee training.

They were teaching you how to cook chicken, and you take the drumsticks and you have to dip it in the boiling oil, you've got to sear it so the skin doesn't peel back. Anyway, one of these pieces of chicken fell out of my hand, and this hot oil burned my hand. So I had a "eureka!" moment. I realized that if any success was going to depend on my cooking ability, it was going to be ill-fated because there's no way I was going to be able to successfully do this and be the operations manager.

So I said, "I have to hire somebody that knows how to do this, who can be an operator." And so I did. I found a guy, a Canadian who had worked for a franchise group in Saskatchewan in Western Canada. I said, "Look, come, I'll make you the operations manager." He did. My job then became, "how do you build the business?" I've never operated one of these stores in the 46 years I've been here. I'm incapable of doing it. I couldn't do it.

So don't try to do it alone. You need people to complement your skills.

You need others to be able to help you do your best. As the business gets bigger, you become dependent on other people. One of the things that I've realized about myself is, you're good at some things, you're not so good at some other things. So if you have a dream of building a business that has size and some substance to it, you need to build a complementary team of management, of people that magnify or compensate for whatever skills you have or don't have. So put together a complementary management team of other people that complement whatever you do. If I'm really good at finance, that's not going to be as important, but if I'm bad at finance, I really need a good strong CFO.

Business is a team effort.

— Jack Cowin #BillionDollarGoldNuggets

In leadership, billionaires use their knowledge of human nature, their relationship and communication skills. It's a skill that you build over many, many years. You will find some elements of effective leadership throughout this book. It would fill another book to describe all the details that make up a great leader and describe the billionaire leadership methods. I may write it one day.

As the business gets bigger, you become dependent on other people.

— Jack Cowin #BillionDollarGoldNuggets

Have you learned all of the Six Skills of Business Mastery, my dear reader? Which of those do you still need to develop to become outrageously successful in business?

- Drifters develop skills that don't generate wealth.

- Millionaires have developed only some of the Six Skills of Business Mastery.

- Billionaires have mastered all Six Skills of Business Mastery at the highest level.

For more stories on this topic, go to:
http://TheBillionDollarSecret.com/resources

CHAPTER 7

The Six Habits of Wealth

*The chains of habit are too light to be felt until
they are too heavy to be broken.*

—Warren Buffett

In the long term, your habits will determine your future. You first need the foundation of the following habits if you want to be really successful in business.

Sergey Galitskiy, the internationally most respected Russian entrepreneur, told me: "The most important thing is the foundation. What you should be most interested in is not the result, but the foundation that you build. Result is always what follows."

Habit 1: Get Up Early

Getting up early is the number one common habit of the most successful entrepreneurs. All my interviewees name it as an important component of their success.

The self-made billionaires that I interviewed get up on average at 5:30 a.m. with some variation to it.

Result is always what follows.

– Sergey Galitskiy #BillionDollarGoldNuggets

Why is getting up early so important?

There are several advantages. Early hours, when the world awakes to life, have something of a primal energy around them. You may have felt this energy at the sunrise. You have time for yourself, time to think in silence, and time to work undisturbed. This, coupled with your fresh mind and body, makes you extremely productive during these hours. And you get this great feeling of doing something, of progressing when others are still asleep. It can even propel you through the rest of the day, giving you additional energy boost.

But keep in mind: It's not the short sleep that makes you successful in business. It's getting up early. Some billionaires sleep for three hours only, some need as much as eight hours, but all of them get up early. Those that need to sleep longer just go to bed earlier.

How to get up early?

The best method I have heard so far is the one Manny Stul, the World Entrepreneur of the Year 2016, gave me:

Do you know what got me out of the habit of long hours? About 40 years ago, I could sleep half the day, no problem. A friend of mine asked me to go to circuit training in the morning, early. He said he'd come and pick me up. He'd pick me up at 5:30 a.m., we'd be there at 6:00 a.m. I said, "No, no, you go." He said he needed me there to motivate him. I said "Yeah, not a problem. We'll do it for a few weeks, and then you'll be motivated." So I set the alarm and I'd wake up and struggle getting out of bed. After about two to three weeks, I was waking up without the alarm, automatically. And I never got out of the habit, ever. Doesn't matter what time I go to bed, I wake up early in the morning and exercise for an hour.

Indeed, a sports commitment in the morning is the best way to get up early.

Habit 2: Keep Healthy

Whether in business or in life in general, health is extremely important. Without health, life is a misery and no amount of success will make it better for you. There is no point in doing business if you aren't healthy.

Jack Cowin told me he had once given a speech with the title "If I knew then what I know now" with 13 different points. "The first one is, if you lose your health, nothing else matters. Your health is the most important. I don't care how wealthy or how important you are or how much power you've got; if you lose your health, nothing else counts. So you've got to look after your health. Include techniques such as meditation or physical training into your life to maintain your mental and physical health."

If you lose your health, nothing else matters.

– Jack Cowin #BillionDollarGoldNuggets

Exercise Regularly

The number one method to keep healthy is a strict exercise regime. Each and every one of the billionaires I interviewed, whether he is 40 or 80, exercises regularly.

Most of them include sports in their morning routine like Petter Stordalen, who believes running with his wife and dog is the best way to start the day.

Years ago, I decided that I will train every morning, and I have no ambitions to compete or anything.

My wife and I are usually up around 5–6 a.m. and out jogging for 10km by 5.30–6.30 a.m. I have always been an early riser. I have never enjoyed sleeping in. Using energy creates energy in my book.

I have always enjoyed it, but when I met Gunhild it became one of the foundations in our life together. It is a good way to update each other on our busy lives, and so many great ideas and beautiful sights have come from this tradition.

On top of that, in winter, I bicycle; in summer, I rollerblade, I paddle and kayak, because I'm living close to the sea. I ski, downhill, cross-country, I go skiing on asphalt with the skis on wheels. And of course, when you're over 50, you have to do some weights as well, because you lose muscles from your late twenties.

We train every day. Regardless of weather, wherever we are. If we have a flight at 6 a.m., we get up at 3 a.m. Compromises are not for Gunhild and I. We like being active in general.

Even older billionaires over 65 or even 80 run or go to the gym daily or at least two to three times a week.

The consistency of your regimen is important.

Lirio Parisotto does the treadmill. "My average is 1,000 calories, three times a week. It's one and a half hour. I do it whenever possible. Sometimes, if I travel then it's difficult. So I pay the bill when I come back. Then I do it every day."

From Sportsmen to Billionaires

A noticeably high percentage of billionaires I interviewed were high performers in sport in their youth and some still are.

Chip Wilson's life was all about sports from childhood on, when he started off as a competitive swimmer. "It was seven or eight practices a week and a swim meet every weekend. At the age of 10 I had a Canadian record, and then by the age of 12 I was one of the best in the world at swimming for my age. So swimming dominated my life." In grade 12 he started playing football. At the university came wrestling.

Then I made up my mind I was going to do the Iron Man, which was at the time the craziest thing in the world anyone could think of. I was always thinking what was more powerful, my mind or my body. I was always trying to see how far I could take my body with my mind.

After triathlons, I started running 10Ks, and I ran my back into the ground. Then I started playing squash, because I could move laterally, so I became a C Level squash player.

And then I got muscular dystrophy in my body. I've had to revolve my life around that. So I started doing yoga, and I did it very consistently. But then I think my mind started moving more to mindfulness, and then climbing mountains started to become very interesting to me.

Frank Hasenfratz was a competitive rower from the age of 16 to 21. If not for the fact that he had to flee Hungary after the uprising that he participated in, he probably would have represented Hungary in the Olympic Games.

Manny Stul loved sports. He loved winning and competing. I asked him which was his favorite sport in his youth.

Anything that I was good at. Sports that I liked were eye-hand coordination. Table tennis, tennis, soccer, badminton, cricket. I was very good at chess. My father taught me. I ended up playing in competitions and representing the school. When I was older, squash became popular. I won a lot of trophies for squash on a state level.

Jack Cowin was selected at high school to the All-Ontario team in American football. At the university he was one of the best players and was the number three draft from all Canadian universities. He went to play professional football for the *Winnipeg Blue Bombers,* which he gave up as soon as he realized he wanted to go into business. He also was a strong wrestler with hopes for the Olympic Games. Unfortunately, this didn't work out for him.

Michał Sołowow is still active in car rallies. It has been his passion for the last 10-plus years, and he became the European WRC vice-champion twice.

Peter Hargreaves was quite competitive in trail running.

Advantages of Sports for Business

Involvement in sports helps you on numerous levels in your business success. The most obvious one is it keeps you in shape, thus giving you vital energy needed in every activity, also in business. But it's more than that.

It helps you think clearly because it freshes up your head, and then you look at things from a different perspective. Peter Hargreaves praises the advantages of running: "I find if you've got lots and lots of things going on in your mind, lots of problems to solve, don't allow them to fester there. Instead go running. I would have huge problems in my mind. I'd go a five- or six-mile run, and when I came back, they'd all be sorted out. I have this theory that during the day, you tax your brain and it puts your body out of balance. You've taxed your brain but not your body. By taxing your body, by actually doing some exercise, you put the two in balance. And you feel more awake and better than you would if you hadn't done it."

Sport teaches you to win and to lose, skills that you need for success both in life and in business. Frank Stronach reminded me, "In sports, you learn sports character and you learn to compete. And you should also learn fair play."

In sports, you learn sports character and you learn to compete.

– Frank Stronach #BillionDollarGoldNuggets

All sports make you disciplined and persistent, help you develop not only physical but also mental strength, and team sports teach you teamwork. The Singaporean billionaire Ron Sim is a marathon runner and a triathlete. He is a strong supporter of sports in education.

Education without sports means nothing, because you basically create the competitive spirit, you create the teamwork, you create the discipline, you create the strength, the endurance, and you learn how to win—and you also learn how to lose.

I think these are the fundamentals of life. Because these are the things that you're going to go through in life. The theoretical classes are not going to teach you much of that. They give you the knowledge that you want in a formal, methodological, and applicable way, that's all. They don't provide you with the intangible substance to run your life.

Sports is probably the only way to understand that you are going to get down with your hands to work, that you need to go through all these elements of life before you are really tested. So I always say the degree is just a license to practice.

You basically create the competitive spirit, you create the teamwork, you create the discipline, you create the strength, the endurance, and you learn how to win—and you also learn how to lose.

– Ron Sim #BillionDollarGoldNuggets

Sports give you confidence and tenacity that are essential in business. It was Jack Cowin's takeaway from his American football career.

I think one of the things that sports give you is confidence. Not physically. You're not going to beat somebody up, but I think you develop a rapport with people. Because it's tough.

You never give up. If you're my opponent, can I wear you down? There's an amazing amount of analogies between sports and business. What would make a successful athlete would make a successful entrepreneur. It's training. Putting yourself through the paces of training to be able to perform.

One of the things that sports give you is confidence. You never give up.

– Jack Cowin #BillionDollarGoldNuggets

Sports teach you to give everything. Chip Wilson's father taught him to give 100% in swimming.

There's no point in doing anything in life unless it's 100%. You might as well just go do something else. That was one thing I learned in sports for life.

Sport instills in you the will to succeed, despite defeats and setbacks. It shows you that you can improve and get better.

I asked Manny Stul what he learned in sports for business or life.

Just the drive to succeed, to keep improving and keep going. In sport sometimes you have injuries, but you've got to play through them. Of course, you have setbacks also in business, but you just need to maintain a positive attitude, always, to overcome them and keep moving forward.

You've got to have the drive within you if you want to be an entrepreneur, if you want to succeed.

There's no point in doing anything in life unless it's 100%. You might as well just go do something else.

– Chip Wilson #BillionDollarGoldNuggets

Let's not forget about other canonical virtues of sport. It teaches you humility and being sincere to yourself. You can't lie to yourself in sports. Your skills are the consequence of your preparation, and your results show you exactly where you are, especially if you compete against others.

Team sports teach to you to assess people and to lead a team.

Healthy Life

Sports isn't the only element of a healthy life. Other elements that billionaires name frequently are meditation, not smoking, and healthy eating habits.

Out of all the 21 billionaires I interviewed for this book, only one was a smoker. All the rest either have never smoked in their lives or gave up smoking long ago.

Habit 3: Read

Books are the treasure chest of the world's knowledge.

When I asked Cho Tak Wong about one message he would like to give to the world audience, his answer was: "I'd ask the young people to read books, read a lot of those about how to do things right, how to be a good person."

Keep in mind, Cho Tak Wong was expelled from elementary school and was illiterate at the age of 14. He never graduated from any school and learned to read and write all by himself. He is a self-taught person who gained all his knowledge from the books he read and the experiences he made. This was what allowed him to become the World Entrepreneur of the Year 2009, the best entrepreneur in the world, so to say.

Reading is, together with exercise, the activity that billionaires spend time on regularly. Almost all my interviewees named reading as one of the habits they follow daily. They usually read in the morning before they go to the office. Some read also before they go to sleep.

You really can't read too much. Manny Stul, the World Entrepreneur of the Year 2016, was a prolific reader in his childhood. He picked it up from his father.

I read about five books a week up to the age of 12. When I was interested, I read a lot. I'd wait for my parents to turn off the lights, and then I'd read under the blankets with a torch [flashlight] till 2:00 or 3:00 in the morning.

Chip Wilson started reading books at the age of 18, but like everything he does, he did it giving 100%. "I was in Alaska on the oil pipeline, and I had a job which was just monitoring this one device. It's very boring, so I read a novel a day for almost a year and a half. So by the age of 19, I'd read probably the 200 top novels of the world, which I think very few people have done."

He instilled the love for books in his wife and his children. "We go to bed early and read. We read. Everyone reads at night."

What Do Billionaires Read?

You may have in your mind the stereotype of a successful businessman reading the economy pages of the daily newspapers or magazines at the breakfast. And you aren't far from the truth. Many billionaires do exactly that.

Some read their national dailies; others read the likes of *The Economist*, *Financial Review*, *Fortune*, *The Times*, or *Newsweek*.

But billionaire reading habits are usually more sophisticated than that. Many billionaires indulge in biographies of the top performers in and outside of business. Sometimes these are books about the greatest leaders in history.

This type of book was decisive in Lirio Parisotto's career.

When I started in business, I read a lot of books. I read all the autobiographies of businessmen which came into my hands.

I'm a self-made man because I read a lot. I haven't graduated in administration or law or something related or electronic engineering.

I was interested in all the times, how they had made the first million. Imagine somebody who has nothing, doesn't have family support, doesn't have wealthy friends, who has nothing but his ideas, and starts to do something and makes a million dollars cash. Of course, at that time it was much more. [chuckles] Maybe it's $10 million today.

I'm a self-made man because I read a lot.

– Lirio Parisotto #BillionDollarGoldNuggets

Industry magazines and domain-specific books are the next most popular reading category among billionaires.

Finally, we come to business books.

For many billionaires, business books were the only guide in their entrepreneurial try-and-fail game. This is how Mohed Altrad learned to do business: "By trying and doing. And very quickly I started reading business books. Whatever aspect, be it sales or anything, I would buy a book and read it and learn."

But you would be surprised to discover that not all billionaires read them. Petter Stordalen has read only one business book in his career. He prefers to read detective novels, and a few other billionaires also enjoy reading belletristic.

A Reading System

It's important to develop a systematic approach to your reading. Don't read random books; read books that give you value. Ideally, keep a priority list of titles to read based on your interests and recommendations of your mentors. Use this list flexibly, and choose the books to read based on the challenges you face at the moment.

Then develop a habit to read at a given time of the day; for example, in the morning, at the lunch break, or before going to bed. Ideally, set off time for reading every day.

The third element is a system to process the reading: marking interesting passages, keeping notes, thoughts, ideas, or maybe even to-dos based on the material you've read.

Go to my website to get the list of books recommended by billionaires: http://TheBillionDollarSecret.com/resources

Habit 4: Contemplate

Billionaires take time during the day to spend it alone to think. Some contemplate by meditating; some do it during other activities like sports.

We will look at this closer with the examples in the next habit.

Habit 5: Routines and Rituals

Routines and rituals are sets of habits that, when employed consistently, will in the long term inevitably produce profound results. Ritualized habits are easier to keep and thus more sustainable. Long-term application brings about a compound effect.

Unfortunately, bad rituals like a cigarette break also will produce profound results but on the negative side. That's why it's essential to set up and follow routines and rituals that support your objectives.

A Morning Routine

A morning routine is the single most important routine for long-term success in business. Almost all the billionaires I interviewed have a morning routine that they follow religiously.

A good example is Kim Beom-Su, who uses his mornings to think deeply and to read.

I usually wake up between 5 and 6 in the morning and go to sleep around 11:30 p.m. I sleep around six hours.

Basically . . . like in golf, there is a routine where you go through certain motions in setting up, like a checklist, without exerting too much energy. And because reading books is part of this routine, I am able to read a lot. And because taking a shower is part of this routine, I am able to think a lot during that time.

After waking up in the morning, I put on my cap and grab my earphones and go for a walk. When I come back from my walk, I take a shower. I walk for around 30, 40 minutes and again take a shower for 30, 40 minutes, thinking about many things. After that I come out to the living room where there are a lot of books and choose one that catches my eye and read that for 30, 40 minutes. The rest of the time I listen to some music in the music room for 30, 40 minutes before having breakfast with my family and going to work.

My first most important habit is the habit of thinking deeply. While taking a shower or taking a walk, I take time to contemplate about things, and this is the most important habit for me because I've organized many thoughts, things have become clearer, and new ideas have developed during those times.

Chip Wilson's morning routine is about sports and information.

I almost always get up at 5:30 in the morning, and I'm old school, so I go get the newspapers, and I read from 5:45 to 6:30. And then I either go to run stairs, or I'll go over to the three mountains in Vancouver and I'll do one hike straight up one of the mountains, or I'll go to a personal trainer. And I usually get home around 8:30, to walk my kids to school and eat something. And I always end up with two cappuccinos in the morning, which sends me off till lunchtime.

Some billionaires have simpler routines, some more complex ones, but as you see above, typical elements of a billionaire morning routine are getting up early, exercising, reading, and spending time alone to think. It doesn't matter that much when you do these activities during the day, but it's important that you do them. Having them in a routine doesn't make you think whether you feel like doing them or not. You just do them, and that supports consistency. Putting them in your morning routine helps you have them "out of the way" straight in the morning when you still have a fresh mind and a lot of energy. Some billionaires add meditation into the mix, some a breakfast or other elements.

"Starting the Business Day" Routine

Billionaires have their usual way to start their day in the office. It's a routine that they follow automatically the minute they enter their office.

What you do first depends very much on the type of business you are involved in and of course the scale of your business. Frank Stronach explains it using manufacturing as an example:

When you are small, you go in the factory. When you are larger, you start with your secretary: "What's new? Anything urgent?" Then you might meet an executive committee or whatever. So it depends on what stage. I went through all these stages.

Some billionaires first want to get on top of the events and see if there is anything that needs their immediate attention. Others are people focused. They first go around the office and talk to key people. Some billionaires check the numbers first.

Chip Wilson approaches every day in a systematic way. Asked what is the first thing he does in the office, he says:

I sit down and I think about what my number one priority of the day is. What is my goal to get done for that day? And I look at my calendar and go, "Okay, is my calendar right?" Actually, do that the night before, so I rearrange things. Then I go, "Has anything changed between last night and this morning, and what do I need to do?" I need to actually insert it into my calendar to give me time to do it.

Habit 6: Discipline

The billionaires I interviewed are the most disciplined people I have ever met. They put a high standard on themselves and on the people around them.

In sports, you can achieve results only if you are disciplined to train consistently. Similarly in business, you can achieve results only if you are disciplined to apply yourself consistently to what needs to be done. You have to show up day in, day out for decades to make it happen.

But billionaires are by no means superhumans or perfect working automatons. They also sometimes feel lazy just like you and me. The only difference is: they are aware of this fact and they don't let themselves slack. They take up the struggle to overcome their weaknesses. This is what Michał Sołowow confessed to me:

I wake up every morning and do things I don't like. I force myself to do them every day. Because I am not hardworking, I force myself to do hard work. I am not systematic, so I have to force myself to become systematic.

I like playing football but don't feel like doing physical exercises. But to keep playing, I force myself to do exercises every day, do push-ups, curl-ups, I swim in a pool. It takes me 40 minutes in the morning, and often another 40 minutes in the evening. I don't like that in principle. But I do it, simply. Generally after doing some exercises I feel better, but I don't like the exercising phase itself. If I could achieve the same effect without doing those exercises, I wouldn't do them. Well, but I do them.

Every day I have to persuade those "lazy bones" that are in me, and they keep telling me: "Today I think I woke up late," or "I am in a hurry, no time," or "I don't feel well enough." But then I respond to myself: "No way, don't cheat yourself, bud, you simply feel lazy . . ." and I do it. In this way I learned about consequence and determination.

What are your habits, dear reader? Have you chosen them consciously? Do they support and enforce your long-term goals? Do you have established routines in your life and business? Do you employ all of the Six Habits of Wealth? It's high time that you do it!

- Drifters don't consciously develop their habits.

- Millionaires choose their habits consciously but don't cover the entire Six Habits of Wealth on a consistent basis.

- Billionaires diligently follow all habits of the Six Habits of Wealth and don't compromise them under any circumstance.

For more stories on this topic, go to:
http://TheBillionDollarSecret.com/resources

CHAPTER 8

Sharpen Your Vision

MEN WANTED
for hazardous journey,
small wages, bitter cold,
long months of complete darkness,
constant danger, safe return doubtful,
honour and recognition
IN CASE OF SUCCESS

—Ernest Shackleton, the greatest adventurer
of all time, whose men were trapped
in the ice of Antarctica for 18 months and survived

Billionaires name having a great vision as one of the keys to success in business. For Cho Tak Wong, the World Entrepreneur of the Year 2009, the way to success has three words: belief, vision, and execution. Many billionaires, like Chip Wilson, consider being visionary one of their strength that determined their extraordinary achievements in business.

Set a Vision and Mission

You need to first know yourself before you set your vision.

Sergey Galitskiy wanted to play soccer professionally when he was still a kid. But he didn't have any talent for it. When he realized this, he set a different vision for himself.

Mohed Altrad says, "My strong point is to have a vision of what I am now, and then projecting this in the future. And for others also."

Your vision should inspire you and others. If it inspires you, it will then drive you throughout your career and help you endure through difficulties and setbacks. If it inspires others, it will help you win them for your causes and remove obstacles in your way.

Every billionaire started with an inspiring vision. For some, like Frank Stronach, it was at first self-centered. He just wanted to be free, also economically free.

Naveen Jain has a crazy vision to go to the moon and by this inspires others for their own moon shots. "I think that it is honestly about coming from that humble background, and to me going to the moon is not just about going to the moon. It is about creating that inspiration to other people in India and around the world to know that it doesn't matter what background you come from. If I can dream and go land on the moon, what would you dream? You are better off than I was. And if I can do that, what would you do? And really inspire everyone to be at their best to find their moon shot. And knowing that each one of us would do something different, it doesn't have to be going to the moon, but they will have their own moon shot."

Right now he is planning a robotic mission to the moon, but there will be a manned mission in the next 20 years as well. "To me, ultimately my goal would be to change the definition of honeymoon to take your honey to the moon. Because it's not called honey Hawaii, so why would you take your honey to Hawaii on honeymoon?"

From all the billionaires I interviewed, probably Petter Stordalen uses vision as a tool in his business most frequently and in the most spectacular way. His business is hotels, and he starts every hotel project with creating and communicating an inspiring vision. Thanks to his magical vision, Petter was able to win the contract for a huge hotel project in Stockholm against many contenders and despite low odds.

They gave me 10% chance of succeeding. I said, "That's not bad. How many are invited to the competition?" They invited 30 or 40 hotel companies, and if they gave me a 10% chance, it's pretty good. Is there anybody who has a 20% chance? No? So I said, "10% means we are 80% ahead of the others." They said, "Why?" "Because most of them had a 2%, 3% chance of succeeding. We have 10%. So we are ahead of the pack already." They said, "Okay, the presentations need to be like that." I told my people, "Forget everything they write. Do what you think is best. Make freaking magic." We went there; we had redrawn everything. Moved one hotel, new hotel there, sky bar, swimming pool, spa, everything.

During the presentation, they were like, "This is something brand new." I said, "If you want to do something that makes people go from New York, from Japan, to see what we have done, do this." They were like, "What?" We had the three best people in the company, and I was supposed to say nothing. But they asked me, "Petter, what are your thoughts around this?" They had told everything about the product, so I told these few people from this huge pension company, "I am not here for the money. I am here with my heart. This is the project which will define hotels in the future. Doesn't matter how much it costs us; we will make magic." I had five minutes. With very strong words, I wanted to show them that this is not an ordinary project for us. This is something brand unique.

I had done that 50 times before.

So when we went out from this meeting, one of the guys in the group said, "Petter, did you mean everything you said?" I said, "Yes, everything." "That was strong." I said, "Yes, that was strong." "But when you say you don't care about the money . . . you do." I said, "Yes, but I wanted those people to understand I'm not here to start with a calculator in my hand. First we'll make magic, and then we see how much do we need to invest. Maybe we need to do some changes, but we don't start with a calculator. We start with passion, enthusiasm, a huge ambition to do something really f--king magic.

If you are sitting there and one guy is telling you "I'll make magic. I'll do something different," you will be proud.

Of course, Petter won the competition and as promised, created magic.

Vision and Mission That Matter

Stand for something important. Set a vision and mission that matter. Focus on creating massive value for people and on improving the world around you, on improving people's lives.

For Chip Wilson, a vision is something that is bigger than one's self and is never achieved; it's always there. "My vision has always been to elevate the world from a place of mediocrity to greatness."

Michał Sołowow, now the wealthiest person in Poland, gave his first public company a proud name, which was also its program: Polish Life Improvement (PLI). "I believed then, and still believe today, that what we do is we raise the quality and standard of living around, no matter the financial outcomes. The truth is we are improving the reality around us, be it by building new flats, office buildings, shopping centers, or by manufacturing something. We improve the life quality for all. And this in some way spreads not only onto the area that we directly affect, but indeed on the whole society."

Hüsnü Özyegin benefited so much from a good education that he is committed to providing those less fortunate with the same opportunity. Next to numerous other philanthropic projects, he created a university in Istanbul. His vision in relation to that is "to make it one of the best research and teaching universities in Turkey, where students, with their professors, invent things that add value to Turkish exports. This is what my goal is from now on. It's not an easy thing to do. I am always thinking of what more I can accomplish, but these days I dream about the university and its graduates and how they will go out into the world and be successful. I imagine our young faculty doing innovative research that will have an impact on our lives. I imagine our graduates becoming entrepreneurs and adding value to our economy."

But his life vision is even greater. "If I can have an impact on another 1 million Turkish people in the next 10 years, I will be happy."

Petter Stordalen's overall business vision also has an environmental and social dimension. "My business goal, which I'm working on every day, and I am not there still and I will not be there in years, is to have a true triple-bottom-line company. That means that you have one area for profit, you have one area for sustainability, and you have one area for social responsibility, and all are equally important, and you release figures and targets on every one of these. We do this today, but we have a long way to go to be a true triple-bottom-line company."

Frank Stronach created a notion of Fair Enterprise and implemented it in his company Magna. It is a system that gives all contributors to value creation, be they managers, investors, or employees, a fair share in the success of the company, also financially. The long-term vision of Fair Enterprise is to eliminate poverty.

What is the primary reason why people get up in the morning? They want to make a better life for themselves and their family.

There's a lot of poverty in the world. I think the two most important things in life are freedom, freedom to be, to live and also let other people live, right? Freedom has very little meaning to a young person or to a kid in inner-city Detroit. There you can be free to be hungry and free. So freedom is the most important thing. But it means also economic freedom. If you're not economically free, you're not a free person. There's very, very few people who are economically free, and that's wrong.

Have you heard of the Golden Rule? Who has the gold makes the rules. The world has always been dominated by the Golden Rule. It still is. I don't want to be dominated by somebody. If I feel that strong, I should not be able to dominate somebody either. So the key question is, how can we dismantle the chains of domination? Not by a violent revolution, but by the revolution of the mind. It's a moral question, right? So the philosophy of Fair Enterprise is driven by the belief that employees have a moral right to some of the profits they helped to generate.

Tony Tan Caktiong is the World Entrepreneur of the Year 2004. His mission is more down to earth, more tangible, but no less important in everybody's life. "I noticed that in many restaurants, fast food is not really that good. It's really hard to find good fast-food restaurants." His mission in business is "to provide a lot of restaurants that serve very good food, where people can really enjoy [the food]."

Cai Dongqing wants to contribute his best to make a better world, to make people a little bit happier. He does it through his enterprises in the entertainment sector. "We have seen an improving living standard of Chinese people over the past several decades. Along with it, people are longing for more mental satisfaction. I wish to bring more happiness to their lives by offering entertaining products such as comics, animation, movies, games, or via other newly emerging forms. This is what I would love to do. Maybe it is my mission."

Kim Beom-Su is pushing the limits of technology. He has invented several business models and introduced new paradigms in the Internet and mobile world. He is literally building the future of the world. He wants to be remembered as somebody who "searched for the future and built the future, as a challenger, with a pioneer feel to it." Success for him is "making the world a better place than when I was born and making at least one person happy."

Tim Draper's mission is "to spread entrepreneurship and venture capital around the world." He wants to be remembered as someone who helped the world accelerate progress.

Mohed Altrad wants to improve the lives of the people he touches. He wants to spread the attitude of kindness across the world.

I'm not interested in having a lot of money in my pocket. Not really. Yes, I can have a few million, but not billions, because I don't really need it.

He wrote a thick charter with a Code of Values for his company and hopes these values will survive him as part of the company and will serve future generations in perpetuity.

And the idea is to save the world. I know that what I am telling you is a drop of water in the humanity. But I'm trying to do something. Well, actually, I'm not trying. I've discovered that's what I've been doing these last 30 years. Because this company grew, I had the opportunity to sell it maybe 13 times, and then have a lot of money in my pocket. But it has never been my ambition.

The central values that he wants to promote are faith and hope.

Faith is the basis you and I and others should act on. Hope is something that transports you to the future. And then just create that and ensure that it carries on and it adapts itself to the size of the group. You hope also that others will be inspired by this thing. If it's the case, 23,000 families will be affected directly by our charter. With maybe four people per family, that's 100,000 people. They have faith and they have hope and they're happy.

Communicate Your Vision and Values Effectively

Having a vision is one thing; being able to convey it is another. In order for your vision to affect other people, you need to learn to communicate it effectively. You need to be able to convey your values to your followers.

For that, communication skill as described in chapter 6 is essential. But there is much more to that.

First you need to be clear on what your vision is, what you want to achieve. If you don't know what you want, how can you get there?

For Ron Sim, clarity is one of the reasons for his success. "What decided my success? I always say that success is a function of two things: what you believe and what you do. I think I always believed in myself, and I have clarity about what I want to do most of the time when I decide on something."

Then you need to make sure you will be understood. You need to clarify your message. Simplicity is king.

This is something, Dilip Shanghvi considers his advantage. "A core strength is the ability to simplify complex issues. I think I always had this capability. I have kept on adding to it because my knowledge base has increased, but the basic skill set existed."

And then you need to express your vision properly.

Sometimes it can be enough to just express what you need.

Michał Sołowow started a construction company shortly after the system change in Poland. Everything was lacking in the Polish economy. For construction, cement is essential, but it wasn't easy to come by.

I came to a cement factory to buy cement. I sat in the corridor. I had a technique for sorting out everything, of course through secretaries, that is flowers, chocolates, smiles. . . .

And some guy was passing through that corridor maybe 10 times, and it didn't even pass through my mind that it could be someone important. I was sitting on that corridor, and in the end that guy asked me, and he was hardly older than me: "Sir, what are you doing here for so long?" I said, "You know, I am waiting for the head of the cement factory" And he said, "That's me." And asked me into his office.

We started talking about what I am doing, what I do for a living, what I need this cement for. And I told him a story, that I am a student, one year after graduation, my company is developing, I don't have cement, and I am in such a trap.

He said, "OK, you will buy from me as much cement as you want under one condition—you will build me, here, a housing compound for the employees of the cement factory and their families." That was what happened in the majority of my contracts. That is when I tried to achieve something; then someone said, "The condition for making it is to carry out such and such work for me." That is how my business developed.

By the way, do you know the saying, "You can have anything you want in your life as long as you help others achieve what they want"? This story is the perfect illustration of this principle.

An important element of the vision mix is to make it durable. Write it down; print it in a book like Mohed Altrad; put it on your website or in the company leaflet, like most billionaires do; paint it on the walls of your company, like Ron Sim did at the entrance to OSIM; or even engrave it into stone, like Petter Stordalen did with his company values.

Every year, there was a convention in Gothenburg, where all employees of Petter's companies gathered to celebrate together. It's a great show, during which Petter took a hammer and a chisel and personally engraved another company value statement into stone, to add one to the Stone Rules of Gothenburg.

You need to rejoice when your vision materializes. "Celebrate your victories" is Petter's credo. "I love celebrations! For example, a hotel opening is not just a party. It is a celebration of the hard and long work that has been put into the project by so many people. It is a BIG thank you to all of the involved, our staff, partners, local community. I believe you have to party just as hard as you work. And in Nordic Choice we work very, very hard."

The skill of storytelling is instrumental in conveying your vision. Be clear about what you want the world to know about you and tell this story. A great story transports your vision more effectively. Petter is a master storyteller. Use the tools of storytelling we were talking about in chapter 6.

Attract People

If you have a compelling vision and you learned to communicate it effectively, it's time to attract people with it and embark with them on your mission. A vision is essential for attracting not only employees, but also business partners and investors.

Attract people and embark with them on your mission.

— Rafael Badziag @BillionairePal #BillionDollarGoldNuggets

How attractive a clear vision can be I was told by Selmo Leisgold, Lirio Parisotto's PR manager. Selmo has known Lirio from the very beginning. Selmo worked for a newspaper in Rio at that time. Lirio operated out of provincial Caxias do Sul in the South of Brazil, where he had started his video rental service. Selmo was sent to him on his 26th birthday with the words: "He is interesting, but he doesn't have a chance." It was the best birthday gift he could get. The encounter with Lirio changed his life and completely changed his world view. Once he talked to Lirio, Selmo never returned to Rio. This one encounter made him want to work to make the vision of this great man real. And I can understand why. Lirio, even at 61, radiates this unbent attractiveness that makes you listen to him and do something for him.

So, a compelling vision not only attracts people, but makes them stick to you.

There is no company without people. As Jack Cowin told me, "Well, you have to have the ability to attract people that are going to be part and parcel of what you're going to try and build."

This ability is what Jack considers one of the keys to entrepreneurial success. "I was able to attract a bunch of young guys who also bought into my vision. Again, it's not my talent, it's just leveraging and getting good people. So I was able to attract some people that were smarter and more capable in various areas than I was. And together we kind of made it work."

The more talented and the more motivated your team is, the better. And a growing company with a great vision attracts top talent and motivates people. I asked Jack how he managed to attract his extraordinary entrepreneurial employees, some of whom had been successful in their own businesses before.

In our case, the biggest factor has been building from zero to a multibillion-dollar business. Being part of that vision. Being part of something bigger than what you could do on your own. Money, as I say, you've got to pay the bills, you want to have a respectable way of life. If that was the number one priority, you'd probably go and do your own thing somewhere. I think it's being part of a bigger dream that this could become. Domino's Pizza that we're involved in right now is an international company now, but this will become a much bigger deal before we're through. And being part of that is much more exciting than "I made a few million dollars on the side. Now what am I going to do to keep myself entertained?"

A compelling vision not only attracts people, but makes them stick to you.

– Rafael Badziag @BillionairePal #BillionDollarGoldNuggets

I asked Kim Beom-Su how he was finding his key employees. His answer shows how important a role the vision plays when you build a team for your business.

At the very beginning it was really hard. Fortunately, although I didn't get the first person I wanted, another friend who was quite famous approached me. After that, it was a very difficult process of gathering employees because at that time it wasn't easy for people to think about leaving a big company to join a start-up, so it was hard to persuade people each time. Even for just a middle managerial role, it was like I was doing the interview and answering all these questions about our company, so it was really agonizing.

After that, as the company started showing some vision for the future and we had some data to back us up, I could show them how much we could grow and show them our future, which made it easier to persuade them, but before that it was hard.

I told them the vision that this would be a big business in the new world and it wouldn't really work if they didn't have some understanding of this.

You have to have the ability to attract people.

— Jack Cowin #BillionDollarGoldNuggets

Vision Gives Direction

People don't need management; they need a common vision. Your vision will give your team a clear goal and a direction. Set a mission and inspire people to move in this direction.

It's quite clear for Cai Dongqing, who set for his company the mission to build the Chinese Disney. "I think for a company, the most important thing is you must set the right strategic direction, which leads a company to go this way or that way. It will enable a company to achieve further progress or suffer a setback. A wrong decision in this point will pose a major challenge for the company."

Great vision attracts top talent and motivates people.

— Rafael Badziag @BillionairePal #BillionDollarGoldNuggets

Your vision will help your team make the right decisions. Why? Because they will adapt to the situation and use their brains to get there. Of course, they will do it only if they are aligned to the mission. That's what Tim Draper calls "a good business."

Vision Changes

Like your dreams, your vision evolves with time.

Jack Cowin told me, "Your vision evolves, it changes. A year ago I had a different vision of where I'd be this year than I am today. But from the start, I think it's fair to say that I had a pretty clear idea that I wanted to build a business. The sales pitch that I gave to the 30 people that invested in me was 'Trust me, I will do my damnedest to make you have a successful investment. I don't know whether it'll be in the chicken business, the hamburger business, making airplanes, who knows where we'll end up, but I'm prepared to sell my house, pack my wife, kids, move halfway around the world, get into a business, and that'll be the nucleus.'" Today, Jack's vision is a multinational pizza empire.

Jollibee is today one of the largest restaurant companies in the world. Tony Tan Caktiong changed the vision of his company several times. The first time was when Jollibee had a few stores, he said that he wanted to be number one in the Philippines. Later he said, "We have been number one in the Philippines. We need to dream bigger, we need to challenge ourselves." It was the time when he said that he wants the company to be number one in Asia. Now Jollibee is already number one in Asia. Tony gathered the team again and told them that they need to dream even bigger because they had achieved it. He said, "It's not the dream anymore if you achieved it." So he said he wants Jollibee to be one of the Top 5 best restaurant companies in the world by the year 2020."

For many of the billionaires I interviewed, escaping poverty was their first vision and then, step-by-step, it evolved to much, much more.

Cai Dongqing's first vision was for his family to become strong in order to not be bullied by neighbors. Then he wanted to be successful in business. Now, his vision is to be the Disney of China.

Another Chinese billionaire, Cho Tak Wong, changed his mission several times.

Our family was very poor it was a fact, but I have never wanted to be defeated by that. Hard life is not a problem. I had to stay on and work step-by-step toward the success in that direction. So I never wanted to give up, never wanted to say, "I will be defeated." That was a very clear mission. First mission, I wanted to get out of the poverty. Second, try to have a good life. That was the direction."

And now he is on a mission to provide the best automotive glass for China and the world.

And what is the mission you are on, dear reader? What is your vision for the future? Have you set one? Have you written it down? How compelling is it? Can you communicate it clearly? Do you attract the best people with it?

- Drifters follow somebody else's vision.

- Millionaires gather limited talent for their vague mission as they fail to create and communicate an attractive vision.

- Billionaires effectively communicate a compelling vision that attracts followers.

For more stories on this topic, go to:
http://TheBillionDollarSecret.com/resources

CHAPTER 9

Don't Be the Flag, Be the Wind

I'm trying to free your mind, Neo.
But I can only show you the door.
You're the one that has to walk through it.

—Morpheus in *The Matrix*

You can have the best knowledge, the best skills, the best conditions, but as long as you don't take action, nothing will happen, and you will never succeed.

Take Action!

So take action!

You can make money only if you act, and sometimes when opportunities are abundant, to act is enough. Michał Sołowow took advantage of such a period in Poland's history in the 1990s. "The opportunities that emerged, almost a free market, were used by many people back then. And then the important thing was to do something, to make something happen. If one was acting, if one was active, then the effect was an opportunity for making money."

> ## As long as you don't take action, nothing will happen, and you will never succeed.
>
> ### – Rafael Badziag @BillionairePal #BillionDollarGoldNuggets

Action is as simple as that, and it really doesn't require a great philosophy. When I asked Tim Draper about advice for people who would like to be as successful as him, he answered: "Choose a goal, and go after it." He should know it as one of the most successful venture capital investors in the world.

But even Tim sometimes fails to act. He told me this story:

*I got into a bidding war over **Facebook**. Facebook was very clever. **Sean Parker** came to me and said, "How about a $20 million valuation?" I said, "Yeah, great." Then they came back a week later and said, "It's going to have to be $40 million." I said, "Okay, great."*

Then they came back another week later and said, "It has to be $80 million," and I said, "Pfft. . . ." I went back to my partners and I said, "What do you think?" They said okay. I said, "Okay, we'll do it at $80 million," and then Facebook came back and they said "No, it's got to be $115 million valuation." I thought "forget it." So by saying "forget it," I left a thousand times [return on investment] on the table.

*Most of my failures were failures to act or failures to invest in companies. We were outbid for Yahoo, too. I made the first offer into **Yahoo**; I should have just gone ahead and written the check with a note and let them convert it into whatever. I almost did that.*

You can make money only if you act.

— Rafael Badziag @BillionairePal #BillionDollarGoldNuggets

Most people are afraid to fail when they act, so they don't act, and this way they fail by failing to act. Don't let it happen to you. Mohed Altrad, the World Entrepreneur of the Year 2015, recommends to do it instead of trying to excuse why you didn't.

Choose a goal, and go after it.

— Tim Draper #BillionDollarGoldNuggets

Recognize and Seize Opportunities

You can't become a billionaire if you don't show up when opportunities arise. Frank Hasenfratz told me an insightful story about his almost partner when he was starting his business that clearly explains this principle.

I wanted to have a partner because I was five years in the country, I didn't speak much English. Enough to get by. I thought to partner with a good friend of mine, and I said, "Bert, do you want to be my partner?" "Okay, how much?" I said, "Well, it looks like we can get the machine for $2,000, so you've got to put a thousand dollars down, I'll put a thousand. 50–50 partner."

But it was only words. Bert was a chemist. He had a very good job and didn't want to quit. On top of that, his check bounced, so their partnership didn't go through.

His thousand dollars would be worth two billion today.

Not showing up to the opportunity can come extremely expensive. You may think, such opportunities never occur in your life. But think about it! How many opportunities have you missed in your life? How many opportunities have passed before your eyes that you haven't noticed? How many opportunities may exist right now that you are not aware of? Are you sure none of those could turn out to be a billion-dollar opportunity?

Most of my failures were failures to act.

— Tim Draper #BillionDollarGoldNuggets

Lirio Parisotto is often known to say, "Saddled horse does not pass twice." I asked him what it meant. "I think sometimes it actually passes two, three, four times, but probably not every year. You need to know where your feeling tells you it's time to take the chance. So don't lose the opportunity. Maybe you won't have another."

And sometimes, like in the case of Michał Sołowow, it is a "once-in-a-lifetime opportunity," where there is a system change in a country and land is up for grabs for those who take it.

Do it instead of trying to excuse why you didn't.

— Mohed Altrad #BillionDollarGoldNuggets

Of course, in order to take advantage of an opportunity you need to be able to recognize it as such.

Naveen Jain was right about several developments in business and was able to capitalize upon them, building several billion-dollar companies. I asked him what quality was instrumental for this. "I think what you really need is good eyesight, not good foresight and not good hindsight. Every one of us has great hindsight. I can tell you exactly what you could have done. Some people claim to have foresight. I can tell you what's going to happen in the future. But I can tell you as a great entrepreneur, what you need is good eyesight. See what's in front of you and be able to say, here's an opportunity."

You can't become a billionaire if you don't show up when opportunities arise.

— Rafael Badziag @BillionairePal #BillionDollarGoldNuggets

A surprisingly high percentage of self-made billionaires are immigrants. It may sound counterintuitive, but immigrants have much higher chances of becoming a billionaire than natives. Frank Hasenfratz believes that's because newcomers can better spot opportunities. "As a newcomer in a country, you see a lot more what's available and what you have to concede and what you can accomplish, much more so than a native, because he sees it every day. He doesn't recognize the opportunities."

Don't lose the opportunity. Maybe you won't have another.

— Lirio Parisotto #BillionDollarGoldNuggets

When you spot a great opportunity, don't hesitate, don't waste time, take action!

Tim Draper learned in his previous experiences as a VC investor how to recognize a great opportunity and quickly act upon it. Now, he doesn't hesitate when he sees one.

When Kazaa got into legal trouble and had to stop the music sharing service and start with something different, Tim smelled a rat.

I thought, "Wow, that technology can be used for anything. File sharing is going to be really important. Not just music, it's everything!"

I asked a guy who worked with my father to go hunt them down and find out what they're doing. He said, "Hey, Tim, you've got to fly out to London. You've got to check this out." So I flew out to London and I met with them, and I made an offer right there on the spot. The business was shared Wi-Fi. Then I brought it back to my partners.

And again the partners were against it. This time, Tim made the deal happen against their reluctance. The team had to change their business model several times. Eventually, they ended up building **Skype**, a several-billion-dollar company. Tim didn't hesitate to bet on the team and won. He was their first investor.

What you really need is good eyesight, not good foresight and not good hindsight.

— Naveen Jain #BillionDollarGoldNuggets

Several years later, the Bitcoin opportunity came around, and Tim again didn't hesitate to show up.

He had been interested in virtual currencies since a Korean friend told him in 2005 that he had spent $40 on a sword for his son.

And he was talking about a virtual sword in the game League of Legends. [chuckles] It was the beginning of something really extraordinary.

Then the crisis of 2008 came.

In 2009, people were just running for the hills, and we needed more heroes. I thought, "Oh boy, maybe we need an alternative to fiat currencies." And I said, "This Bitcoin is a really interesting alternative." HTTP became the leader in Internet even though there were many other protocols, so I just figured there would be one leader, and that Bitcoin was the leader. So I backed it.

He invested in one of the first Bitcoin companies: Coin Lab. It was a mining company that unfortunately lost all the Bitcoin in the Mt. Gox crash.

But in 2014, the U.S. Marshals Office confiscated Bitcoin from Silk Road and was offering it in an auction. Tim didn't hesitate to buy all 30,000 Bitcoin offered in the auction and paid around $20 million for it.

The price was about $600 at the time of the auction. There have been some technical snafus and the price went down to $180; lots of other things have happened. I looked very stupid for a couple of years there.

This changed dramatically in 2017 when the Bitcoin price started to skyrocket. And even after a decline in 2018, the value of these Bitcoin at the time of writing is around $200 million.

Immigrants have much higher chances of becoming a billionaire than natives.

— Rafael Badziag @BillionairePal #BillionDollarGoldNuggets

Kim Beom-Su considers using the opportunities that arose his biggest success. He was able to capitalize on a paradigm shift when the Internet/web era was opening. He created popular Internet games and introduced a freemium business model that made them highly profitable. Then, when smartphone/mobile era was starting, he also took advantage of this opportunity and created the Kakao messenger, which practically monopolizes private communication in South Korea. "I jumped into that world and contextualized what was important, then worked as a team with gifted friends and grabbed a great opportunity, and did that two times. I think that is my biggest success."

Better Fast than Perfect

In business, it's better to be fast than to be perfect. Trying to be perfect keeps you from taking action. Don't wait for the right conditions to come before you take action.

There is never a right moment to start a business or have a child. But if you don't do it, nothing will happen. So don't wait for the right moment. The sooner you do it, the better.

Ron Sim has a similar perspective:

When I first started the business, friends were always saying, "Business? Good times are over. This is not the time for business," 35 years ago. Today, people still say the same thing. 1997 crisis comes, there you are. 2008 crisis comes, people say the same thing. To me, "No. Good or bad is a function of how you see things perspectively."

Today, Ron is a billionaire, and his friends still complain about bad times.

Be first if you can. This will give you a competitive advantage.

Dilip Shanghvi told me, "One of the reasons why we are successful is that we entered all the businesses before our competitors did. They were all more difficult businesses. When we went into psychiatry, it was a very small market. Same with cardiology. So we never had big competition. It's only when we became successful and started growing very fast, people started getting into these areas. So getting into business before it becomes fashionable is useful." With this strategy, Dilip Shanghvi built the greatest pharmaceutical company in India and became the wealthiest person in pharmaceuticals worldwide.

For Kim Beom-Su, there are two decisive factors for success in the early business stage. "One is, can you be the best in the field you have started in, and the second is, are you the first in this field? You need to carefully consider these two things. If you are the first in the field, because it's something no one has tried before you need to get in there fast and keep it up until the business grows."

Speed is important. Speed of action is a quality of most billionaires. They follow the motto "act now and think later."

Develop the attitude of urgency.

Chip Wilson doesn't want to put away anything in his life.

It doesn't matter whether you're going to die in an airplane crash tomorrow or you're going to die 80 years from now; you've got to treat every day and every second as though you're going to only have a day to live. And there's no time to waste. Especially talking to boring people, or to people that are complainers, or people that aren't going to be great in life. There's only one life to live.

I asked Chip about one message he would like to give to the world audience. His answer: "40,000 days and then you're dead." It should give you the right perspective on your life and provide the feeling of urgency. His life philosophy has two cornerstones: "There's no time to waste. It's got to be great or nothing."

Treat every day and every second as though you're going to only have a day to live. There's no time to waste.

— Chip Wilson #BillionDollarGoldNuggets

Make fast decisions. It's better to be wrong fast than to be right too late. But there is a flip side: pay attention to carefully weighing the irretrievable decisions. What do I mean? Dilip Shanghvi explains it as follows:

There are retrievable decisions and irretrievable decisions. I don't take irretrievable decisions fast, because once you take that decision, you have no ability to correct it. For example, investing $4 billion is a decision I can take. That is easy to take because I can live with it. But some decisions like firing a person or breaking a relationship—I reflect a lot before I take that decision.

40,000 days and then you're dead.

— Chip Wilson #BillionDollarGoldNuggets

Sell the Strawberries You Have

One of the most valuable lessons in this book is the **Strawberry Philosophy** I have learned from Petter Stordalen, the Hotel King of Scandinavia. When he was 12, Petter liked hanging out in his father's grocery store. But one thing he loved even more was selling strawberries at the local marketplace.

The competition was very hard at that time because there were four or five other strawberry sellers. They had huge stands with roof, and I had this small round table which I had from my mother. I didn't even have a shade. I was standing under a small personal umbrella, but I was selling strawberries with a lot of energy and a lot of enthusiasm.

I knew that I had to sell every strawberry, because the day after they were nothing. You couldn't sell it. You need fresh strawberries.

But sometimes I would envy the other competitors because they had bigger sales stands; some had a camping wagon behind. Some had flowers on the side; they had apples and everything. I only had strawberries. That was my segment, strawberries.

I had long hours, the sun was burning, and sometimes I would complain to my father, "I envy them for all this, and my berries are smaller, my sales stand is smaller, and I don't have this, I don't have that." One night, he told me, "Petter, I'll teach you one thing: sell the strawberries you have, because they're the only ones you can sell."

That night, before I let my head on the pillow and fell into sleep, the last thing I was thinking about was, "My father is a genius, and one day I will take over his store."

This advice was a game changer in Petter's life.

At the age of 12, I was named by the local newspaper "the best strawberry seller in Norway." It was not official, but they wrote it. And I felt I was the best strawberry seller in Norway. And probably at that time I was, because I was selling three, four, five times the volume of my competitors at that time.

On a good day, Petter was able to sell 2,400 strawberry boxes and make more revenue selling strawberries than his father did in his two grocery stores.

And I would be saying to you, "If you want to make jam, if you buy two cases, I'll give you some extra." My customers were coming back to me, and I was always treating them like: "I have some really nice here, super fresh, this is the biggest and best berries."

The strawberry philosophy is the biggest reason for my success. Because you can always say, "If I had that hotel, if I had that shopping center, if I had that car, if I had that much money, if I had. . . ." I mean, it's endless. You can always envy your competitors. Sell your hotel; everyone can sell the Ritz.

My success thinking is to always start with what you have. Never focus on what you don't have. Focus on what you have and make the most out of it. Do the best out of what you have.

This mindset became Petter's Strawberry Philosophy, and it led to his extraordinary business success. His companies carry the name Strawberry, and his life motto is "Sell the berries you have, because these are the only ones you can sell." Petter likes to refer to himself as "The Strawberry Seller." The Strawberry Philosophy is also one of the Stone Rules of Gothenburg.

Be like Petter; sell the strawberries you have instead of waiting and saying "If I only had. . . ."

Sell the strawberries you have, because they're the only ones you can sell.

— Petter Stordalen #BillionDollarGoldNuggets

Other billionaires call It resourcefulness. Ron Sim considers it one of his strengths to be able to do something with nothing, or as he puts it, "resourcefulness without resources."

Focus on what you have and make the most out of it.

— Petter Stordalen #BillionDollarGoldNuggets

Don't Be the Flag, Be the Wind

Most people think life happens to them, that they are the product of circumstances. A billionaire sees himself as the driving force, the creator of circumstances, and not their victim.

Frank Hasenfratz is quite cocky. His favorite saying is: "I don't get headaches, I give headaches." It describes his life attitude well.

I don't get headaches, I give headaches.

— Frank Hasenfratz #BillionDollarGoldNuggets

Billionaires are proactive, not reactive.

Jack Cowin's motto is, "Don't wait for your ship to come in; row out to meet it." It manifested itself in numerous situations in his career, and it applies also to negative events. In his life lessons, Jack says: "Don't wait until the dogs are barking at the door to do things."

Don't wait for your ship to come in; row out to meet it.

— Jack Cowin #BillionDollarGoldNuggets

Being proactive takes less time. It will become clear to you if you calculate the time cost of being reactive. You will realize that being proactive is actually easier than to react.

Don't wait until the dogs are barking at the door to do things.

— Jack Cowin #BillionDollarGoldNuggets

Proactivity is also how billionaires approach the future of the world.

Tim Draper wants to see Bitcoin succeed, so he invested in over 50 Bitcoin companies to help this future to come. "You can actually drive something to happen if you have a strong enough force behind you." At the entrance to his Draper University, he features **Elon Musk**'s quote: "Instead of witnessing the future, you can create it."

Be "Lucky"

I often get the question how much luck is involved in a billionaire's success. How important for the billionaires was it to be in the right place at the right time? This element certainly plays a relatively big role in the fast-living tech industry, but keep in mind that the vast majority of my interviewees became winners in traditional industries against strong incumbent competitors.

Nevertheless, if you ask me, "Do you need to be lucky?," I will have to give you an unsatisfactory answer: "Yes."

Yes, you need some luck in order to succeed in this extraordinary way in business as billionaires do. Success can't be guaranteed; only failure can. Even billionaires themselves admit they were lucky, although in a different way than you may assume.

When asked about his success secret, Hüsnü Özyegin said, "I believe that success is not down to one single secret or factor but a combination of several things. In my case, hard work and luck would be up there at the top of the list."

Frank Stronach sees luck and knowledge as the main differences between a millionaire and a billionaire.

Also, Manny Stul considers luck as the main difference between them, but he stresses you can make your own luck. "Difference between a millionaire and a billionaire? Luck. Being in the right place at the right time. But you make your own luck through hard work, through perseverance, passion."

Instead of witnessing the future, you can create it.

— Elon Musk #BillionDollarGoldNuggets

You can make luck happen if you take a chance. And the more chances you take, the higher the probability of a lucky strike. So, taking action drives your luck.

This is how Hüsnü Özyegin got involved in banking:

I very much believe in the film Sliding Doors. You can open one door versus another one in a building, and they're different. Your life can change completely. I also very much believe in luck. Being lucky is important. Whoever tells you about sell when the market is high or buy when the market is low, that is all baloney, as Americans say. It's luck that drives you through success.

It was luck that I became a board member of a bank at 29.

When I came back from the States, I had written job application letters to three prominent businessmen. One of them offered me a job, and I was on my way to sign the employment contract when I looked up and saw a building that said Cukurova Holding.

I remembered this as the company of my classmate Mehmet Emin Karamehmet, whom I hadn't seen since high school. I still had time until my appointment and decided to see if Mehmet was around to say hello to him. By chance he was in and welcomed me enthusiastically.

When I told him that I was about to sign a contract, he said, "Why don't you come and work with me, I need smart people like you, you can be a board member of Pamukbank, we can learn together." I was struck by his enthusiasm and made the decision then and there to accept his offer.

Imagine, I knew nothing about banking, I hadn't seen Mehmet in 12 years, but I accepted. That is why I say luck. Some people may say fate or kismet. If I hadn't walked down that street that day and dropped in on Mehmet, my life may have been very different. Who knows?

But Hüsnü did take action, did act upon this opportunity and did visit Mehmet. What was the outcome of taking this chance? After three years on the board of the bank, he became the managing director at the age of only 32 and was earning millions. And after four more years, he took a chance to become a shareholder. As his request was rejected, he then again took action, sold his houses, borrowed money, and founded his own bank.

In 2006, 19 years after founding Finansbank, he again "got lucky," selling it for $5.5 billion.

The timing was meticulous. Banking, especially in an emerging market, is sometimes like a roller-coaster business. The market value of Finansbank was $711 million in September of 2000. Only nine months later, we had a financial crisis in Turkey, and in June 2001, the market value was $84 million. At the end of 2004, it was $3.5 billion. It went from $84 million to $3.5 billion. I decided to sell. By the time we closed the deal, it was $5.5 billion, after another eight months.

This was the highest company sale in the history of Turkey, and it made Hüsnü a billionaire

Taking action drives your luck.

— Rafael Badziag @BillionairePal #BillionDollarGoldNuggets

Even if the probability of success is low, you should take the chance. It may work out. But only if you try it.

Billionaires believe they are lucky and assume everything will work out well. Tony Tan Caktiong, the World Entrepreneur of the Year 2004, told me, "I think I am born with luck, so everything I do it will be okay. It will turn out okay. And then we do things, and if it's not okay we just keep on tweaking along the way."

And yes, sometimes you will have bad luck, like Manny Stul during his first stock market experiences. Manny was into gambling in his youth, and that's why the stock market had this magical attraction for him.

I was playing the share market. At that time, nickel stock went from 20 cents to $280 in a matter of months. Everyone else was doing it. It's pretty hard to go wrong in a market where the shares go through the roof like that. I was actually making quite a lot of money.

And then I decided I wanted to get involved in the stock market directly.

First step would be the chalkie. In those days, it wasn't electronic. There was a chalkie that would write on the board. I was living in Perth; I got a job in Melbourne as a chalkie. So I sold out all my shares, and I shifted to Melbourne.

It wasn't big bucks. Maybe five, six thousand dollars. But I'm going back 45 years ago, so for me, then, that was a fortune.

While I was traveling from Perth to Melbourne to settle into Melbourne, the stock market collapsed. I thought, "Wow, how clever am I? I sold out at the top of the market and I got out before it crashed. What a brilliant investor I am." It's utter nonsense. I just happened to be in transit. I just happened to be out of the market. I would've been in the market. If I'd have been a couple of weeks later, I would've been in the market. But in my mind I thought how clever I was.

I arrived to Melbourne and the job was gone. There was no job because the market collapsed. So I didn't want to go back to Perth, because that means that I've failed. "The boy comes to Melbourne and then goes back to Perth."

The stock market collapse shattered all career dreams of Manny, and the money he made ran out after eight months. But it didn't stop him on his way. He got up, got a day job auditing, and a night job pulling beer at a pub. He started earning and trying to save up enough money to start a business. Forty-five years later, he became a billionaire and the World Entrepreneur of the Year, the best entrepreneur in the world if you will.

And you, dear reader? Will you let bad luck stop you on your way?

Are you taking action or waiting for life to happen to you? Are you the flag or the wind? Can you see the opportunities around you? Are you taking advantage of them or waiting for the right conditions? Are you selling the strawberries you have? How are you helping your luck?

- Drifters see themselves as products of circumstances, don't take action, and let life happen to them.
- Millionaires wait for right conditions to take action.
- Billionaires never wait; they sell the strawberries they have.

For more stories on this topic, go to:
http://TheBillionDollarSecret.com/resources

CHAPTER 10

Be Bold or Be Broke

*What would life be if we had no courage
to attempt anything?*

—Vincent van Gogh

There is no way around taking risk if you want to be successful in business.

When we were in his house, Jack Cowin told me, "You have to take risk to achieve something that is worthwhile. If you don't take some risk, then you'll have moderate success, if any." Of course, you shouldn't exaggerate, "everything in moderation. But you've got to take risk. You've got to be prepared to accept risk. If it doesn't require risk, it's not an opportunity."

For Mohed Altrad, the World Entrepreneur of the Year 2015, risk is a necessary component. "I took risk every year and up to now, because there is no success without risk."

Ron Sim, the Singaporean creator of the OSIM empire, is a true fighter. During the interview in his office, he told me, "Prepare to lose if you want to win." For him, progress in life is a learning process. "If you don't take risk, you will never learn."

You have to take risk to achieve something that is worthwhile.

– Jack Cowin #BillionDollarGoldNuggets

For Hüsnü Özyegin, entrepreneurship really means taking risks.

And indeed, every company starts with a big risk. According to Naveen Jain, "Every company you start is a risk to your reputation, is a risk to your wealth, and is a risk to the number of people who believe in you and they quit their job and come and join you. Their life depends on my not screwing up. So to me, it is a massive burden on me to make sure I don't fail because their lives will change. And I have looked at their wives' eyes and they're looking at me saying, please don't f*ck it up."

If it doesn't require risk, it's not an opportunity.

– Jack Cowin #BillionDollarGoldNuggets

Kim Beom-Su makes clear that due to social change, our times are predestined for risk-taking. "When you are young, you tend to think getting hired at a good company is the safest way to go, but I think that era has passed. Because working for a good company doesn't guarantee a secure retirement or any long-term security. Now, it's an era where it's very important to take risks and try different things, and from that find what you really enjoy doing and are really good at."

There is no success without risk.

— Mohed Altrad #BillionDollarGoldNuggets

Interestingly, billionaires don't see intelligence as a prerequisite for their extraordinary business success. They stress that entrepreneurs are adventurous rather than intelligent.

This is what Sergey Galitskiy noticed when he had been working for a bank, before he got involved in his own business. "When I communicated with clients in the bank, who were businesspeople, I felt how intellectually weak they were. But I was impressed by the way they think. So these were people not of a smart mind, but rather of an adventurous mind. And this made a big impression on me."

Prepare to lose if you want to win.

— Ron Sim #BillionDollarGoldNuggets

Don't Let the Fear Stop You from Doing Things

Courage is one of the most important character traits for an entrepreneur.

Fear of failure is a huge force, so use it to do it right instead of having it limit you.

If you don't take risk, you will never learn.

— Ron Sim #BillionDollarGoldNuggets

Jack Cowin's father kept telling him he could achieve what he wanted if he wasn't afraid of difficult challenges and was brave enough to follow his dreams.

Chip Wilson had the courage to take the greatest risk of his life when he started Lululemon. "I had two children. When you start to bet on the children, that's the tough part." Yes, he had some capital after he sold his previous company. "I had a house, I had security. I could've gotten a job as a barista at Starbucks, and anything would've been fine." But he put all his money into the company, mortgaged the house, and kept borrowing every cent he could to put into it. "I really was risking. Could I pay my alimony to my ex-wife? Are my kids going to get fed? It was a big concern."

Entrepreneurship really means taking risks.

— Hüsnü Özyegin #BillionDollarGoldNuggets

Act despite the fear of rejection. You can't please everybody. If you do something, there will always be people who don't like it.

Naveen Jain told me these insightful words when we met in the Shelbourne Hotel in Dublin:

When you are a people person, you put yourself out there; you're always afraid of being rejected. And then being an immigrant, obviously my English is not as good. Sometimes people look at you as if you're crazy because they don't understand what you're saying. So in some sense, you're always afraid that people may not like you.

But to some extent, I have gotten over it. I have realized that you can't get everyone to like you. If you want everyone to like you, you have to do nothing, be nothing, and stand for nothing. But if you do something, there are people who will hate it. So you know what? It doesn't matter.

Every company starts with a big risk.

— Rafael Badziag @BillionairePal #BillionDollarGoldNuggets

Are you afraid of ridicule? Get rid of it. Billionaires don't hesitate to do things that might look foolish or go wrong.

This willingness to fail is what Tim Draper considers his success secret.

I think if I am willing to take a chance on something and willing to either lose my money or get embarrassed or lose face or have some problem and still be willing to wake up the next day and go to work, I think that is the strength of becoming successful. I think you have to be willing to do something that might look stupid and might fail.

That's how he became a legendary Silicon Valley venture capital investor.

Our business is remarkable in that way because we often fail. We fail, in fact, maybe more than half of the time in the venture capital business, and still somehow continue to be in the business.

Now, it's an era where it's very important to take risks and try different things.

— Kim Beom-Su #BillionDollarGoldNuggets

Billionaires are also humans. They weren't born the greatest risk-takers, defying all fears. I asked Jack Cowin about what he would have changed if he turned 20 again.

I'd probably be bolder. I'd probably have taken more risk. The fear of failure makes you more conscious. The fear of debt makes you more conscious. So I would have more confidence in myself that I could find my way through the maze.

And caution, because you don't want to go broke. Rule #1 in business: don't go broke. If you make a mistake, you make a misjudgment; it's easy to do. We could've gone broke a couple times due to high interest rates. The truth is in the restaurant business you're constantly not that far away from the danger of someone dying from food poisoning if someone did something very mistaken regarding procedures which requires constant diligence. It's a risk that you live with all the time, so you've really got to manage it properly.

Rule #1 in Business: Don't Go Broke

We were sitting in front of Jack's house and he expanded on this topic, warning against betting the farm and giving me some of his life lessons:

You don't have to go for broke every time. Don't bet the farm. Things go wrong with the best-laid plans. Spread the risk. In baseball terms, you don't have to hit a home run every time. Singles and doubles will get you there. Babe Ruth hit the most home runs; he also struck out the most. So you don't have to take huge risks to get there, everything in moderation. Don't underestimate the power of compound interest.

The number one priority of a CEO is to make sure that the company stays in business and survives. What threats can take you out of the game? What decisions, if wrong, could be terminal? What is your margin of error?

Accept that without risk, and the possibility of failure, success will be limited.

You can't please everybody. If you do something, there will always be people who don't like it.

– Rafael Badziag @BillionairePal #BillionDollarGoldNuggets

Risk can kill your business, so don't bet the shop, protect your downside.

Manny Stul, the World Entrepreneur of the Year 2016, likes risk like nobody, but he wouldn't risk everything even on a bulletproof venture.

I like taking risks. It's in my nature. But don't bet the farm on anything! I don't care how good it is and how it appears to be a no-brainer and how it appears to be guaranteed.

I asked him if that would also be the case at the beginning, when you don't actually have anything.

Well, then what have you got to lose? If I lost everything when I started, there wasn't much to lose. I was probably taking bigger risks then. But certainly nothing that would ruin my life, if you know what I mean.

And yes, Manny was betting the farm at the beginning of his first business with gift articles called hurdy-gurdys that were manufactured in Japan.

I brought some in, and they were very successful. Round about end of April, when I was going to place another order, they said, "We have huge demand. We can supply you whatever you want, but you have to get us the order now. And the order you give us now is all the stock you will get for Christmas. You won't get more, you won't get less." I didn't sleep for three nights, because I knew I had a winner, and I didn't know what the potential was. I put everything into that. The whole lot, all the liquid assets that were available to me at that time. I didn't have anything. If I had a house, I could've possibly bet the house, but I didn't have one.

It paid off well for Manny, but as his company grew, he paid attention not to take risks that could ruin him.

You can't get everyone to like you. If you want everyone to like you, you have to do nothing, be nothing, and stand for nothing.

— Naveen Jain #BillionDollarGoldNuggets

You should always have a margin of safety. It's essential to never run out of cash.

Hüsnü Özyegin, typically for somebody with a banking background, is very conservative about protecting his downside. For him, "assessing the downside is really, really important."

Entrepreneurs are adventurous rather than intelligent.

— Rafael Badziag @BillionairePal #BillionDollarGoldNuggets

When I asked Frank Hasenfratz what he avoids in business, he answered with just one word: "overextending." Don't shy away from risk, but don't stretch your business too much financially. It could break and go down under the burden. "You may be lucky two times or three times, but one day you may stretch too far. So I take risk every day, but the risk I take I can afford to lose. It's really important to keep your debt so that it's manageable."

You have to be willing to do something that might look stupid and might fail.

— Tim Draper #BillionDollarGoldNuggets

Watch the Risk/Reward Ratio

One of the most important qualities of an entrepreneur is being able to assess risk. That's how Jack Cowin sees it: "Risk can kill you. So judgment in how much risk to take, when, where, that is all a very fine line. Because without risk, you're not going to go too far. You have to take risk. It's part of the deal. If you don't have some risk, you're wasting your time."

Rule #1 in business: don't go broke.

— Jack Cowin #BillionDollarGoldNuggets

As Lirio Parisotto puts it: "I need the risk. If I'm alive, I'm at risk to die. You risk all the time. But if I make a choice in business, I need to be able to afford it if things go wrong."

Cho Tak Wong, the World Entrepreneur of the Year 2009, recommends to "do an analysis and estimate what risks could be in a given project," and take only risks that you can deal with.

Accept that without risk, and the possibility of failure, success will be limited.

— Jack Cowin #BillionDollarGoldNuggets

It is also foolish to take unnecessary risk that doesn't bring you closer to your objectives. I asked Jack Cowin what he avoided in business. His answer: "Unnecessary risk. Risk is necessary, but don't do things which are superfluous to what the end game is."

Don't bet the farm on anything! I don't care how good it is and how it appears to be a no-brainer and how it appears to be guaranteed.

— Manny Stul #BillionDollarGoldNuggets

Billionaires look at the potential of things, not only at the downside.

Many billionaires, like Kim Beom-Su, always "choose opportunity over risk."

Jack Cowin warns of the dangers of too much education: "One of the problems of getting too much education as an MBA is you find out all the reasons why you shouldn't do something. You become too cautious. You find out all the things that can go wrong. You measure the downside much more than you do the potential."

Assessing the downside is really, really important.

— Hüsnü Özyegin #BillionDollarGoldNuggets

So what is the winning formula with regard to risk?

It's quite straightforward: take calculated risks with the best risk/reward ratio instead of "betting the shop." Or in other words: take the risks you can afford that have the greatest upside and the smallest downside.

One of the most important qualities of an entrepreneur is being able to assess risk.

— Rafael Badziag @BillionairePal #BillionDollarGoldNuggets

The risk perception is subjective and doesn't necessarily correspond to the amount of money in question. Dilip Shanghvi risks literally billions every day, but he is unfazed by it. "People perceive that I take big risks, I honestly don't really take big risks. I'm able to manage risk effectively. So I have an internal mechanism of rationally distributing risk, and I always appoint risk with the return."

It may sound pretentious to you, but in reality it's quite obvious. With growing size, your approach to risk changes. Ron Sim explains it clearly: "As I age, I become more cautious, I become more careful. When I was young, I would do it first. Now I consider it a bit more. There's more to lose now, but now I'm more prepared to play bigger games with bigger stakes."

> ## Without risk, you're not going to go too far. You have to take risk. It's part of the deal. If you don't have some risk, you're wasting your time.
>
> **— Jack Cowin #BillionDollarGoldNuggets**

Business is a continuous risk-taking.

Tim Draper internalized risk into his business to the degree that he even wrote a song, "Riskmaster," a eulogy on entrepreneurship. As a seasoned venture capital investor, he developed strategies to peg his risk. He used these strategies when he became an **early investor in Tesla** even before **Elon Musk** took over as the CEO, as the following story shows.

I went out and I got this ride in an electric car that this guy had put together with PVC tubing and just jerry-rigged together. His name was Ian Wright. He put me in the car, we took off, and I couldn't believe how fast it was or how fast it stopped. So I got very excited about the idea of an electric car. I thought, Oh my gosh, these lines are going to cross. You're going to see electric cars getting better than the combustion engine because they're so much faster and they stop better and they perform better.

Later, Tim found out that Tesla solved the problem of exploding batteries that killed Fisker, an early electric car. He met **Martin Eberhard**, the founder of **Tesla**, and made a small investment.

I wanted to make a big one but my partners were smart; they said, "Just make a small investment, because this is going to be capital-intensive."

*Later, **Elon Musk** came in with $10 million when the company was out of money, and he said "I'm going to take it over," and everybody said, "Yeah! Awesome."*

> ## If I'm alive, I'm at risk to die. You risk all the time. But if I make a choice in business, I need to be able to afford it if things go wrong.
>
> **— Lirio Parisotto #BillionDollarGoldNuggets**

"Indecent" Offers, Audacious Moves

Billionaires are not scared to make others "indecent" business offers.

In 1986, the 28-year-old Tim Draper was just out of business school. "I went to the board members of Activision at Sutter Hill Ventures and asked to become the CEO, and told them that as CEO, I would use the public stock to buy up Microsoft and Lotus and a bunch of other software companies that were all private and valued low. In retrospect, they should have done it, but they looked at me with cocked heads and politely showed me the door."

And Manny Stul, the World Entrepreneur of the Year 2016, follows the same strategy:

I have always had and still do have the attitude of "ask for the world and work your way back from that" in negotiating. So there was no limit to what I ask for because you never know for sure how other people will react until you begin the process.

Take only risks that you can deal with.

– Cho Tak Wong #BillionDollarGoldNuggets

Hüsnü Özyegin, now the wealthiest self-made man in Turkey, was the president of the student body at Oregon State University. He made a bold move and invited Senator Robert "Bobby" Kennedy, the American president's brother, to visit OSU during his trip to the western states. Hüsnü wrote him a letter and, surprisingly, he accepted. This audacious move paid off big time for Hüsnü, as he was then personally hosting this rock star of a politician at his university. Hüsnü showed me with pride a picture of him with Robert Kennedy on stage together. But it paid off even more in the future, when Hüsnü applied for Harvard Business School.

I was actually quite surprised that Harvard Business School accepted me, because I barely graduated from Oregon State with a grade average of 2.17. You have to have a 2 average to graduate from school. But then again, the president of the university wrote my recommendation letter. He told me that it was the only recommendation letter he wrote for anybody that year, for the graduating class of some 3,000 students. [laughs] I stuffed all my photos with Bobby Kennedy and my student body presidential campaign material into my application envelope.

Harvard is a business school that requires four years' job experience, but despite those very low grades and no job experience, they accepted me.

Apparently, the pictures with Bobby Kennedy made an impression on the admissions.

Risk is necessary, but don't do things which are superfluous to what the end game is.

— Jack Cowin #BillionDollarGoldNuggets

To achieve big things you often have to take a leap of faith. You should try to do things far beyond your comfort zone. Billionaires take on outrageous challenges or even try to go for the seemingly impossible.

Naveen Jain founded Infospace when there were no smartphones, but he was on a mission to build services for mobile Internet. "People thought it was the absolutely craziest thing to do and that it would never happen. When I was creating an information commerce business of selling information on the Internet, they thought that was the absolute craziest idea. And now, think about it, I want to go to the moon and they think it's a crazy idea. So point is if people don't think what you're doing is crazy, then you're not thinking big enough."

Look at the potential of things, not only at the downside.

— Rafael Badziag @BillionairePal #BillionDollarGoldNuggets

Don't be scared of big numbers. If you do one BIG thing, people will start approaching you.

For Tim Draper, one of the turning points in his career was the Hotmail deal. Hotmail was one of the first web-based email services, and Tim was the first investor in it. It was one of the fastest-growing services of the 1990s, and quickly became the largest such service in the world. Tim sold Hotmail just 1.5 years after launch for $400 million to Microsoft. "That was a big deal. It put us on the map. It was a big enough media deal that they started to focus on us. That ended up being a really good launching pad for us; we were able to raise the next fund fairly easily. We put that to work in the Internet. From then to five or six years from then, we were near the top of the heap. That was really very exciting."

Choose opportunity over risk.

— Kim Beom-Su #BillionDollarGoldNuggets

Don't Be Afraid to Be Different

Petter Stordalen recommends to go the road less traveled if you want to be successful in business, and not to be scared to be different.

Take calculated risks with the best risk/reward ratio instead of "betting the shop."

— Rafael Badziag @BillionairePal #BillionDollarGoldNuggets

But what do you do if you are the only man in the room who shares your specific conviction? Billionaires don't get bogged down by this detail.

Naveen Jain fights for his convictions. He told me this story when we met in Dublin:

*I was in my first few months at Microsoft, and I had a meeting with **Bill Gates** about Windows NT. I'm a mid-level manager, the dumb young guy, and all the top guys are in this meeting. And Bill is an extremely intense person. Somebody is presenting about this Windows, and Bill looks at me and says, "What do you think about this operating system?" And I said, "Bill, I think it's going to be big, fat, and slow." Everybody in the room is quiet now. And Bill looks at me for 10 seconds intensely and quietly, and he says, "Exactly!"*

The meeting adjourns and the guy who is my manager says, "Do you know you work for me and what you did is absolutely going to cost you." I looked at him and said, "Martin, it may come as a surprise to you. Slavery is long gone. I do not work for you. I work for the company and I work for myself, so don't you ever tell me I work for you." And he said, "I'm going to put you on probation, and that will show you who you work for." And he did.

And guess what happened. They changed everything in that operating system to become a lean mean operating system because I was able to go say, Bill, this is exactly what's going to happen if you go down this path. So now, the cost was I almost got fired. But that is how entrepreneurs are. They don't care. They're going to go out and say what it is, and they're going to go out and do it themselves. So that's my entrepreneur way.

Ask for the world and work your way back from that.

— Manny Stul #BillionDollarGoldNuggets

Six Strategies to Develop Courage and Not Worry

Billionaires generally consider themselves limitless, sometimes even fearless. They never stop risking.

If people don't think what you're doing is crazy, then you're not thinking big enough.

— Naveen Jain #BillionDollarGoldNuggets

It's easy to say "Be Bold," but how do you develop courage?

1. You need to accept that you may fail. In the next chapters, I will show you actually must fail and fail many times before you become a success.

2. Realize that you are a tiny, unimportant speck of dust and your life is very limited. So why worry?

    Cho Tak Wong, the World Entrepreneur of the Year 2009 from China, explains it as follows:

    Everybody's life is limited. It is very short, and each individual has very limited power, no matter how hard you work. Compared to the world, compared to the history, a person is very, very small.

3. Realize that risk in business comes from your ignorance. It's the fear of the unknown. Your experience will help you get rid of it.

    Naveen Jain explains it clearly:

    Well, risk is in your mind and your belief because risk comes from ignorance. Risk is like the fear of the unknown. If you know what's around the corner, it doesn't feel risky. When you are in a dark alley, you're afraid to make a turn. If you have a flashlight, you don't feel afraid.

    So if you're an entrepreneur, if you started three companies, there is no risk in the fourth company. You know every single thing you're going to go through. You know you're going to have a near-death experience, you know the hurdles are going to come, you know the business deals that you thought were almost done are going to fall apart. And the deals are going to come together you never thought would come together. So point is you have seen it all.

    Mohed Altrad told me he was "very, very anxious in the beginning, but courage comes with experience."

Risk is in your mind.
It comes from ignorance.
Risk is the fear of the unknown.

– Naveen Jain #BillionDollarGoldNuggets

4. The more risk you take, the better you can handle it. Stay foolish!

Chip Wilson got his risk affinity from his grandparents, who were entrepreneurs initially selling furniture. They had been caught up in the first computer fraud in mutual funds and had to move into a trailer.

But it was always part of what I loved about what I call the American Dream. You risk big, you can get big, and you fail and you start all over again, and you don't let it get you down.

These early experiences allowed Chip bold moves already in his teenage years. When he was 14, he got on a plane on his own and went to Antigua with about $47 in his pocket and was trying to live there for $3 a day. Then at 17, he went to Alaska to work on the oil pipeline, a decision that made him wealthy before 20. He gave up the university and education to do it. From the outside, it looked like trading his life in for short-term gain, but it turned out well for him.

You risk big, you can get big.

– Chip Wilson #BillionDollarGoldNuggets

5. See life as an adventure and a challenge. Regard risk as fun.

Risk is an integral element of Petter Stordalen's life philosophy: "Live life like you mean it. Take risks; don't be afraid of failing or falling down. Every bruise tells a story, and someday you might even laugh at it."

Jack Cowin gave me a quote from his life lessons: "Be prepared to take some risks. Life is an adventure and a challenge. When you are young, you can afford to fail because you can start over again. When you are old, you need the stimulation."

Chip Wilson shares his interesting approach:

Creativity and risk are fun, and might actually be one of the reasons for living.

Courage comes with experience.

– Mohed Altrad #BillionDollarGoldNuggets

6. Have some sort of a safety net. Have your back protected and something to fall back on. It will help you to spread your wings, worry less, and be bold.

    For Naveen Jain, this protection is his family:

    It's really about the joy of having a family where whatever happens, someone will always be there at your side, who will love you, trust you, and be there for you. And always have your back protected. And that gives you so much inner strength to do things that you would never do.

    For Peter Hargreaves, the safety net is the profession he learned: chartered accountant.

    It was a very, very good, solid qualification. Very useful to me. And it gave me the security. If you have something to fall back on, you worry less about failing, because you know you can go back to that.

Live life like you mean it.

— Chip Wilson #BillionDollarGoldNuggets

Are you willing to take risks, my dear reader? Are you courageous enough to go for what you want to achieve, or do you let your fears stop you from taking bold steps? Are you afraid to be different, to make "indecent" offers and audacious moves? Do you handle your risk consciously? How?

Creativity and risk are fun, and might actually be one of the reasons for living.

— Chip Wilson #BillionDollarGoldNuggets

-   Drifters play it safe.

-   Millionaires aren't proficient in handling risk. They either bet the house or take risks with limited upside.

-   Billionaires know how to handle risk and take risks with huge upside and low downside.

For more stories on this topic, go to:
http://TheBillionDollarSecret.com/resources

CHAPTER 11

Stumble Forward

Mistakes are the portals to discovery.

—James Joyce

Billionaires see life as an adventurous journey.

For Jack Cowin, "part and parcel of any journey are obstacles. Life is an obstacle course."

Michał Sołowow likens his life to a roller-coaster ride:

My life is a ride on a roller coaster, which moves fast, very high in the Alps. And I, the engine driver of that roller coaster, keep solving a dilemma: either the wagon will derail or I will miss the next turn. The stations are awfully short. If you blink your eyes just for a moment, you could miss a stop. Besides, when you board the roller coaster, you can get out only in the mountains, and you have a chance to enter the next roller coaster. When I entered into that roller coaster for the first time, I didn't realize how tall those mountains are, that there are so many turns and stations. . . .

Part and parcel of any journey are obstacles. Life is an obstacle course.

— Jack Cowin #BillionDollarGoldNuggets

Obstacles Are Often an Opportunity in Disguise

If something bad happens, look for the good in it. You never know what it's good for. Sometimes it's actually a blessing.

Frank Stronach, founder of Magna, an auto industry giant, had an experience in his life that made him realize that sometimes a failure is a blessing in disguise. When Frank was 22, he applied for work at the Ford company as a tool and die maker.

They were hiring for their new factory. They interviewed me and said, "We don't think you have enough experience." And later on I met the president of Ford, and I said, "You're lucky I wasn't there; otherwise I would be the president of Ford."

On the other hand, if Frank had become a Ford employee, he might have become a very successful manager, possibly a CEO, but he would never have founded Magna and become a billionaire.

Mohed Altrad considers being chosen the World Entrepreneur of the Year 2015 his greatest success. But it wouldn't have happened if not for an unexpected mishap. The event takes place every year in Monaco. And Mohed is also the owner and manager of the Rugby team Montpellier Hérault.

I was not supposed to go to Monaco. I told them I am not coming, because our rugby team was playing the playoffs that were the same week as the World Entrepreneur of the Year event in Monaco.

Unfortunately for us, or fortunately for me, we were eliminated the day before I had to be in Monaco, so I told them, "I'll go." That's why I was in Monaco.

You can find good surprises in bad situations.

The judge committee has a file, and then they read this file, and then you enter this impressive room in the Hermitage Hotel in Monaco. The head of the railways in Canada, the head of Mitsubishi. And then they start, and you have only 20 minutes. You tell them what you want to tell, and then they listen to you for 10 minutes, and then 10 minutes later they bombard you with questions and you have to be very brief in your answers.

It's difficult. It's not difficult to tell something. It's difficult to tell a good story. You have to tell a story in the minimum number of words.

Mohed, of course, is an excellent storyteller. And as an award-winning author, he knows how to deliver a short but good story.

I was some sort of prepared. I understood that there were things that made them know, "This is the best company."

And that's how he was chosen the best entrepreneur in the world in 2015.

You can find good surprises in bad situations.

— Mohed Altrad #BillionDollarGoldNuggets

Where most people see a problem, billionaires see an opportunity in solving it. They use obstacles to their advantage. For example, in the pharmaceutical industry, psychiatrists are served poorly by distributors. Dilip Shanghvi explains why:

Psychiatrists are the most difficult people to meet, because they make you wait for one or two hours at a stretch. Because each patient takes half an hour or one hour. In that time, a representative can do five visits to general practitioners.

We took this business which was not very attractive for our competitors, and we structured our strategy accordingly. Our people had no choice but to succeed with psychiatrists.

If you see all successful companies, they have all solved a problem. Facebook, LinkedIn, Google, they all solve problems, even if people didn't know the problems existed. So if you solve a problem, that creates an opportunity.

This attitude was one of the reasons Dilip became the world's wealthiest person in the pharmaceutical industry.

If you solve a problem, that creates an opportunity.

– Dilip Shanghvi #BillionDollarGoldNuggets

Billionaires see even crises as opportunities.

Mohed Altrad sees a crisis as an opportunity to buy. He expanded his company by acquisitions in the scaffolding industry whenever there was a crisis. "It was easy because most of the businesses were in trouble, all European companies. So it was easy to buy them." Initially, he was buying only businesses that were losing money and were cheap to buy because he himself didn't have much money. That way, Mohed managed within 30 years to add over 230 companies to his Altrad Group and became the world leader in his industry.

Peter Hargreaves believes recessions have a cleansing effect on the economy and free up good people who are locked in bad companies, "and some of those people actually succeed in business."

A crisis as an opportunity to buy.

– Mohed Altrad #BillionDollarGoldNuggets

In crises and adverse experiences you learn the most.

Peter gave me this great advice: "You should always learn from everything. And I think you learn more from adverse experiences. You learn more from bad experiences, and I think you learn more working for bad companies than good companies, strangely enough." You just learn what not to do.

Experiment, Be Willing to Fail, but Learn from Your Mistakes

Don't expect success to appear at the very first try. You need to try over and over again and fail over and over again. And you need to do it right only once. Once you finally succeed, you become an "overnight success."

I asked Manny Stul, the World Entrepreneur of the Year 2016, what were his greatest failures. He replied, "There's lots of failures along the way; it's part of the process. You can't be successful without having failures. It's not possible. The only people that don't make mistakes are the people that don't do anything. If you want to stay out of trouble, you can go and work for the government."

On your way up you will fail many times. Only if you accept your failings, will you be able to challenge yourself in the long run. And only by challenging yourself can you succeed. That's what I learned from Petter Stordalen.

You can't be successful without having failures. The only people that don't make mistakes are the people that don't do anything.

– Manny Stul #BillionDollarGoldNuggets

Tim Draper, the legendary venture capital investor, is even more radical on this point. For him, "success is continuing to be willing to fail."

Sergey Galitskiy is absolutely unfazed by mistakes. I asked him what he would do differently if he started again. He replied, "Nothing, because life is not interesting without mistakes. Life is not interesting without trying. Life cannot consist only of positive emotions. You have to, however, make sure that there are more positive emotions and that they dominate over the negative ones. But you can't eat ice cream and cake 24 hours a day. Sometimes you have to eat onions."

Be prepared to fail many times. You will make a lot of mistakes, especially in the beginning. Make sure you can afford it.

Ron Sim recommends:

If you want to do business, you've got to get your hands dirty. You've got to be prepared to walk it "come what may." And you've got to tell yourself that you're going to fall many times, and you're going to fail many times, and you're going to lose many times. And those are not problems. Those are testing moments for you to overcome. If you take that with the right mindset, it's a piece of cake.

Success is continuing to be willing to fail.

– Tim Draper #BillionDollarGoldNuggets

Mistakes will happen. It's okay to make mistakes, but learn from them and avoid repeating them.

Manny Stul, the World Entrepreneur of the Year 2016, learned everything about business in the first years of his first company when he did everything by try and error and naturally made a lot of mistakes. "Nothing, nothing, nothing do I not know about business as a consequence of those days." He made so many mistakes, he can't even remember. "But I never made the same mistake twice."

For Manny, mistakes are okay, but failures not necessary. "The most important thing is to learn from your experiences, and don't make the same mistakes twice."

Life is not interesting without mistakes.

– Sergey Galitskiy #BillionDollarGoldNuggets

Many billionaires use experimentation as a business tool. They experiment with their ideas, test them in their businesses, willing to try things that might not work.

At his Draper University, Tim Draper teaches his students entrepreneurship by offering them a safe environment where they can experiment and also make mistakes.

We're encouraging more of the risk-taking, the failing. People realize when they're there, they're safe, they can try stuff. In other schools, they can't make any mistakes or they don't get an "A," which is wrong. This is much, much better.

I want students to learn to be willing to fail, willing to try things that might not work. They come out going, "I'm going to try it. I'll try stuff. If it doesn't work, it's okay." They don't worry about losing face or not being like their neighbors. We make them independent souls that can work really well in teams, and I think that's a really powerful thing.

Kim Beom-Su approaches this concept in a structured way. For him, business is setting a hypothesis and then proving it. "I usually try various things that I thought of, so I've had many experiences where I make a hypothesis and then it didn't work out." He takes the rate of growth as the main criterion on whether he should continue with the project at hand or not. "You try it out for 6 to 12 months, then you have the data to see how people are responding to it and you can make the decision."

You can't eat ice cream and cake 24 hours a day.

– Sergey Galitskiy #BillionDollarGoldNuggets

Some billionaires use a simple rule of thumb: "If it doesn't kill you, go for it!"

Mohed Altrad's company went immediately abroad in its acquisition spree. I asked Mohed if it wasn't too risky to do it in the very beginning. "It was easy. The targets in Spain and Italy were small companies, such as 1 million Euros. You are not taking a big risk. So the idea is to go abroad, assuming what happens if these two go bankrupt? Nothing. You will have a hit on your head and you'll overcome it. That's the thing."

You're going to fall many times, and you're going to fail many times, and you're going to lose many times.

– Ron Sim #BillionDollarGoldNuggets

You just give it a try. If it doesn't work, you improve.

Tony Tan Caktiong, the World Entrepreneur of the Year 2004, went abroad very early. "We opened Jollibee in Singapore. It failed. So we went to Taiwan. It failed. And this probably was bold when we were not ready because we had the dream that we want to be a global company. So after those we just kept on thinking, how do we make it better?"

Tim Draper's action plan is simple: "I experience. I adjust. I act."

Business is setting a hypothesis and then proving it.

– Kim Beom-Su #BillionDollarGoldNuggets

Be a Problem Solver

Entrepreneurs are problem solvers.

Naveen Jain has an interesting theory about entrepreneurship:

Let's just start with the basic thing of what's an entrepreneur? If you look at all the humans in the world, you categorize them into three types of people.

One group of people who say I can think about the problem. I can tell you what the problem is. And all of us are very good at it. So we call them human beings. Everyone is the person who can tell you what problems are.

The second group are the people who would come up with the solutions. They will tell you what the solution to this problem is. These are the visionaries, and these are the people we would call the professors.

There's only one type of person who goes out and does something about it. And he says, "To hell with it. I'm going to go out and do it." And those are the people who are entrepreneurs. You can be an entrepreneur inside a company, inside a personal relationship, or starting a company. So, entrepreneurship is not necessarily about starting a business but about solving a problem.

Many billionaires consider solving problems as one of their strong points. Michał Sołowow considers himself a crisis manager. "I am rather useful for such difficult situations."

I experience. I adjust. I act.

– Tim Draper #BillionDollarGoldNuggets

Problems are a treasure trove for business models.

When I asked Dilip Shanghvi for advice for people who want to be as successful as him, he answered: "I think the most important thing would be to find a problem to solve."

Dilip also learned from his father to always confront his problems, instead of running away from them:

When I worked with my father in the pharmaceutical wholesale business, if I received a phone call from someone I didn't want to speak with, I wouldn't answer. My father would ask me, "Why didn't you talk to him?" I'd say, "We need to pay him. I can't pay him today; I plan to pay him tomorrow, so I did not talk to him."

My father said, "No, you should call him first, tell him that you cannot pay him today, even though you promised, and that you will pay tomorrow. Don't avoid a difficult situation. You have to face it, because if today you have an issue and you run away, then you will not learn to solve problems, and people will not trust you."

Problems are a treasure trove for business models.

– Rafael Badziag @BillionairePal #BillionDollarGoldNuggets

For every adversity there is always a solution. Don't complain; find a solution instead.

Mohed Altrad's life was dominated by adversity.

If you look at my life, it's a series of adversities. It starts from the beginning, the death of my mother and the fact that my father didn't want me to live with him so he cast me away. Then coming to France, you have another problem, which is *language. You can't communicate with people. Cultural difference. And then later on, to succeed at the university, and the fact that you don't have money during your early years in the university. I used to have something like 20 Euros ($25) a month and had to live on that, to eat, to dress, to walk.*

Later on, when I started a business, I needed banks, and no bank wanted to open a bank account for my company because "you are an immigrant, you are Syrian, you are an Arab, you are a Bedouin, and you have a computer science education and you are trying to do business in scaffolding or concrete mixers." It's a combination [leading to] disaster, according to them.

Whatever the adversity, whatever the stage in which this happens, there is always a solution to get out of it. It's not always a good solution, but when you are at this stage, it's not a matter of having a good life or a very good life, it's a matter of life and death. This is the thing, you see. It's about surviving.

I went through this all my life. Now, things [have] improved, but believe me, this is still flowing in my blood, in my heart. I don't forget this.

Don't avoid a difficult situation. You have to face it, because if today you have an issue and you run away, then you will not learn to solve problems, and people will not trust you.

— Dilip Shanghvi #BillionDollarGoldNuggets

Unsuccessful people first look for the culprits when problems arise. This is not what billionaires do. They look for solutions. Michał Sołowow codified it as one of the rules for his companies: "We solve problems; we don't search for the culpable."

For billionaires, problem solving is a source of motivation.

Manny Stul just loves problem solving.

The more complicated the problem is, the more I enjoy it. The reality is our whole business life is like a game of chess. And it is only a game. People need to be mindful of that: it is only a game, and not to take it too seriously. All that happens as you get bigger is the numbers get bigger, but it's still the same game.

Michał Sołowow shares a similar attitude:

I am motivated by problems. Every day I want things to work better. Those problems that I encounter in everyday life lead me to solving them. In other words, it's a self-propelling mechanism. I like my work, I like what I do.

**The more complicated the problem is,
the more I enjoy it.**

— Manny Stul #BillionDollarGoldNuggets

After a Failure, Get Up, Improve, and Never Look Back

It's okay to fail. But quickly pick yourself up and get back into the game. Don't let a failure or a mishap stop you on your way.

Michał Sołowow pretty much sums up billionaires' attitude toward failures: "Determination is needed, an ability to stand up after defeats is needed. You need the ability to accept those defeats because they keep happening all the time. They happen daily. Every day something happens in a way that we would not like it to, and one needs to accept that and do one's best to improve it. One important thing is also the ability to draw conclusions from those defeats. To continuously learn and after all self-improve."

**Whole business life is like a game of
chess. And it is only a game.**

— Manny Stul #BillionDollarGoldNuggets

Petter Stordalen gives a perfect example of how you get up immediately after you fall. He was fired from the shopping center development company at the peak of his success. Just in the moment when he thought he knew it all and became invincible, he lost it all.

"Okay, what do I do? Definitely not shopping centers. I'm done with shopping centers."

I was looking to different possible options, and I thought, "Okay." Private health care was in the early beginning in Norway. That could be something. Then I saw hotels. Hotels. Not much had happened in the hotel industry in the last 20 years. It's the same players, run by old men in dark suits, more than 50 years old. I was around 30. So I decided hotels.

I set up a press conference and I told them, "I'm here to tell you." Everybody thought I would talk about shopping centers. "My new business is hotels." They started to laugh. "I know why you laugh, because my ambition is to make the biggest hotel company ever in Norway." They were like, "Ah ha ha." Then I said, "I know why you are still laughing, because it will be the biggest one in Scandinavia," and they literally had to carry people out. One guy asked me, "So Petter, how many hotels do you have?" I said, "I have one. Bought it yesterday out of a bankruptcy."

And from that day, we added on average one hotel and 50 people every 14 days. I went from one hotel to 100, from a few employees to 5,000 in less than three years. And people stopped laughing.

As I am writing this book, Petter has close to 200 hotels in his Nordic Choice hotel chain including the brands Clarion Hotel, Comfort Hotel, and Quality Hotel. It is the largest hotel chain in Scandinavia. Nobody laughs at Petter's claims anymore; they call him the Hotel King.

I am motivated by problems.

– Michał Sołowow #BillionDollarGoldNuggets

Jack Cowin's attitude is, "If you have not had a few failures, you haven't tried enough. You've been slack and lazy."

So never look back. Don't dwell on your failures. Instead, focus on what you can do now to improve the future.

I asked Jack what he would do differently if he were 21 again.

My basic make-up and attitude is a positive one. I look on the positive side of life. If I was 21 again, there wouldn't be too many things I'd do different. Sometimes I might've gone harder or things like this, but I think it's really important not to dwell on things that didn't work. Get on with it, next. Let's put our energy into something that's going to work. And I'm not trying to be dismissive, because I say we've made lots of mistakes, from the start.

If you have not had a few failures, you haven't tried enough. You've been slack and lazy.

– Jack Cowin #BillionDollarGoldNuggets

Hüsnü Özyegin recommends to learn from your mistakes instead of dwelling on them:

I have missed more opportunities than I grabbed. I never regret that, because I'm very satisfied with what I've done, and my character is such that I don't look back at what I missed; rather I try to learn from my mistakes, not dwell on what I missed but try to understand what I did wrong, so to speak.

Frank Stronach is even more radical with respect to this: "I see nothing as a failure. If something doesn't work out, you learn from it. Don't look back. Don't get angry. And just look forward."

Frank Hasenfratz likes to say: "If you're looking back too often, you're going to trip going forward."

It's really important not to dwell on things that didn't work. Get on with it.

— Jack Cowin #BillionDollarGoldNuggets

Accept and Embrace Change

One of the recurring concepts during my interviews with billionaires was the concept of change. Most people have trouble with the fast-changing world we live in. They want things to stay as they are, do the things as they did yesterday. Most of us have difficulty accepting change and adapting to it.

Billionaires have a completely different approach. They not only accept change and are prepared for it, they embrace it and take advantage of it. In most cases, they are the change agents who cause the world to change.

I don't look back at what I missed; rather I try to learn from my mistakes.

— Hüsnü Özyegin #BillionDollarGoldNuggets

That's what Jack Cowin likes about business: "One of the beauties of business is the fact every day is different, it's a challenge."

I see nothing as a failure. If something doesn't work out, you learn from it. Don't look back. Don't get angry. And just look forward.

— Frank Stronach #BillionDollarGoldNuggets

For Frank Hasenfratz, "Every day, you've got to change. If you don't change, you die." Frank is well aware of the changing world. And of the need to adapt to changing conditions.

One thing is sure, things will change. Does business change? For sure. If you don't change, you won't be around. And I can show you something; I just got it now. The Chamber of Commerce puts out a publication. I asked my assistant, "Get me the 1964 book if you can find it." That's when I started a business. She found it in the library. There were probably 100 manufacturing plants in this town. How many do you think are left?

Three. They've all gone by the wayside. And why? They didn't change.

I've been here for 60 years. And if you're not a little bit apprehensive, if you don't think, "I've got to do better tomorrow, I've got to get a different product or a more advanced product"—if you don't do that, you won't be here for long. To me, have I got it made? Absolutely not! Don't even think about it.

If you're looking back too often, you're going to trip going forward.

— Frank Hasenfratz #BillionDollarGoldNuggets

Manny Stul says you need to constantly adjust to what's going on, and adapt. He considers innovation to be an imperative element of his success secret.

Every day, you've got to change. If you don't change, you die.

— Frank Hasenfratz #BillionDollarGoldNuggets

Lirio Parisotto is the master of metamorphosis. In the course of his business career, he managed to change his business model several times, going from a small company with revenues much below a million dollars to a multibillion-dollar industry giant. At first, he was in electronics retail. Then he went into video rental. With his Videolar, which initially was just a video recording business, he was constantly surfing on the wave of disruption. As different carriers came and went, starting with VHS, through CDs, DVDs, blu-rays, he reinvented Videolar over and over again, spotting the decline of one technology just in the right moment, to be on time for the next opportunity. Simultaneously, he was moving his focus from the video recording business to industrial media production. When it came to the final dematerialization of storage media, Videolar was confronted with the risk of bankruptcy. Lirio had to mobilize huge financial resources from his stock market investments and make an enormous effort to move ahead and change the focus of the company to the petrochemical business. He once again managed to reinvent his company and move to large-scale production of plastic materials and products.

Let's end this chapter with the strong warning I got from Kim Beom-Su when I asked him about a message he would like to share with the world.

The future is something that the history of humanity has never lived before. You need to be prepared to move on from your previous world and space to a new world in the future. You must prepare to move on because just settling in the present could become a very dangerous decision.

There were transitional, revolution periods before, but with the emergence of the fourth industrial revolution, an unpredictable and uncertain future is fast approaching, and we need to get people ready to adapt, find jobs, survive it in a safe manner, but I think we are weak at that, so I'm looking for a way to help people do that.

The digital and virtual world is becoming more and more important, and in reality it's becoming more important and more influential than a minister. In addition to that, another completely different world, the world of artificial intelligence and robotics, is opening up, and we need to seriously think about this, more deeply and more diversely.

There's going to be a whole new future and whole new world that we are not prepared for, and I believe that there's not enough serious and important discussions going on, on how to prepare for that future, and I see a lot of people are very unprepared.

Someone who is able to securely and adventurously go with this world will adapt well, but those who can't will experience an even bigger gap; whether it be gap in income or gap in living standards, it has the possibility to become extreme. These people have never seen this world, learned about this world, heard about this world . . . perhaps they've heard about it . . . but if they don't adapt to it, they will face existential challenges.

What is your attitude to problems and obstacles in life, dear reader? Do you see them as opportunities? Are you willing to experiment, to fail and learn from your mistakes? Are you a problem solver? Do you get up after every failure to move forward without looking back? Finally, do you accept and embrace change?

- Drifters don't act, because they are afraid of making a mistake.

- Millionaires act but try to avoid mistakes, and they spend too much time dwelling on their past failures.

- Billionaires are willing to fail, accept their failures, learn from them, improve, move on, and never look back. They test their ideas and know that mistakes are inevitable to tell their good ideas from the bad ones and to move forward.

For more stories on this topic, go to:
http://TheBillionDollarSecret.com/resources

CHAPTER 12

Keep Fighting to Win

Our greatest weakness lies in giving up.
The most certain way to succeed is always
to try just one more time.

–Thomas A. Edison

Realize that creating anything of note can't be easy. When building a business empire, you will have to demonstrate grit, determination, and resilience. You will encounter numerous obstacles that you will have to overcome. You will have to persevere through hardships. You will have to fall and get up many times. You will have to keep fighting until you reach your goals.

Get Serious and Commit to Success

If you want to achieve great things in business, you need to commit to success. Stop playing games and get serious.

I asked Manny Stul, the World Entrepreneur of the Year 2016, what advice he would give to young people around the world who dream of becoming a winner. His answer was about passion and love for what you do, and "the commitment, the sacrifices you have to make. In sport, for example, it's training; if it's a business, it's long hours. You can't be half-pregnant in this. You've got to be fully committed to it. So the advice to young people: find something that you love doing, be passionate about it, and commit to it totally."

You need to put yourself in a situation where you are challenged to succeed. This is what Jack Cowin did. His early life had been taking place within a 100-mile radius of where he had lived in Ontario, Canada. And then he went to Australia, to a far-away continent, to start a business. This was a great challenge but also a big commitment.

Cai Dongqing says "If you set a goal, there is no other choice than to achieve it."

> ### You can't be half-pregnant in this. You've got to be fully committed to it.
>
> **— Manny Stul #BillionDollarGoldNuggets**

Be Willing to Compete, Fight!

Nobody will give you anything in this world. You need to fight for what you want but also fight for your right. So you should not only dare to dream big, but also dare to fight for your dreams.

Have a strong will and know what you want.

This is how Frank Hasenfratz got his first contract and started his own business:

I worked at Sheepbridge Engineering. I went to our general manager and said, "I want you to fire my boss. I can't work with him. He is intelligent, and I admire a lot of the things he does, but he doesn't recognize when he's wrong."

Stubbornness is good, but not to the point where it's detrimental to your job. And my boss was so stubborn. We were manufacturing a part for Ford Motor Company, and we machined it the wrong way. But you've got to do it like this because my boss wanted so.

I said to the general manager, "I want you to fire him, or I quit." He said, "I guess you quit."

Frank knew a much better and cheaper way to manufacture the part.

I said, "Contract me with the job for the cost of the scrap you have." He said, "Not a bad idea." It was my first contract. In the basement I set it up. At my house, and the garage and basement. He supplied the material, I bought a machine. So we were in business.

Put yourself in a situation where you are challenged to succeed.

— Rafael Badziag @BillionairePal #BillionDollarGoldNuggets

If you want to win, you better be strong.

I asked Sergey Galitskiy about his success secret.

The most important thing is that you are stronger than your competitors. Business is a game of minds.

As Petter Stordalen points out, it's not physical, but mental strength that helps you prevail.

If you set a goal, there is no other choice than to achieve it.

— Cai Dongqing #BillionDollarGoldNuggets

So, develop strength and never let others put you down.

Cho Tak Wong, the World Entrepreneur of the Year 2009, sees the business environment as a never-ending battle:

Sometimes you will be criticized or even taken advantage of by other people. Such is life; it all belongs to life. That's how people are. If somebody is a little bit more advanced than other people, then he tries to put you down and it's very normal. If you are small, you'll be put down by big people. It's not easy to stay up, as they will put you down again. You can get up, but you can't stay up all the time. Before, we were being put down by some big people, and then we started to work very hard, we started to build ourselves until we were really doing well and those people will not put us down anymore.

The most important thing is that you are stronger than your competitors. Business is a game of minds.

— Sergey Galitskiy #BillionDollarGoldNuggets

Don't shy away from competition.

Frank Hasenfratz really likes to compete. I asked him what he dreams about.

I want to win a card game. I want to win in golf. I want to win at everything. That sounds egotistic, maybe, but competition is good. We shouldn't shy away from competition. Competition makes us stronger, makes us think "how can we do things better?" So I like competition.

It's not physical, but mental strength that helps you prevail.

— Petter Stordalen #BillionDollarGoldNuggets

Billionaires not only are competitive, they first of all like to win.

Manny Stul, later the World Entrepreneur of the Year 2016, always had fun competing.

I won a scholarship that was available to all students, and it was based on your exam results when you were 15. I wasn't good at school but I did study for that, because I wanted to win the scholarship, for no other reason. I know it sounds crazy. I did it for no other reason than the competitiveness. I wanted to be one of the few kids in our state that had the scholarship. It was prestigious. Like if an athlete went to competition, he's held in high esteem by other students, girls, etc. I wanted to have a scholarship because I wanted to be a winner.

Only 1% of the students were granted the scholarship.

Then, at the university, instead of studying, his competitiveness could only be satiated by billiards, snooker, and five-card stud.

Never Accept a "No"

Petter Stordalen is probably one of the most tenacious people I know. And it means something. I am an ultra marathon runner myself. He is proud that he never in his life took "no" for an answer. The two of us were having lunch at his fabulous hotel The Thief in Oslo, when he told me the story of how he was fighting for his future wife Gunhild.

I was trying for two years, but she didn't want to date me because she had read so much in the tabloids about me. Then I said, "Okay, you need to give me something. One chance." Then she said, "Okay, if you beat me in running, you will get a dinner date." I said, "That's fair." She was thinking, "Petter is this short, chubby guy," and she is tall, she runs like a gazelle. She runs every day. She thought, "I've been running all my life. This will be easy. He is 16 years older than me."

So we started to run, and she started very, very fast. Very fast. I thought, "OK, I'm about to lose." But not today. I was running, and in the beginning, I thought, "I just have to keep on the same pace." I was following her half a meter behind, and she had the same pace.

Then there was a small ascent, and I thought, "Okay, I have to test how much capacity there is." I was increasing the speed slightly, and then I heard the breath was coming like. . . . Then I thought, "Okay. You start to feel it." Then I told myself, "When the longest hill is coming, start to increase the speed a lot in the bottom."

So we were coming down and then it starts, it's not very steep, but it's like 400 meters long, a nice size. I am starting with a quite high speed, and then I hear her breathe heavily. So I increased quite a lot in the middle of this uphill, and suddenly she just started to slow down. Then I turned around, jogging backwards, and said, "Is something wrong? Do we have problems to follow here?" She said, "Okay, I've lost." [laughs] It was maybe 6 kilometers into the race and we were going for 10.

So I won. But the thing also was that she didn't only give me the date, because I said, "The dinner, you have to lose something. Because if I lose, I will not get the dinner date. But if you lose, you need to lose something. So she had to follow me as my secret fiancé to a wedding in Finland two weeks later. [laughs]

She has asked me a few times, "Petter, honestly how much longer could you go?" My answer is always the same. "I don't know." I only knew one thing: "I just have to win. Doesn't matter what it takes."

But she was rock hard. She gave everything. You could hear it in her breath. She really was at the limit. A red zone. She had been red zone for the last one, two kilometers. I was saying something like "Now I like the speed. Now it started to be the speed I like," even if I thought I was close my red light as well. But I thought I could manage to be in that red zone at least two maybe three kilometers. If I really go to the bottom, I can be there. It will hurt like hell, but I can manage.

I was in the red zone myself. But I said, "Yeah, speed is good. Feeling good." And then you literally take out the energy from the people you are competing with.

If you want to read the story in full detail, go to:
http://TheBillionDollarSecret.com/resources

Lirio Parisotto has had spectacular success in almost everything he did.

I asked him about the secret of his success. His answer: "Never accept a no."

If you accept, you lose. When you hear "no," don't just accept. You need to find another way.

When I started the business, I came from the province into the biggest city of Brazil to do business with the studios from Hollywood. Can you imagine it?

It wasn't easy. I didn't know anybody. The people were a little arrogant. I was a salesman, and it was difficult to arrange an appointment because people didn't want to talk to me.

Lirio wasn't deterred by this.

One client I wanted very much when I started was Warner, and the guy who worked there was a Brazilian man, very complicated, arrogant. So I heard a lot of no's, for years. But one day I convinced him. He worked with me; until I closed the recording business last year, he was here. But at the start it was very difficult.

At the end, Lirio managed to convince all six major film corporations to work with him exclusively, thus holding over 90% of the Brazilian market in his hand.

He told me it helps to understand "no" as "maybe."

Never accept a no.

— Lirio Parisotto #BillionDollarGoldNuggets

Persevere with Grit and Resilience

It's easy to have ideas; it's very hard to turn an idea into a great business. It requires long years of grit, determination, and resilience. In our interviews, billionaires often compared business to a marathon.

And there is a great advantage in it, as Hüsnü Özyegin points out:

You have to believe and then work very hard and not give up. These days I give young people the example of a marathon runner, because life is a marathon, not a 100-meter dash. You can fall and still win the race in 42 kilometers. I tell them these things because that's my life also. It's been a roller coaster, a marathon.

Life is a marathon, not a 100-meter dash. You can fall and still win the race.

— Hüsnü Özyegin #BillionDollarGoldNuggets

Going from zero to billions is a long process. There are many turns on the road, and when you start, you don't see the road behind the next turn. You don't even realize how long the road is. The task at hand seems unsurmountable. It's like eating an elephant. Petter Stordalen asked me:

Do you think you can eat an elephant? You can, but take it piece by piece. Don't think about that big freaking monster of an elephant. Piece by piece.

Mainstream media always present shiny events and dramatic turning points that lead to spectacular success in billionaires' careers. But the reality is that success on that level rarely comes from these dramatic breakthroughs. It comes from many, many small steps in the right direction.

Becoming a billionaire is a process; it's never an overnight success. It's doing the right thing over and over again for long periods of time. So prepare for decades of hustle.

Frank Stronach puts it in simple words, "You don't get success overnight. You've got to work, you've got to work, you've got to work, you've got to work."

Business success does not come to you; it needs to be built. As Mohed Altrad points out, "You should have to produce what's necessary to succeed. Success is not something that will fall from the sky. It's not something you wake up one morning and you have success. It's not like this. It's something to be built. This is one thing. The other thing is, to build a successful organization, it takes a really long time. Successful, sustainable, brilliant organization. Nevertheless, this same organization could fall very quickly. That is the rule of the game."

You don't get success overnight. You've got to work, you've got to work, you've got to work, you've got to work.

— Frank Stronach #BillionDollarGoldNuggets

This long-term performance is what makes it so difficult. This is what most millionaires don't manage to sustain. So be persistent and keep watching the ball.

I asked Michał Sołowow how his business attitude is now different from the one at the beginning of his career.

Back then I fought daily for survival and for life, and today I continue doing it. In some way that has not changed. Every day in the morning, I come here into my office to do something and use my time to the max. Back then, at the beginning, it was the same.

Asked about the message he would like to give to the readers, he said:

Have plans, dreams, and make an effort to realize them consistently; don't give up easily; fight above all else, with your weaknesses and limitations.

Success does not come to you; it needs to be built.

— Rafael Badziag @BillionairePal #BillionDollarGoldNuggets

Jack Cowin stresses how important it is to keep showing up.

You show up every day. You show up. For the average guy, eventually it gets too hard. Over time, most people failed. They didn't show up. They didn't make it.

Success is not something that will fall from the sky. It's not something you wake up one morning and you have success. It's not like this. It's something to be built.

— Mohed Altrad #BillionDollarGoldNuggets

There is a difference between a failure and the final defeat. You can only be defeated if you give up after a failure. Don't do it. Don't take the easy way out; instead—persevere. The difference between defeat and success is the thin line between giving up and continuing to move forward. In case you fall, don't sacrifice your goal; just choose another way. If you failed once, try again until you succeed. As long as you don't give up, you haven't really failed.

I asked Naveen Jain about his attitude toward failures.

First of all, failures are such a wrong way of looking at it. It's about the things that you're trying and may not work. Failure only happens when you give up. Everything else is just simply a pivot. So when things are not working out, it's not a failure; it simply says that particular idea is not working.

Have plans, dreams, and make an effort to realize them consistently.

— Michał Sołowow #BillionDollarGoldNuggets

Resilience is necessary not only in the later stages of your business, but also at the start, where you have to endure through harsh beginnings.

And the conditions were even harsher for the entrepreneurs in Eastern Europe, when the socialist system fell apart. Sergey Galitskiy, who now reigns over an empire of 17,000 supermarkets in his Magnit, remembers:

In the first years, we were not making money and I had to feed the family, so I had a lot of stress. You're young, this is your first life experience, and you're always concerned whether you can manage or not. So from time to time I was giving up and thinking, "I can't make it. I overestimated my abilities."

Distribution business at the time wasn't a very profitable thing. Because we paid taxes and had to compete with players who didn't. And we also made a lot of wrong decisions, which of course did not improve the condition of the company.

In Russia, there was no entrepreneurial culture, no examples. What is left for you is to learn from your own mistakes. Additionally, at the time, the atmosphere was very complicated. When society is breaking, then here we've got gangsters, and sometimes the government and authorities behaved like gangsters too.

On one occasion, somebody put a funeral wreath at Sergey's door, on another somebody fired a grenade into his office, and in yet another case people appeared with automatic weapons at one of his shops.

So, briefly, that was not an easy time at all. But youth can overcome everything. You are not smart enough to be scared.

Failure only happens when you give up. Everything else is just simply a pivot.

– Naveen Jain #BillionDollarGoldNuggets

You just have to hang in until you succeed.

Naveen Jain, before becoming a serial entrepreneur and a billionaire, had been an early Microsoft employee. In these early days of Microsoft, he was able to spend time with its founder, **Bill Gates**, who later became the wealthiest person in the world. When we met in Dublin, Naveen shared with me his personal perspective on Bill that is very different from the stories known from the mainstream media.

Bill was a man who I knew, who's self-made, somebody who created the whole industry out of nothing, who was able to see something that other people would laugh about.

Everyone knew the main frames and mini frames and he was the guy who was saying, "The computer can be on your desk." And you looked at these large companies that were in the marketplace, and they were all asking their customers,

"What do you want?" And the customers were just saying, "I want better, faster, cheaper of what you built, not something different."

But breakthroughs never happen that way. And every smart person will tell you, every great idea is a crazy idea until the breakthrough happens, then it becomes obvious. Duh, of course, everybody knew this is going to happen.

So point is, here was this guy who was able to push through all that and create a totally new industry. And he was very down to earth. Obviously, in the early days of Microsoft I was able to spend time with him, and I found him to be driven, passionate, and full of belief.

Most people would have given up on many of the things that he pursued relentlessly. When Windows came out, Windows 1.0 was a total flop. Windows 2.0 was a total flop. Windows 386 was a total flop. He didn't give up until the version Windows 3.0, and life never looked the same again.

"Never give up" is the life motto of several self-made billionaires I interviewed.

Mohed Altrad's life always was an uphill battle

All my life is adversity, from the start. You have a lot of areas where life could stop for you. My life is a sort of miracle, and if you look at the origin of my life, a Bedouin in the desert, you have nothing. The number of days is enormous where you wake up in the morning and have nothing to eat, nothing to drink, in the middle of the desert. But you survive.

If it doesn't kill you, it will make you better.

Never give up.
— Rafael Badziag @BillionairePal #BillionDollarGoldNuggets

Suffering is for Mohed an indispensable element of success. "There is no success without suffering. You have to suffer to succeed."

And you need to follow through despite adversity.

It's the same with writing books. How many heads of the companies read economic books? Not all of them.

What's the percentage of these who read books on the economy, read novels? It's not a huge percentage, maybe 10%, 20%.

How many of those write something about the economy? You find another percentage. Small.

How many of these write novels, literature? It's near zero.

But Mohed Altrad, in addition to becoming the world's best entrepreneur in 2015, became an acclaimed author. He wrote several books on business and the economy and five novels. His autobiographical novel *Badawi* won several literary awards and became obligatory reading in many French schools.

> ## There is no success without suffering. You have to suffer to succeed.
>
> **– Mohed Altrad #BillionDollarGoldNuggets**

Know When to Hold and When to Fold

Often in business and life you are faced with the following dilemma:

What to do if the road to your goal is paved with failures? When to give up and when to hold on?

First, realize that every successful company almost failed at some point. So if you believe in the project, don't give up.

Naveen Jain gave me the example of Infospace, which he founded:

Every business has obstacles. A business that has not gone to the valley of death has never been successful. Every company will tell you that they almost had a near-death experience. And when you come out of it, you're stronger, better.

Infospace was a great example of this. I started it with my own money, and we had less than one month of payroll left in the bank, and I told every employee, we have one month to turn around; either we make something happen, we find a way to do business, or we're going to die.

We were trying to build classified services for people to find homes for sale. And my business person comes to me and says, "Hey, there's a guy, he wants to give us all the home listings for free and we can make all the money we want from it and he didn't want any piece of it. We should just go out and take it, and we can do advertising and we can make money on it."

Now, I was stuck on having to make money because we had no money left. I told him, "I want that guy to pay us for it." And he said, "He's giving it to us for free, why would he pay us?" And I said, "I want the damn money. Tell him he needs to pay us if he wants his listing there, he needs to pay us."

My business guy on the phone told him, "My boss wants you to pay. If you want this listing to be taken, he wants you to pay." And silence. Silence is golden, silence makes people uncomfortable. And the response on the other end was "How much?" Now, I had a business. We were burning $10,000 a month. He said, "Boss says $10,000." Thought for a second, "Can I pay $5,000 in the first month then *second month I'll pay $10,000, starting second month?" And I said, "We have a deal."*

But my point was when you are near death, you come up with a business model that you would never do if you had lots of money. If you have lots of money, you would never ask the guy how much?

Until then, nobody would pay for the content he provides. But Naveen realized that the home listings were actually advertising, and it saved his company. Infospace became one of the giants of the dot com boom, a $40 billion enterprise.

Second, analyze the cause and then take the appropriate steps.

Cho Tak Wong, the Chinese auto glass giant, explained to me his approach:

If any business starts losing money, then I will admit that we must have made some wrong decisions. However, in order to set it right, I have to correct it right away. But before I do it, I will look for the reason. Is the reason the strategy, or was the reason the execution, or was it an environment change. If the reason was the environment change, then we didn't do good study, so it was wrong decision; so I will correct it, including stopping it.

Sometimes it's wiser to give up one limb in order for the whole body to survive. Hüsnü Özyegin recommends to cut the losses in unsuccessful projects:

Make tough decisions. If you think that there is no end in sight to the road you are on, you have to get out. You cannot insist on a business where you're not successful. Of course, you have to be patient, but if you cannot see the light at the end of the tunnel, you have to cut your losses. It's difficult, but once you make the decision, you feel better. In Turkish we have a saying, "Cut the arm," you know? The body doesn't go away. You have to cut the arm sometimes.

If you think that there is no end in sight to the road you are on, you have to get out.

— Hüsnü Özyegin #BillionDollarGoldNuggets

Cut your losses if you can't win. Don't lie to yourself. Take the losses if there is no straight line to profit.

Peter Hargreaves stops a project immediately as soon as he realizes it won't work, and he has a method to spot it relatively early.

I once started a venture in the firm with a guy, and I told him I would give him two years to make it profitable. What he didn't know was that if after six months it didn't look as though it was going to make a profit, I would have closed it down then. Big companies when they give something two years never appraise whether it's actually likely to be successful and run it for two years when they should have known it wasn't going to happen within the first year. As soon as you know something isn't going to work, you should cut it immediately. You know when something isn't going to work when suddenly you spend an inordinate amount of time discussing it.

Don't spend more time on things that don't work than on those that do.

Are you prepared for the long fight against adversity, dear reader? Are you serious about your goals and committed to success? Do you accept "no" as an answer? Do you have the grit and resilience necessary to persevere through the valley of death? Do you know when to hold and when to fold?

- Drifters accept their failure as the final defeat.

- Millionaires don't give up as easily, but sometimes aren't persistent enough and often spend more time on things that don't work than on those that do.

- Billionaires are extremely tenacious but are able to cut the losses immediately when they realize a project won't work.

For more stories on this topic, go to:
http://TheBillionDollarSecret.com/resources

CHAPTER 13

Do Not Conform

The reasonable man adapts himself to the world, the unreasonable one persists in trying to adapt the world to himself. Therefore all progress depends on the unreasonable man.

—George Bernard Shaw

It's a fallacy that learning all the rules and then proficiently applying them or complying with them will make you rich. Jumping through hoops established by other people might make you the perfect cog in somebody else's machine, but it is a sure formula for mediocrity and financial failure.

Billionaires choose their own way and stick to their own rules. They do not conform to norms established by others. They don't follow trends, nor do they follow others. They are the ones who create the trends for others to follow.

Self-made billionaires quite naturally are great individualists. Some describe themselves as loners or "lonely wolves." You may say, "Well, it's lonely at the top." But it is their independent thinking and reliance on their own judgment that brought them to the top in the first place.

Have a Rebellious Spirit

Billionaires' rebellious spirit and healthy disregard for authority often first materialize during childhood.

Sergey Galitskiy, now the largest food retailer in Russia, recalls: "I can say that I was abused by the life conditions in the Soviet Union, and I always thought that this is not comfortable for me, and I was always thinking about it." Once, he skipped the obligatory First May parade and ended up in big trouble at school as a result of it. "In fact, I had a very strong defiant spirit, my school results were not the best. So I was in conflict with the teachers. I didn't feel that they were authorities. I didn't see any people that may share with me some intelligent things that can surpass my individuality and make me do what they want."

For Chip Wilson, a billionaire Canadian sports apparel manufacturer and retailer, defiance became a necessity when he was 12 and struggling with hunger due to a money shortage while his parents were getting divorced. He forged his mother's signature on a check in order to buy some food for lunch. He realized at this moment that in order to survive he needed to do things for himself and couldn't rely on anybody else—not even his parents. That independent attitude became his "winning formula," which led to the founding of several successful businesses.

Manny Stul, the World Entrepreneur of the Year 2016, found school boring and stupid. "Don't get me wrong; I was good at it. I just wasn't interested.

I was always in trouble." He was notorious for his cheekiness and for talking back. "I can remember being given the cane across my hands or across the back of my legs in those days." Once, when he was 16, he disappeared from home for several days. His strong will constantly sparked conflicts with his father, who punished him regularly.

Some billionaires, such as American software billionaire Naveen Jain, demonstrated disdain for the status quo from an early age.

While studying for his MBA in India at a Jesuit school, Naveen disliked that the entire city was under strict alcohol prohibition. Naveen never drank alcohol, but he didn't like the regulation and decided to stir the pot by having a drink with the dean (whom he referred to as the "warden"). "I decided I'm going to take on this one, this is just not right," Naveen explains. "They can't be telling me what to do and what not to do. I should be the one making a decision I don't want to drink. I don't want them to be telling me that I can't drink."

The result? Naveen was called in to meet with the school principal, Father Megrat, who asked him if he had been drinking. He confessed that he had. The principal informed him that he was going to be expelled for his misbehavior. But the young Jainist (an ancient Indian religion) played the system: "Father, you're probably right. But I am not Christian. You are. You asked me as Father and I confessed to you, and if you want to use my confession for whatever purpose you want, that's entirely up to you."

This caught the principal off guard: "You know I can never use your confession." "I know that," Naveen shot back. "Why do you think I told you?"

His deed went unpunished.

Lirio Parisotto wasn't as lucky when it came to pursuing his career as a priest in a seminary. His strong temperament and behavior didn't fit the religious standards of the Catholic Church. He was too much of an anarchist, which had a detrimental influence on other students, and was kicked out.

Break Social Norms

Billionaires seek to stand on their own feet and not be dependent on the roles assigned to them by society. They are people who break the norms, break the rules, and break out from the beaten path.

Mohed Altrad, who became the world leader in scaffolding, was born a poor Bedouin in Syria. His tribe was determined to force him to fulfill his destiny as a shepherd. Yet he resisted his fate, starting with attending school even though his grandmother had prohibited it.

Mohed's family arranged for him to marry a poor Bedouin girl who matched his class, which would have cemented his shepherd status. Mohed went to court to cancel the arrangement, arguing that it was against his will. His tribe wanted to decide everything about his life: whom he should marry, how he had to dress, what he ate, and what he needed to do. He refused to allow others to decide his destiny and broke from his tribe's practice.

Frank Hasenfratz, a Canadian auto parts manufacturer and another rebellious soul, remarked: "You know, we are oddballs." Frank grew up in Communist Hungary. While serving as an apprentice in a factory, he once cut out the picture of Hungarian dictator Matyas Rakosi from a dozen newspapers and put the pieces in the factory restrooms as toilet paper. Frank was incarcerated for 30 days; he never confessed, despite being interrogated and abused.

When Frank became interested in rowing, he wished to train with rowers at another factory who were about to go to the Olympic Games. However, all of the training centers were company clubs that restricted play to their own employees. In order to join, he needed to be hired by them. He applied and went to work for the other company. But changing your workplace wasn't permissible in the communist system, and he was dealt with severely. The regime at the time believed that if one person broke the rules it would jeopardize the factory's "five-year plan." His punishment included: being banned for life from continuing his education; a 10% wage cut; and he had to return to working for his previous employer. The wage cut wasn't as much of a problem as the education ban. Still, Frank managed to complete his education during his time in the army, where he won the support of his colonel, who made it possible for him to study again.

His military service was riddled with instances of insubordination. He was jailed when he called an officer an "idiot." His failure to follow the rules during a military exercise almost resulted in his shooting down a Soviet plane with a flak.

Even an army jail couldn't hold Frank back from doing what he considered to be right. When his sister was getting married, he convinced the man in charge, Sergeant Yanush—who happened to be his earlier rowing buddy—to allow him to escape. He even managed to borrow his sergeant's uniform. If he were to have been caught, it would have meant being charged for two more severe military crimes: desertion and impersonating an officer.

He attended the wedding and everybody was happy. Not only did he keep his family in the dark about his jail stay, he fooled them into believing he was a sergeant.

He was having such a good time he decided to stay in Budapest three days longer than planned.

On his train ride back from Budapest, he was spotted by his captain. "Where have you been?" the captain remarked. "I thought you're locked up. And you got promoted in jail." As Frank searched for an answer, the captain said, "Okay, I will talk to you later" before walking away. Apparently, he knew exactly what was going on but generously overlooked it and never mentioned it again, except for an occasional look that said, "I know about you."

Perhaps the best proof of Frank's nonconformity was fighting in the Hungarian Uprising on the side of insurgents against the communist Hungarian government and the Russian army.

Break Out of an Unsupportive Environment

Immigrants account for a strikingly high percentage of self-made billionaires on the Forbes List. Many of my interviewees left their countries to escape an unsupportive environment and break out of the roles assigned to them by their initial society before they became the people they were meant to be.

Out of 21 billionaires I have included in this book, five are immigrants:

- Frank Hasenfratz: left Hungary after the Uprising was suppressed by the Russians.

- Frank Stronach: exited impoverished postwar Austria for Canada.

- Naveen Jain: left India to find a better future in the United States.

- Mohed Altrad: was one of the best students in Syria, he became an immigrant to France when he won the right to study there.

- Jack Cowin: left Canada for Australia, where he was convinced he would find business opportunity.

Sometimes—as was the case with Tony Tan Caktiong, Lirio Parisotto, and Manny Stul—it was the children of the emigrants who sought to rise above the level of their struggling parents and to make it big in their country.

It is ingrained in the mind of a self-made billionaire that he will not base his future on anything he cannot control: the social background he was born into; the circumstances he has encountered; the role assigned to him by his family; or the social stigma of society.

Be Unemployable

Many billionaires always avoided being employed on a permanent basis; they are always independent, preferring to work on their own account. Due to their untamed natures, billionaires are often useless as regular employees. And those who started out as employees felt an undeniable urge to break free and become sovereign business players.

Lirio Parisotto is a good example here. After 20-year-old Lirio was fired from his job in Brasilia, he was hired at a meat processing company in Nova Bassano as a human resource official. This wasn't enough for his restless spirit, and he studied to complete his secondary education. At the same time, he transported people in his newly purchased Volkswagen Kombi to the city of Passo Fundo, which was located 100 kilometers away (about 62 miles). A round trip today takes three-and-a-half hours—and it was longer back then.

Lirio usually returned late at night, and, as a result, he was so tired the next day that instead of working he slept in the back room of his friend's office. Whenever the plant director searched for Lirio, people told him that Lirio was at the plant talking to employees. It took the director two years to discover the truth and fire Lirio.

Lirio subsequently won a competition for a job at Banco de Brazil, which offered him a top salary, a lifetime employment, and a full pension retirement guarantee. It was a dream job that everyone wanted but few could land. He gave it up for the dream of becoming a doctor. He quit the job that so many people dreamed about.

Lirio graduated from the university and became a physician, but even this didn't work for him; he found himself unable to work at a hospital.

He finally came to the realization that he wasn't meant to be an employee. He gave up on having a job and instead focused on his business, which he had begun while he was a student.

Go Where No One Has Gone Before

Billionaires are not afraid to be different or first in a new field, no matter how much controversy they stir.

Cho Tak Wong was one of the first entrepreneurs in his country when the Communist Party began to reform the system in the early 1980s. Cho Tak Wong was among the first private factory owners in China, acquiring a factory no one dared to take over as it was run by the Communist Party. In 1993, he became the first in his industry to list a company on a stock exchange and, two years later, the first in China to install an independent board of directors. In 2004, he became the first Chinese businessman to win an anti-dumping case in America. He was also the first—and probably only—entrepreneur in China to give a state subsidy back to the government, as it was unused in the 2008 financial crisis.

Tim Draper, the legendary Silicon Valley investor, adeptly taps into virgin areas of business. He is considered the inventor of viral marketing, which revolutionized the start-up scene. He was the founding investor in **Hotmail**, the world's first webmail service. While the founders searched for a way to grow their customer base with virtually no marketing budget, he told them to add the following sign-up link below each email sent via Hotmail by its users: "P.S.: I love you. Get your free e-mail at Hotmail."

The founders were reluctant. Tim needed weeks to convince the founders of the merits of this strategy. The team finally agreed to include the line without the "I love you" part. This created a so-called "viral loop." Each email sent using Hotmail became a simultaneous invitation to use the service. Hotmail's growth became exponential within a few hours. After six months, the company went from zero to 1 million users. The next million only took three weeks, and it rose upward from that point on.

Hüsnü Özyegin was the only Turkish student while he studied at Oregon State University, and became the second Turkish student ever to enroll in Harvard Business School. He was also the only person in Turkey to ask the Treasury for a banking license as a professional, even though he had little capital to operate a bank. Nobody had accomplished this before, but he was granted the license and achieved astounding success.

Kim Beom-Su—the Korean mobile tycoon whose Kakao messenger is used by virtually 100% of smartphone owners in his country—ventured several times into undiscovered business territory. Back in the 1990s, when there were no fixed web standards, he invented a gaming system in which players were connected over the Internet and could play Tetris or Korean Chess against each other. This revolutionary concept was a precursor of today's online games.

When the dot.com bubble burst and money became tight, his company was in dire need of a revenue stream. He came up with the "freemium" business model in gaming, in which gamers could play for free but paid for additional features. "People could do most of the things for free, but if they wanted premium functions or service, they could pay $4 per month," he explains. When they launched the premium membership program, they were nervous about how it might perform, since paid online games that existed at that time weren't well received and were struggling financially. "But on the day we opened this service we hit $79,000 and knew it was a success."

His status as a pioneer became solidified with his company's next ventures. The Hangame portal became the first to offer virtual items and avatars in games. With Kakao, his next company, he found a way to monetize a mobile messenger by offering a platform for third-party games and charging a commission for it. The Korean game market grew more than 20 times, and his concept became a successful new business model around the world.

More recently, Kim Beom-Su solved another industry problem by figuring out how to sell content to mobile users when they were accustomed to receiving everything for free. After two years of searching for a solution, he created KakaoPage—a platform on which users may read comics and books or watch cartoons and videos generated by other site visitors for free. The catch: If customers want to read the next chapter or see the next episode one week earlier than the no-charge users, they need to pay. The model was a win-win for users, creators, and for Kakao.

Create Trends

Chip Wilson created four companies that manufacture different types of clothing. At first, the focus was on general fashion, but then he set up Westbeach to produce beach and surf clothing five to seven years ahead of this trend. Next, he forged a skating business, once again before it became trendy. As he describes: "I'd put the concept out there and nobody would believe it. So I've always been in a world where I've had to just do it, what I wanted."

Westbeach Surf Company had been known as a surf/skate company, but Chip began to see that sales were starting to decline and snowboarding was coming up. He wanted to make snowboard clothing for this newly emerging customer base. "But the people in the company were so ingrained in surf and skate that they didn't want to change."

Chip changed the company name to Westbeach Snowboard and initiated the manufacture of baggy snowboarding pants with a "gangster" look. Chip's statement puts in perspective how far ahead of the trend they were: "Snowboarding had gone from three companies in 1987 to about 500 companies in 1993."

He then discovered that nobody paid enough attention to women's sportswear. That's when he stumbled upon yoga and went with a gut feeling. In 1998, based on his experiences with technical fabrics and sportswear, he developed a tightly worn fabric that looked great on women's legs and butts. Thus Lululemon was born.

Chip set up the first yoga store in Vancouver, where the only yoga classes in town took place. Several years later, Lululemon became a major sportswear brand with over 300 locations and billions in revenue, competing with brands such as Nike and Under Armour. With this venture, Chip became a billionaire.

He is unrelenting when it comes to anticipating "the next big thing." Despite his track record, he once again encountered fierce resistance when he sought to evolve Lululemon into the realm of mindfulness. That's how the idea for Kit and Ace was born: a brand that takes the best principles of athletic wear and applies them to clothing that can be worn all day.

But Chip is also a great innovator in the realm of business models. In 1980, he invented the vertical business model in clothing retailing. "There was nobody doing it," he recalls. "Almost everyone said what I was doing was not right, but it always seemed to work."

Think Different

All billionaires think different as part of their DNA. They think independently, challenge the status quo, and refuse to accept the old truths. Billionaires look for their own truths outside the mainstream.

Petter Stordalen advises people to "be scared when everybody is satisfied and there are only blue skies, and be brave when everybody's scared. Because if you do what everybody is doing, you will never succeed. If you came up with a new toothpaste, it's too late. You need to do something differently. But you can also change an old industry, like I did with hotels." Petter told me: "Don't be afraid to be different. Sell yourself as best as you can and don't listen to others."

Billionaires view things from their own perspectives. They see things as they could be instead of seeing them exactly as they are.

When Petter Stordalen, known as the Hotel King, saw the old post building in Gothenburg, he said it's perfect for a hotel. The objections were powerful: "No, no, no, it's the old post office. It's over 100 years old. It's been closed for 15 years."

Petter held his ground: "It's a hotel."

"No, Petter, it's not, and it's under strict rules. You can't do anything with it, you can't change anything."

Petter bought it anyway. After eliminating all of the bureaucratic obstacles and remodeling the building and area, it became a huge success. In fact, the area has become the new center of town.

It is unlikely you will reach the billionaire level if you are a follower and go head-to-head against the harsh competition. Instead, find a hole in the system and exploit it. Also, don't follow the seemingly obvious truths, and steer clear of options that are "apparent."

Sergey Galitskiy has a sober view: "You should not believe in obvious decisions that are important. You should not take faith in simple decisions. You always have to doubt everything, even the most obvious decisions, and this is the key to success."

Vladimir Gordeychuk, Sergey's business partner, confirms that "Sergey never believes in anything. He always doubts everything. He has his own opinion about every single situation."

Billionaires never let the opinion of others decide their actions or self-worth. As Lirio Parisotto puts it: "Of course, everybody prefers applause instead of complaints. But in some way, I think for the billionaires it doesn't matter whether they get applause or discouragement. They have their own inner standards, and they are their own judge. They are prepared for criticism. They know today you get applause, and it's possible tomorrow you are in trouble. If people complain today about you, tomorrow maybe they applaud. So billionaires have personality enough to stand over it. I don't need anybody to tell me I do the wrong thing when I do it. I know I do the wrong thing. So the greatest criticism comes from me."

Live Your Own Life

Personal independence seems to be an important component of billionaires' lives. Not only do they insist on this for themselves, they also look to pass their independent mindsets onto their children. They want them to become free-thinking persons in their own right.

Contrary to what most parents say to their children, Petter Stordalen repeatedly tells his own kids that grades in school aren't important. He stresses to them: "Be happy with all the things you do. Choose your way, not my way. Not the way your mother wants you to take. Choose your life. Live your life the way you want to live it. Do whatever you want as long as you are happy with what you do."

Tony Tan Caktiong has a similar philosophy with his children: "I think I want them to know how to enjoy their life and live their life based on their own needs and passion. You don't live your life to follow somebody's beliefs or society's beliefs, so whatever is your passion you live toward that passion."

As Hüsnü Özyegin often mentions during graduation ceremonies at his university: "Don't do what your parents tell you, but do what you want to do in life; otherwise you will regret it. If you do what you want to do in life and you are unhappy, you take the responsibility. But if somebody else tells you what to do in life and you end up unhappy, then it's your mistake to listen to them."

Caution: A Potential Downside

There is also a flip side to billionaires' individualism.

Earlier in this chapter I addressed how billionaires do it their own way and don't take advice from others. But you shouldn't give up cooperation in favor of individualism.

When Hangame became the number one gaming company in Korea, there was a tight competitor, Netmarble, that offered Brian Kim Beom-Su an opportunity to develop some joint projects. "I thought we were the top company at that time, so we didn't need their help and coldly sent him away."

Brian thought the gap between them would increase, but it didn't. Hangame struggled to stay at the top. If they had partnered, they might have performed better. "But I couldn't break out of the bias of thinking what I have is bigger and that I could do it on my own, so I learned that instead of doing things on your own, sometimes things could be greater if you do it together." Brian considers this one of the biggest mistakes in his business career.

On the other hand, don't shy away from seeking help or advice when needed, especially if it falls into an area of weakness. You must know yourself and act accordingly. An aversion to assistance may lead to making simple mistakes or being overwhelmed with the amount of work on your hands.

Chip Wilson believes this can become a major limitation. "I wanted to do it all myself and I wanted to make all my mistakes. I didn't want to be responsible to anybody else for the mistakes that I'd made. It's been a real limitation, because I find that people really do want to help."

As you've seen in this chapter, billionaires are nonconformists who demonstrate individualism at an early age when they break more than a few rules. Over the years they learn to trust their instincts and go against the grain, even when everyone around them thinks they are out of their minds and advise them against taking chances.

Knowing when to make the leap versus when to run in the opposite direction often means the difference between bankruptcy and billions. Are you bold enough to become a nonconformist?

- Drifters don't know or don't understand the rules, and they fail to follow them.

- Millionaires know all the rules and excel in applying them proficiently.

- Billionaires know all the rules, but they are aware those are created by men. They look for a hole in the system and exploit it to their advantage. They create new rules, new paradigms.

For more stories on this topic, go to:
http://TheBillionDollarSecret.com/resources

CHAPTER 14

Outwork Them All with Passion

It has been my observation that most people get ahead during the time other people waste.

—Henry Ford

There is no way around hard work. The more effort you put in, the higher your chance of being successful. So be diligent.

People say things like "work smart, not hard." It's nonsense. You should work smart and hard in order to be able to compete with those who do. Your only advantage is the effort you put in.

Sergey Galitskiy built Magnit, with 17,000 supermarkets the largest food retailer in Russia. When I interviewed him in his mahogany office, I asked him for advice to somebody who wants to be as successful as him. His advice: "Don't think that you are better than others. Only by working harder can you achieve more than the others." For him, one of the top three most important qualities for a businessperson is diligence. "You have to be very industrious because your intellect will never supersede that of other people too much. And only by working harder can you defeat those."

> ## Don't think that you are better than others. Only by working harder can you achieve more than the others.
>
> — Sergey Galitskiy #BillionDollarGoldNuggets

Be Diligent

Mohed Altrad, the world leader in scaffolding and the World Entrepreneur of the Year 2015, argues along these lines as well:

You could be talented, you could be a visionary, but you have to work. I have a rugby club here in Montpellier, and one of the most important rugby clubs in Europe. Last year, we won the European Cup. You have talented guys, talented players, but they don't work hard. I tell them, "You have to work hard, because talent is not enough." So work hard!

Jack Cowin got the right attitude from his father, who used to tell him, "You can achieve whatever you want to achieve if you work hard enough at it."

> ## You have to be very industrious because your intellect will never supersede that of other people too much.
>
> — Sergey Galitskiy #BillionDollarGoldNuggets

It may sound like a cliché, but most billionaires name hard work as an essential part of their success secret.

Hüsnü Özyegin's life motto is "hard work." He told me that in his classes there were always people who were smarter than he was. But he was always able to outwork them. Even now he never thinks of himself as the smartest guy in the room. But he believes he can prevail by his effort. This is also the core of the message he shares with his students: "If you believe and you work hard, you can be successful like me."

You could be talented, you could be a visionary, but you have to work.

— Mohed Altrad #BillionDollarGoldNuggets

Lirio Parisotto thinks "the value is made of character. You win if you work and study."

Ron Sim had to learn this great life lesson when he failed his secondary school entry exam. He learned that without diligence there is no result.

Everybody went to secondary school, and I had to repeat. So I woke up, and I topped the class when I repeated. Because I was determined to say "I've got to come back."

You can achieve whatever you want to achieve if you work hard enough at it.

— Jack Cowin #BillionDollarGoldNuggets

ABW = Always Be Working

Hard work may be a vague concept for you, and different people may associate it with different intensity. Let's make it concrete.

You win if you work and study.

— Lirio Parisotto #BillionDollarGoldNuggets

Working hard has two dimensions: working with high intensity and working long hours.

At the peak of their performance, many billionaires work every waking hour. It means up to 18 hours a day and 8 hours on weekends. They don't take days off and work also on weekends, especially in the first years of their business. A 105-hour workweek has three times as many hours as a 35-hour workweek. It is clear you accomplish much more in the first case. So invest the time and keep on grinding. Always be working.

Sometimes, you will need to work for three days straight or sleep at the company, like Frank Stronach did at the beginning of his business.

When I had my first factory, or the second, there were times when I made a commitment to deliver the product on time. The most I did was worked 72 hours straight through to get it done. I had very good stamina.

In the first few years, I worked weekends, Saturdays, and Sundays also. I had one desire: never to be hungry anymore and to be free. And I could see, I could see the progression. So I said 10 years, then I'll be free, and then I can do whatever I want to do.

Cho Tak Wong was selling fruit with his father before he started with his own business. His mother had to wipe away her tears when waking him up at 2 a.m. He remembers the lack of sleep and his huge work quota:

At that time, I had a little more than five hours of sleep every day. Then, the first 20 years in my career in Fuyao Glass, I had no more than six hours a day. It was 24/7, no free Saturday, no free Sunday. Every day it was the same.

Manny Stul was working on weekends in his first company. Even today he works a lot: "Most nights I'm working, and when I come home I continue working."

Mohed Altrad works on weekends even today.

All three of them became World Entrepreneur of the Year, in different years. Apparently, if you want to become the best entrepreneur in the world, working 24/7 is what you need to do, especially in the first years of your business.

With time, when you have organized your top management, you may allow yourself to not work on weekends, but certainly not at the beginning of your business.

Maybe the billionaire attitude toward hard work is best carried by Frank Hasenfratz's saying: "I only work half days—from 7 a.m. to 7 p.m." Frank is over 80 and still very active in his company, when other people his age have been enjoying their retirement for over a decade. Billionaires over 70, like Hüsnü Özyegin, regularly work over 60 hours a week.

You need to put in time if you want to be successful in business.

Mohed Altrad told me, "If you want to succeed, you can't succeed with two hours of work a day. It's not possible."

Billionaires always want to work more. When I asked Tim Draper what he would like to change in his life, he said he would like to have more time, so he could work more.

I only work half days—from 7 a.m. to 7 p.m.

— Frank Hasenfratz #BillionDollarGoldNuggets

In the beginning, there is no job too simple for you.

Fran Hasenfratz's first job upon arrival in Canada was washing cars.

Frank Stronach was a dishwasher at a hospital before he found a job at a factory.

Naveen Jain believes it's better to have any job than no job, and he speaks from experience.

When I was in Silicon Valley, one of the companies that I used to work for was shutting down because it was moving to LA. And I did not want to move to LA, so I was essentially not going to have a job, and I had just gotten married.

So I applied for every job. It didn't matter at what level the job was, how low paying it was, how dirty it was. And my wife looked at me and said, "You are an educated person. You are a senior manager, why would you apply for this job?" And I said, because this job is better than what I have now, which is no job. Once I get this job, I'm going to find one that's better than the job I have. And until I get the first job, every job is better.

And then I'm going to keep applying until I get the job I want. And that is having self-respect to know that you have dignity of work. And even if I make a dollar, honest living is more important to me than taking unemployment insurance and living off that. I would never do that.

If you want to succeed, you can't succeed with two hours of work a day. It's not possible.

— Mohed Altrad #BillionDollarGoldNuggets

ABB = Always Be Busy

There is always something you can do to progress your business. Billionaires use their time to the best to do these things. They make their diligence their competitive advantage.

Jack Cowin explained to me how sports had ingrained it in him:

I did very well as a college football player, got recognized on the all-star teams that they chose. I wasn't the greatest athlete, but I think I tried harder than anybody else did. Training's really important. You're not the best, but nobody's going to out-train you. You're going to push to be as physically fit as you can be.

This job is better than what I have now, which is no job.

— Naveen Jain #BillionDollarGoldNuggets

Hard work promotes your luck. Peter Hargreaves likes to say, "The more I work, the luckier I am."

When I met the American celebrity billionaire Mark Cuban in Monaco, he told me business was an ultimate sport. It is played without end, without interruption, and without rules; and there is always somebody who is trying to knock you out. So if you want to win in this game, you can't afford to stop competing even for a second.

The more I work, the luckier I am.

— Peter Hargreaves #BillionDollarGoldNuggets

Sergey Galitskiy shares these views:

In many sciences, scientists manage to explore something to the end and are done. There is nothing similar in business. What works here is that as soon as you fall asleep, somebody is coming to eat you. It's impossible to say, okay the next year I am fine, I will feel good. You can't feel relaxed at any time.

Take the Hard Route and Don't Make Shortcuts

The way to success is to do hard things rather than to take an easier route.

This is what Tim Draper shared with me:

I always felt like the way to become successful was to do all the hard things. Do everything you feel is hard rather than try to take an easier route. If you just keep doing that and take the next step forward, that usually works. Easy paths don't usually lead you to a good outcome. So, do the hard things, and then you can do easy things after the hard things are done.

Do everything you feel is hard rather than try to take an easier route.

— Tim Draper #BillionDollarGoldNuggets

Ask yourself, are you choosing a life of ease or a life of service and adventure? Life in ease is a life of vanity. But if you take the hard route, you will be rewarded.

When Naveen Jain got his engineering degree and MBA in personnel management and human resources, he stumbled upon the hardest aptitude test he had ever heard about. Some of his friends took it.

And the friends said this was the hardest test they had ever taken. I looked at them and said, "Oh, come on. I mean we are all here. We are pretty smart kids. How hard can this be?" And that guy, I swear I looked in his eye and he said, "You know, you have never taken a test like that. You won't know." And I said, "Goddammit, I'm going to just go. . . ." I finished my lunch and I said, "I'm going to go take the damn test and see how hard it is."

One day I took a test, aced it. Next morning I got a call from this company called Barous Corporation, which is a computer company. He said, "We looked at your test scores and we'd like to offer you a job of computer programmer." I said, "I'm sorry I have never seen a computer in my life. I don't even know what a computer is. How would I program something like that?" And they're looking at my score and they're saying, "No, but you have an absolute aptitude for computer programming. Do you know the difference between a bit and a bite?" And I said, "Of course I do." And he said, "What's that?" I said, "Small is a bit." He said, "There you have it." [laughs] And next thing I know, they say, "Well, we're going to teach you computer programming. And we're going to hire you. We're going to take you to the United States. But we're not going to pay you much. We're going to pay you $500 a month."

Five hundred dollars a month seemed a lot from the perspective of India, but it turned out to be hardly enough to survive in New Jersey, where he ended up. On top of that, he had never experienced a winter before.

There's no insulation in the house, the cold wind is blowing, and now, I have no clothes, I have no boots, I am walking in snow with my leather sole shoes. I have decided that I have had it. This is not a country I can live [in]. This is a nightmare and I want to go back to my country, and I'm done with this experiment now.

But Naveen stayed and was greatly rewarded for the challenges he took. Soon, he went to California. Later he got hired by Microsoft and started earning good money. Then he founded Infospace, one of the giants of the dot.com era that made him a billionaire. And since then he has started numerous other companies. He became a visionary, a role model for legions of ambitious entrepreneurs around the world.

Do you want to drift aimlessly through life or do something of importance? Do you want to just consume, or do you want to create something of value? Do you want to observe from the back row, or do you want to participate in the game of life yourself?

Chip Wilson, the Lululemon founder, shared these thoughts with me:

I think it's a matter of, what's my life worth? And do I want to cruise or do I want to create? I want to create as much as I can before I die.

Do I want to cruise or do I want to create?

— Chip Wilson #BillionDollarGoldNuggets

Go Full Speed, Give 100%

If you want to outcompete others, don't slack. Go full speed; give everything you have. Be willing to go the extra mile. Only this way are you going to win in the game of business.

Petter Stordalen is probably the most energetic person I know. I asked him about his secret of sustaining such a high energy level.

That's a very good question, because if you give a lot of energy, you get a lot of energy. It's like training. People think training takes a lot of energy. No, it's the opposite; it gives a lot of energy. So after I've done my exercise, the running in the morning, both mentally and physically, I'm filled up with good energy. It's a good way to start the morning. The dog is happy, my wife is happy, I am happy, and it doesn't matter if it's cold, warm, snow, rain. So when people say, "But you work a lot ...," it's because of that.

Tim Draper gives everything each and every day, doesn't hold back anything, and falls asleep completely depleted.

When I hit the bed at the end of a day, I have done as much as I felt I could.

If you give a lot of energy, you get a lot of energy.

— Petter Stordalen #BillionDollarGoldNuggets

If you don't want to spend your life wondering "what would happen if," always give 100%. This is what Chip Wilson learned when he was a competitive butterfly swimmer.

I always tell the story about being at the end of a swimming pool when I was 10 years old. And at that time people always tried to sprint to the end and to make themselves look good at the end of a race. My dad said, "Why don't you go full-out right from the very start? And if you can't make it, then you can't make it. But try that." It was really him telling me not to hold anything back, to give it and do it right from the very start. Of course, I broke a Canadian record because of that.

And then because of that, I always think that if I don't give 100% on everything, if I only gave 98% and I failed, would I regret that I didn't give the other 2% my whole life? Would I go to my grave going, "I wonder if. . . ?" And I never want to be in a "wonder if" position.

Key to Diligence and Resilience: Passion

Passion is one of the most important qualities of a businessperson and part of the success secret for many of my interviewees. If you have passion for what you do, you will be self-motivated, driven, and relentless. Only passion can help you endure through the harsh beginnings and overcome the many obstacles that you are going to encounter. So better be driven.

Following Peter Hargreaves, "the biggest advantage that you can have in business is loving the industry you're in because you're not working then. It's almost a pleasure to come to work. It's almost a hobby. And I do love this business, and I do love this industry. I have other small ventures outside this business, but I don't love them, whereas I love this. So that makes a big difference."

It is also important for Tony Tan Caktiong:

You have to make sure that whatever you do, you have a passion for it. You have to have some interest.

Jack Cowin concurs:

If you're interested in something, you can't tell the difference between work and play. If you're interested in it because you really like it, then it comes easy to you. Because if you don't enjoy it, eventually you'll fail. That's the most important thing. Being able to identify where you belong and what makes you happy.

The biggest advantage that you can have in business is loving the industry you're in because you're not working then.

— Peter Hargreaves #BillionDollarGoldNuggets

You don't need time to relax when you enjoy what you do.

Because of that, Manny Stul can work up to 18 hours a day:

I don't get stressed. There's good stress and bad stress. If you love what you're doing and there's passion in what you're doing, you can work 18 hours a day and it's not stressful. If you hate what you're doing and you hate being there, you can work three hours a day and you'll probably end up sick because you're miserable or you feel trapped.

Make sure that whatever you do, you have a passion for it.

— Tony Tan Caktiong #BillionDollarGoldNuggets

If you like what you do, you will become good at it and inevitably successful. I got this advice from Frank Stronach:

You must do something that you like, that you enjoy. If you like something, then you're gonna be good in it. If you put in that extra effort, you could be one of the best men or women. Whatever it is, be one of the best. Then money is always a by-product. Whatever you do.

How to Find Your Passion?

If Naveen Jain could call his 20-year-old self, he would advise him to find his passion.

And the best way to find your true passion is imagine if you had everything in your life, a billion dollars, a lovely family, everything that you always wanted, what would you do? And always remember making money is a by-product of doing things that you love doing because if you love doing something, you do it for long time. You become really good at it. And then when you're good at it, you obviously make a lot of money.

Imagine if you had everything in your life, a billion dollars, a lovely family, everything that you always wanted, what would you do?

— Naveen Jain #BillionDollarGoldNuggets

Would you do what you are doing for no money?

This is the question Chip Wilson, like most other self-made billionaires, answers with a clear "yes."

I would've done everything I did for no money. It was really the absolute love of going, "I have an idea. I have a concept. I wonder if people really want it." And being able to want to take that to fruition, and being able to stay up those extra five, six hours a night to make something nobody else would make, and being able to get into the store in the morning and look at people's eyes and see if they actually want it, and then what price they want it at.

Billionaires love and enjoy what they do. Frank Hasenfratz is a typical example:

Let me put it this way: in all fairness, there is nothing—nothing—I would rather do than what I'm doing. There is nothing. If you ask me to be prime minister, no. I have the best job in the world, and I did all the years.

Be Proud of What You Do and Create

Billionaires are proud to do business and proud of what they create.

Peter Hargreaves gave me this perspective:

People forget that without business, and without the profits it creates and the jobs it creates, they wouldn't be able to live the lifestyles they do. And I think people ought to be prouder of their businesses. I mean, in a lot of countries, athletes and footballers and singers and actors are given far more acclaim than businessmen, and to me, that's really quite sad.

And indeed, Peter is extremely proud about his unique expertise in his industry.

I have the best job in the world, and I did all the years.

— Frank Hasenfratz #BillionDollarGoldNuggets

Tony Tan Caktiong, the World Entrepreneur of the Year 2004, is proud when customers say: "Wow, your food tastes very good."

We are so happy when we receive those kinds of comments, like "well, we went to your store and your food tastes very good."

Cai Dongqing, similarly, is proud of his achievements and the value he brings his customers:

I feel proud of turning the company from a toy manufacturing company into a pan-entertainment group engaging in comprehensive businesses including toy manufacturing, comic, animation, licensing, movie, game, and smart science. And I am proud that the characters we create bring happiness and memories to people and become part of their lives.

Enjoy the Process, Not the Result

You need to enjoy the process more than the result. Billionaires like the process of building a company more than having a company. They enjoy making money more than having money.

Cho Tak Wong, the World Entrepreneur of the Year 2009, has achieved a lot of fame and riches. For him, "it's not the most important thing. In reality you enjoy more the whole process how you build up enterprises. This is the real enjoyment."

Naveen Jain likens business to having sex:

Think of making money as having sex. You can't focus on the end goal. You have to enjoy the process.

In reality you enjoy more the whole process how you build up enterprises.

— Cho Tak Wong #BillionDollarGoldNuggets

The path to success and happiness is thus to find something that you are good at and passionate about and want to do and then enjoy your life doing it.

Peter Hargreaves shared this insight with me when we met at his office in Bristol:

I was never very good at anything. I mean, I did the running, but I was never very good at it. I never won anything. I never won anything at squash or tennis. I was never in the school teams or a sport or anything like that. The one thing I found I was good at was business, and I think if you find something you're good at, it's wonderful if you can do it. I mean, some people are good at things and they don't want to do it, and that's really sad. I've known people who are just natural athletes and didn't want to do it. But I found something I was good at, and I enjoyed it. I think it's as simple as that.

Think of making money as having sex. You can't focus on the end goal. You have to enjoy the process.

— Naveen Jain #BillionDollarGoldNuggets

Not Enjoying? Get Off the Train!

But what if you don't enjoy what you do?

The best advice in this point I was given by Jack Cowin, when we talked on the porch of his house in Sydney:

I think probably the most important thing is you have to want to do it. If you're swimming against the current, it's hard. If you're making yourself do something, it's tough. You have to really want to be able to do it. You're going to run into obstacles, and if you don't really enjoy what you're doing, you're going to get sick of it, you're going to get tired, you're going to quit because it's too hard. But if you enjoy it, you're probably going to be good at it; if you're good at it, you get positive reinforcement, and the positive reinforcement makes you want to do more of it. Success is contagious; so is failure. So enjoy what you're doing, and if you're not enjoying it, you're probably on the wrong train. You're going in the wrong direction. Get off the train.

The one thing I found I was good at was business, and I think if you find something you're good at, it's wonderful if you can do it.

— Peter Hargreaves #BillionDollarGoldNuggets

Sometimes you achieve everything you wanted. Manny Stul reached that point with his first company in 1993.

I wanted to get out. I tried to sell the company. I wanted to sell for six, seven million. For me in those days, that was a fortune. I couldn't sell for a variety of reasons. Going public was the last option.

I asked Manny why he wanted to sell.

I'd had enough. I'd accomplished everything that I wanted to accomplish. I didn't necessarily want to retire; I just wanted out of the gift company. You set yourself certain goals—everything I did up to that point, up to about a year before, I did with passion and drive.

It's like climbing a mountain. You really want to climb that mountain, and you do everything in your power to achieve impossible things to actually get there. Once you get to the top of the mountain, in your eyes, now what? That's the way I felt.

Manny was bored to death. Fortunately, he was able to list his company on the stock exchange, and after an escrow period of 18 months, he got out with a lot of cash.

He wants his children to find what they love to do, find their passion.

So many people spend their lives going through the motions, where they're in a job that they hate or they're doing stuff that they dislike. That's no way to live. You have to really enjoy what you're doing. It's very, very important. You lose a lot of your life energy if you're expending it doing stuff that you don't like and don't enjoy.

Enjoy what you're doing, and if you're not enjoying it, you're probably on the wrong train. You're going in the wrong direction. Get off the train.

— Jack Cowin #BillionDollarGoldNuggets

And you, dear reader? How do you want to outwork your competitors? Are you enjoying your business? How passionate, how proud are you about it? How diligent are you? Do you work long hours going full speed? Are you taking the hard route or trying to shortcut it?

You lose a lot of your life energy if you're expending it doing stuff that you don't like and don't enjoy.

— Manny Stul #BillionDollarGoldNuggets

- Drifters are lazy and passionless; they take the easy route.

- Millionaires are hardworking but inconsistent; they don't give 100% and are distracted by consumption; their passion often isn't aligned with their business.

- Billionaires are passionate about what they do; they are diligent heavy-lifters who outwork everybody around; they create instead of consuming; they take the hard route and go full speed.

For more stories on this topic, go to:
http://TheBillionDollarSecret.com/resources

CHAPTER 15

Are You F.A.S.T.?

Efficiency is doing things right;
effectiveness is doing the right things.

—Peter Drucker

To be particularly successful, you have got to have done a lot of things right. You have got to run a great operation; you have got to be efficient and know how to treat your employees. That's how Peter Hargreaves sees it.

F.A.S.T. means Flawless execution, Absolute focus, Speed, and Time management, in short: efficiency. How efficient, how F.A.S.T., are you in your execution?

Execution Is King

Everybody has ideas, but what counts is the execution.

In real-life business, it's not the most brilliant idea that wins; it's the company that can perform best in the marketplace.

Petter Stordalen, the Scandinavian Hotel King, likes to say, "Execution is everything. You can be a professor at Harvard Business, but if you don't have the execution, you will never succeed. People think a strategy or a market position is the most important thing for success, but I say no. That's maybe 15%, 20%. Eighty percent of your success is execution, the ability to actually put your ideas into life, into reality."

Execution is everything.

– Petter Stordalen #BillionDollarGoldNuggets

One of the most important qualities of a businessperson is the excellence in execution.

As I wrote before, for Cho Tak Wong, the auto glass manufacturer from China, his success secret has three words, and execution is its final element: "belief, vision, and execution." Execution power is central to his business philosophy.

Eighty percent of your success is execution.

– Petter Stordalen #BillionDollarGoldNuggets

Time Is Key, Speed Is Critical

Realize that time is your most important asset. It's not money. You can always make money even if you lose all of it, but you can never bring back the time you have lost. It's better to save time than to save money.

Billionaires realize how important speed is in their business, and they excel in it. Michał Sołowow, the wealthiest person in Poland, told me, "Speed in business is in my view one of the critical parameters."

This is how being fast helped Frank Hasenfratz win General Motors as a customer and got a multimillion-dollar contract:

I was introduced to a manufacturer's rep who represented General Motors. That would be fantastic, to get into General Motors. And he walked me through the shop, and he said, "This is what we want outsourced. We're not going to make it in-house." They were the spindles for the cars. "How many?" "8,000 a day." Holy shit! How many machines will I need? So I gave him a price. I said, "Do you want to think about it?" "No, the price is right." We got the job. First automotive job, big job. We built a brand-new plant for it.

That's the power of speed in business.

One of the most spectacular feats Petter Stordalen pulled off happened in 1992, in the deepest recession, when the famous Steen & Strøm department store in Oslo filed for bankruptcy. Steen & Strøm is the Harrods of Norway, an institution with almost 200 years of history. It defines retail business in this country.

Petter decides to make a bid for the store. His plan is to divide the store up into 52 departments and rent them out to tenants within nine months.

On Monday noon, the decision is announced. Petter wins and celebrates the victory with his team.

Then the phone rings again: "Petter, you need to go down to Steen & Strøm right away. The old management, assuming their victory, had gathered the employees and wanted to present their plans. When they learned the news, they left leaving the employees gathered on the ground floor. You need to go there now and present them your plan."

Employees demand quick solutions and ask when the store is going to reopen. Surprised, Petter, in his youthful zeal, announces to reopen on Wednesday, 3 p.m. and promises a great opening campaign.

I think: I will not even be able to get an ad in the newspaper. It's like 1 p.m. Monday already. How shall I manage?

He also realizes he spent all the money for the inventory and the brand already. His team gets nervous as there is no chance for a successful opening with no budget and within 48 hours. He tells his team:

The good thing now, we have two options. Both options will give you a place in the Guinness Book of Records. The first one: If you only sit here on our ass doing nothing, we will be the fastest bankruptcy ever. We will go bankrupt before we open the store.

They certainly don't want this to happen.

The second one, when I told the investors what we should do in nine months, we have to do it before Wednesday.

Within these two days, Petter manages not only to sign the tenants for the 52 departments, but also to make them move in and prepare the opening sale.

By selling the inventory and the store equipment to them he manages to regain almost all of his investment on day one. For Petter, it is like selling strawberries again.

The next hurdle is the advertisement for the opening campaign. He manages to place a double broadsheet opening ad at the biggest newspaper way past the deadline by promising he will place 50 colored pages over the next six months. Petter even gets interviews in the headline news. He says it's going to be the biggest opening sale in Oslo's history.

The opening is indeed a fantastic success. There are more people in the store than ever before. So many that the escalators stop working due to overheating and the fire department orders to open all the outside doors due to the danger of fire.

At the end, Steen & Strøm goes from losing $6.5 million a year under the old management to $5.5 million profit in the first year under the new owners.

Petter with his team manages a complete turnaround practically in 48 hours! An epic performance, never achieved before or after. It is something business schools in Norway analyze and marvel about to this day!

Get this exciting story in full detail on my website: http://TheBillionDollarSecret.com/resources

For me, the most impressive billionaire in regard to efficiency is Sergey Galitskiy, the founder and CEO of Magnit, the largest food retailer in Europe. They have 17,000 stores now, and when I interviewed Sergey in Krasnodar, they were opening five new supermarkets each and every day. Can you imagine that? Do you realize what is needed to open just one supermarket? First you need to find land, then to negotiate and buy it, then you need to get all the permissions, then build the store, then install all the systems, hire and train people, organize supply and logistics, then actually supply it and market it to the customers, then you can open it. And they do it five times each and every day? How is it possible?

It wasn't in the beginning, but Magnit was steadily increasing its capabilities, skills, and efficiency. At the end, they managed to reach this velocity.

The never-ending increase in efficiency is deeply rooted in Magnit's culture. Sergey's business partner, Vladimir Gordeychuk, says you have to move faster and faster; otherwise you die.

If you stop, you die. You have to move. You have to run. And right now you have to run quicker and quicker. It's very difficult to be upper position, to take upper position.

Six Billionaire Efficiency Strategies

Efficiency means also to care for the outcome and not do something just for the sake of doing it.

That's something that Ron Sim has paid attention to since his school times.

When I was in my primary and secondary school, I used to look at something and I'd process it. "What if I do this? What if I do that? What if I don't do it?" And my friends would say, "You think too much. Just do it." Which is not wrong, but not right either.

As I aged, I noticed that is actually my sense of analytical power. It's the source of the thought process that helps me to decide whether to do something or not.

I ask myself, "How to do it to achieve the best result?" Whereas they don't think of the best outcome. But I think of the best outcome. And is the outcome sustainable? A lot of people just do it, but they don't care about the outcome.

These are the six efficiency strategies that allow billionaires to achieve more in less time and with less effort:

1. Set Goals

Have your goals written down. Chip Wilson stresses the importance of deadlines and "conditions of satisfaction."

I do everything with "by when" dates, so there's got to be a conditions of satisfaction with a "by when" date on everything I do, even for myself, so I know that if I'm promising to do something by a certain date, I'll do it. And I have to have integrity even with myself, so if I say I'm going to do something by a certain time, then I have to do it, and I have to do it in the way that it's expected to be done.

There's got to be a conditions of satisfaction with a "by when" date on everything I do.

– Chip Wilson #BillionDollarGoldNuggets

This is the advice Ron Sim gave his children:

Life is a long journey; if you don't stay focused, you've got no goals, you're a lost man. If you're not hardworking, you're going to be a useless person. If you're not disciplined, you're going to get yourself in trouble. So keep focus.

2. Plan Regularly

Michał Sołowow, like every billionaire, prefers planning over dreaming.

On the lower level, I don't have dreams, I have plans. I have plans of various kinds, which relate to the companies, things we do. I have all sorts of plans that are not surprising or above average, which are rather being realized. I mean, they are in the domain of plans.

Most billionaires, like Jack Cowin, plan daily.

I have a day timer, a calendar which dictates where you are, what you're doing for the year, and then you kind of reflect back. I do daily planning as to what I'm going to do today, and over top of that, probably three or four bigger goals of things that I want to do.

> ## Life is a long journey; if you don't stay focused, you've got no goals, you're a lost man.
>
> **– Ron Sim #BillionDollarGoldNuggets**

3. Prioritize

Billionaires use various prioritization strategies. It's important to set your priorities, then choose a prio strategy that fits you and be consistent in using it.

Prioritization Strategy: Most Important Stuff First

This strategy is probably the most popular among the efficiency gurus, and it is broadly applied also by many billionaires.

Kim Beom-Su, the Korean mobile services dominator, belongs to those billionaires who use this strategy to prioritize their projects and tasks.

I tried to continuously question what I do. What is the most important thing right now? What is the most important person, what is the most important task I need to deal with right now? I'd think in those terms and try to do those things and delegate the rest, so that's kind of my style, and so I don't feel the need to manage my time. If I have a lot of time on my hands, that means the company is doing well, and if I get busy, that means things aren't going so well.

Prioritization Strategy: Most Difficult Stuff First

This strategy, which Brian Tracy calls "eat that frog first," is used by even more billionaires than the first one. They do the hardest tasks first.

Lirio Parisotto describes this strategy as follows:

The first things I need to do are the things I don't like to do. Why? Because it makes the other things easy. When you delay it for tomorrow, then if you have to do it tomorrow it's even worse. So if you have something to do you don't like, someone you need to call and you don't take this call because you know that person would complain, or you have trouble or you don't like the person or you need to fire someone who's disgusting, then it's the first thing to do. At the end, we need to stay with just the easy things to do, things that are pleasurable.

Peter Hargreaves asks himself two questions every morning: "Who do you least want to speak to?" and "What task do you least want to do?"

Invariably, those are your two top priorities of the day. You should immediately speak to the person you don't want to speak to and complete the task you didn't want to do. Those two things were clogging your mind, and you will have a great day from then on.

> ### The first things I need to do are the things I don't like to do.
>
> **— Lirio Parisotto #BillionDollarGoldNuggets**

Prioritization Strategy: Most Urgent Stuff First

You would think this is the old-style way of doing things, but this strategy is actually used successfully by some billionaires.

Ron Sim's prioritization consists of three steps: "Urgent—Sensible—Logical."

Cai Dongqing told me, "Normally I will deal with things according to how urgent it is."

And some billionaires switch to the urgency mode if needed.

Prioritization Strategy: Higher Potential First

Some billionaires have developed a more sophisticated strategy to prioritize their projects and tasks. They give priority to things with bigger upside.

Tony Tan Caktiong is the World Entrepreneur of the Year 2004. He describes this strategy quite clearly:

Sometimes it depends on urgency, if it's really needed. But most of the time it's more about what are the projects. Then we will look at the big ones that have the bigger potential rewards, and we go for them.

Sergey Galitskiy goes one step further. He keeps an eye on the risk/reward ratio and recommends to differentiate the strategy depending on the size of the company: When small, focus on the things with most upside. When big, focus on the things with most weight.

4. Focus

Every entrepreneur has hundreds of things to do and thousands of ideas to follow. If you don't focus on what you want to do and push through to finish them, then the things you want done just don't get done. So it's important not only to prioritize and decide what you need to do, but also to decide which things not to do. Also, don't get distracted by urgencies.

"Be a rifle, not a shotgun," as Jack Cowin puts it. "Beware of prettier girls, new theories, and diversions."

Tim Draper told me:

Something my dad taught me was you go after one thing hard and do it till it's done. Just focus until it's there, until you've achieved what it is that you wanted to accomplish. I believed in that, and I do believe in that.

Michał Sołowow learned two important principles in his business career.

You know, there are several things that a person learns in life, and they become principles. The first one is: "Decide on which of the things you don't do," that is, in fact, to concentrate on important things. Often the ability to say "no" to something that potentially looks attractive is difficult, and doing everything is impossible and simply causes a distraction. And that distraction, that is, the lack of concentration on important objectives, indeed means that you do everything but nothing comes out of it in the end. The second principle is that, if you cannot understand something, then you simply shouldn't do it. I mean, if I cannot understand something, for example some market, things, events, and I cannot understand that quickly, that means that I shouldn't engage myself with that.

Decide on which of the things you don't do.

— Michał Sołowow #BillionDollarGoldNuggets

Chip Wilson reflects about his focus every day.

I really have no problem letting stuff go that isn't working. I'm talking day-to-day type of thing. I go into the business every day, and I go, "If I was to compete against myself, how would I do that?" That helps me prioritize what it is that needs to occur and helps me drop things that aren't important that maybe people think are important, and move into things that are important.

If you cannot understand something, then you simply shouldn't do it.

— Michał Sołowow #BillionDollarGoldNuggets

Cho Tak Wong learned that you should focus on what you are good at in the 1990s when his company started to prepare for the IPO. His company almost went bankrupt, because despite his lack of expertise in development, he built an industrial village for the local government and got caught in the crisis of 1994.

I spent many, many years to restructure and to deal with all the losses. And I learned through these things that if any company wants to be successful, it needs to be a professional company. You have to do extremely good work. Do not diversify. Be good at what you do, focus on it, and be very strong in it, then you can become big.

5. Leverage Your Time and Energy

Realize that you have a limited amount of time and energy every day. You can't scale your own work. That's why time management and productivity strategies work only to an extent. As your company grows, they quickly lose steam and become the bottleneck. That's where leverage comes in. You can leverage time, energy, skill, and even finances by getting help from other people.

Be good at what you do, focus on it, and be very strong in it, then you can become big.

— Cho Tak Wong #BillionDollarGoldNuggets

Jack Cowin explains:

You have to get into a business where you can put a multiple on what the earnings are rather than personal exertion. I say to people, do not be a dentist. They say, "What do you mean?" I say, when a dentist is not drilling teeth, he's not making any money. It's all built on his ability to drill teeth. Get into something where there's no eighth day of the week, there's no 25th hour of the day. Get into something where you can leverage your time and energy by being able to have other people work with you and for you.

You have to be able to put a leverage on what you earn rather than personal exertion. Do not be in the personal exertion business. You have to be able to get some leverage on your time and energy.

6. Measure Everything You Do

Whatever you measure gets done. That's why it's important to measure everything you do in business.

A champion of efficiency for me is Frank Hasenfratz. His Linamar has roughly double the profitability compared to other auto parts manufacturers. Frank's life motto is, "Measure everything you do."

He introduced in his factories a never-ending measurement and cost improvement process that is performed by the Cost Attack Team (CAT) led by him personally.

The most important for me is that we measure everything. From Day 1, I measured everything. If I can do that in 1 minute and 20 seconds, how can we do it better? Not that you work harder, but a better way.

For instance, when we do a CAT, there's a short guy, and the night shift is a tall guy. Now, what kind of table do you put in front of him? You put a table that the tall guy bends down all the time, the short guy can't reach it. Why not make a table that's adjustable? Nobody thinks of that. "This is a factory; why do you want to do that?" Yeah, it costs a little more. But think about it. That short guy doesn't have to step on a stool.

Frank was a competitive rower in his youth. When I asked him what he learned in sports for business, he answered:

You must time everything, you must measure everything, and you've got to be disciplined. You cannot row in a rowing team without being disciplined and being a team player. Even if you're a leader, you have to be a team leader. And why would you want to get into a race and not measure how well you do? Business is like that. Measure, measure, measure.

For instance, I measure how many strokes I need to shave. It looks like you don't measure, because you've got a beard. [laughs] But I measure.

I couldn't believe it and asked him how many strokes he needed.

I needed 78 strokes to shave. But now I'm a few years older, my face is bigger and I have more wrinkles. I'm going close to 83, 84.

I asked, "And time? Do you measure it as well?"

Of course, I measure it. It's about two-and-a-half minutes. It takes me 15 minutes to shower and shave. And I'm right on time, all the time, because I measure it.

Measure everything you do.

— Frank Hasenfratz #BillionDollarGoldNuggets

Work Smart

It's not only about working hard, it's also about working smart. My interviewees shared with me some of the efficiency tools that they apply.

Get on Top of the Emails

Billionaires, like each of us, have to cope with the never-ending influx of emails. Some of them have developed explicit strategies to cope with them.

Mohed Altrad manages over 200 companies. Nevertheless, when I wrote him an email, I was getting an answer within an hour or two. Surprised by that, I asked him how he manages his mailbox.

I see something like 300 emails a day, which is really huge. If I don't treat them, I have a problem the day after. Most of them, fortunately, I have to transfer to somebody else. I go through them very quickly, but nevertheless you still have something like 5% or 10% of the emails. I have to treat them. Every two hours I look at my folder and see what's urgent, what's not urgent, what needs to be transferred. For instance, for yourself, I know it's important for you, so I try to consider it as priority. I treated it as such.

Similarly, Manny Stul surprised me with his quick answers.

I try to do stuff in sequence. Like emails, I try to answer the most recent emails first rather than the other way around. Sometimes you can get a chain of emails, like several people, and I want to be talking about the last result. You can make a comment on something or give advice, but there's been 10 more emails since in the same day that there's more information that's come in that's relevant.

So I always try to go top-down. That's the wrong way, normally the way people do, but that's certainly the way I do answer my emails. That why I'm always up-to-date with what's happening. I try to keep on top of my emails, which is the reason why I work at night.

Interestingly enough, both Mohed Altrad and Manny Stul became World Entrepreneurs of the Year (in different years). Their email processing strategy is apparently a sign of their excellent skill at structuring their world and their work.

Replicate What Works

If you find a way of doing things that works especially well, do it again and again, as many times as you can. Replicate this method to take the most advantage of it. This is how Frank Stronach went up from 1 factory to over 400 factories.

When I started out, I hired somebody that was my foreman. After two years I asked him, "How come you're so different?" He said he's thinking of starting his own factory. So I said to him, "Let's talk tomorrow." At that time, I had already some money in the bank. So the next day, I went to him. I said, "Look, why don't we open up a new factory. I pay the initial cost. You own one-third; I own two-thirds. You have a base salary, no more overtime. At the end of the year, we take equal out, one-third, two-thirds, leave some of the profit for growth." He said, "Do you mean it?" I said, "Yes," and we went to a lawyer and we signed. [laughs] Then I took the next foreman, and the next foreman, and the next foreman. All of a sudden, we have over 400 factories now.

Keep It Simple

But Frank Stronach is also the master of simplicity. Keep things simple. Reduce complexity as much as possible. This increases efficiency. When I asked him about his success secret, he answered:

Keep it simple. Don't make it too complicated. We are so big, I have 25 lawyers in my department. They gave me a 100-page contract. I said, "Write me down the same thing in 25 pages."

Use the Force of the Current

Dilip Shanghvi recommends to flow with the current, to take advantage of its force, instead of expending your force against it.

If you are flowing with the current, the force required to move is very little. If you're flowing against the direction, you will need a lot of force. I am a strong believer in finding a way to minimize effort-to-output ratio. If you put X amount of effort, and if you get 10X amount of output, that's a much better solution than when you put X amount of effort and get 1X amount of output.

Apply the Maximum Velocity Principle

If you wonder how billionaires manage to grow their companies so fast, to create unimaginable value within decades when others would need millennia, this principle is the answer.

Sergey Galitskiy explains how it works:

I always think, I took maximum risk in my life. Although, as time goes by, when you get older, everybody including myself wants to take less risk. It needs the sum of accumulated experience and intellect to understand how much risk you can actually take on. That's what I call preparedness for the business. Give the thread the most strain without breaking it. That's how you achieve the maximum velocity.

For example, in the first five to seven years we didn't make any money, but we were opening new branches. And every month we would open P and L Statements, and we were scared to see that it would be either loss or zero, but we continued to open new branches. But I was only 25, 27 back then.

> ## Give the thread the most strain without breaking it. That's how you achieve the maximum velocity.
>
> **– Sergey Galitskiy #BillionDollarGoldNuggets**

What about you, dear reader? How F.A.S.T. are you? How efficient are you in your execution? Do you set goals and plan regularly? Do you prioritize and focus? How do you leverage your time and energy? Do you measure everything you do? Do you work smart? Only by doing this do you stand a chance of reaching billions.

- Drifters have ideas, but they can't execute them.

- Millionaires execute their ideas, but they aren't efficient in doing so.

- Billionaires execute their ideas efficiently; they are fast and focused.

For more stories on this topic, go to:
http://TheBillionDollarSecret.com/resources

CHAPTER 16

Be Smart with Money

Frugality includes all the other virtues.

—Cicero

There is a huge misconception that most people have about billionaires and money. They think billionaires sit on mountains of money and don't do anything but invent new ways of spending it. Nothing could be further from the truth. In the introduction, I explained that keeping $1 billion in cash would cause up to a $135,000 opportunity cost each and every day. It just doesn't make sense. Almost all of the wealth billionaires own is in the companies they own, in the stock of other companies, in real estate and other assets.

Billionaires don't see money as something to spend on themselves. Money is there to invest and create. It is a form of universal energy in business that allows them to make things happen, to turn their visions into reality.

The Right Attitude

Naveen Jain thinks of himself as a trustee of his money rather than the owner.

There is an extremely interesting way of looking at success in life.

I was at this event where there was some really smart group of people and I'm walking and I say, "Hello. How are you?" And the guy responded back said, "Well, I am depressed." I'm already five feet out, really, you don't expect someone to answer that question other than "Fine, thank you. How are you?" [laughs] So when someone answered that, you take five steps back and say, "Oh, I'm so sorry. What happened?" And the person says, it was just when the crash happened, and he said, "I lost half my money in the stock market and I'm not feeling good." It was in the 2008 crash.

I took a deep breath and I said, "Well, money does not belong to you. Anyway, you are simply a trustee of God's kindness. And God still believes in you because he still left half with you, and he expects you to do something good with his trust. And as a trustee you are not giving him the kindness that he is giving you. You're not going out and using that to help other people. And if he didn't believe in you, he would have taken it all. So he still believes in you to leave with a half. And hope you will go and do something with it. And then he may come back and say, you know what? You're a good trustee, he'll give you more."

He looks at me funny and he says, "Why do you believe God has anything to do with it?" And I said, "Well, have you tried being kind to people and tried just using as if it's not about money, it's about genuinely wanting to help people? And see the kind of kindness you get in that and maybe God might even be kind to you."

I left and I met him, three, four years later. And I said, "How are you?" And he said, "I do remember and I'm doing really, really well." And I said, "Oh, how so?" He said, "Not only I'm happy but I made everything back that I have lost."

And I said, "What had changed?" And he says, "My outlook on life had changed. I no longer worry about when I talk to people what they want. I want to help them just like you said. And it's amazing how much happier I am and how much more money I have."

On TV you hear the stories of lavish billionaire lifestyles filled with luxury and extravagance. In reality, many self-made billionaires are modest and frugal in their private lives.

Frank Hasenfratz doesn't need much for himself. "I eat a cheese sandwich a day and a Diet Coke. Most days, that's what I do. My requirements are not excessive. I don't think I changed much since I was 10 years old."

Peter Hargreaves, the founder of Hargreaves Lansdown, learned to be extremely careful with money from this father.

My father had a small business. He was brought up in very austere times. People weren't wealthy, especially after the Second World War. This country was bankrupt for many years, and so were almost every country in Europe. And my father was exceptionally careful with money. I saw how careful he was, and I saw how each week, he put so much money away for the gas bill, so much money for electricity, etc., and it brings business to the very basic level.

Peter applies extreme frugality in his business. There are no company cars in his company, and privately he was driving an eight-year-old Toyota Prius when I interviewed him in Bristol. He passed his modesty on to his children.

I'm very proud of my two children, and the reason I'm so proud of them is they're completely untouched by the money. They are two normal, natural children who live very modest lives. My daughter had a year's placement in London, and she had a flat in London, and she used to go walk behind me, switching the lights off if I left them on because she had to pay the electricity bill.

They drive very modest cars; they both have a car that's seven years old. They both have quite modest flats. And if they go on holiday, they go with their mates, and they go to the back of the plane. By the way, because I live 10 minutes from Bristol airport, it is so much easier to fly budget airlines from Bristol; we fly budget airlines in preference to driving the two hours to Heathrow.

Peter told me a story that he once went to Zara in Mallorca and bought a pair of shoes from the counter with a discount.

They were about 35 Euros, these shoes. And I still love them to this day. I've worn them for 10 years, and it's still my favorite pair of shoes, and clean and polished. They look like new. I bet they're the only pair that are still in existence of that shoe that they made.

But probably the most humble of all my interviewees is Narayana Murthy, the founder of Infosys, one of the largest software companies in the world. He still lives in the modest three-bedroom apartment in Bangalore that he moved into with his wife when he founded his company.

Lirio Parisotto knows Narayana because they were competing the same year for the World Entrepreneur of the Year Award. At the gala event, there is a dress code requiring you to wear a tuxedo. Narayana Murthy won the competition and became the World Entrepreneur of the Year 2003, but, as Lirio told me, he was the only man not wearing a tuxedo. Narayana said he didn't own one since he didn't really need it. He wore just a regular suit.

Narayana told me the only luxury he allowed himself were books.

This is not exactly the type of spending habits you would expect from somebody with a net worth of over $2 billion, would you?

Learn How to Handle Money

If you don't know how to handle money, you can't succeed in business. Learn about money and finance.

A good exercise in handling money is keeping track of your personal spending.

Hüsnü Özyegin, now the wealthiest self-made man in Turkey, developed a budgeting habit early in his life, and he used bookkeeping and money-handling skills later at the university.

I became treasurer of the fraternity. I used to keep the books of the fraternity, and they paid me $80 a month, which was pretty good money for me. So summer jobs, winter jobs. I kept a record of every penny I spent. I still have that columnar notebook that shows it. I kept records of everything.

Hüsnü brings out his old columnar notebook and reads: "Scrapbook, $3. Notebooks, $1.75." His script is very precise. "Carbon paper, plastics for campaign. I used to run for office. You see, $2. Homecoming. Gillette shaving, $1.55. Mail Christmas cards, $1.96. Lottery for house dance, $1. After I had some money, I started dating girls. Date with Sally, $2.15. Even Socks, $1.79. Shoes, $11.95. Everything was cheap in those days."

The most important lesson that I can give to anybody is keep track of your money or have a budget early in life. It also renders you to have a tremendous amount of self-discipline.

Some self-made billionaires learned how to deal with money and how to save it up early in their lives.

Tim Draper learned to invest and understand money as early as age nine.

My dad got me investing when I was nine years old. I was able to buy one share of a stock with my pocket money. It was Mutual of Omaha.

The stock didn't move much. Then I also put $10 in the bank and watched that, and not much happened to that either. I got 5% a year or something. I think it was 10% a year for a little while. I thought, "Wow, that's pretty good. It was a dollar, and now it's $1.10."

He got me going early as an investor, and that turned out to have a big impact on me, because when I got started in the venture business, I borrowed money from the SBA, a small business investment company. And when I was trying to borrow the money, I was 26 years old or something, and one of the conditions was you've got to have 10 years of investment experience. I said, "I've been investing since I was 9." The guy goes, "Okay!"

So it helped that I got started early. I think it was great that I had an allowance. Allowance was really important so we understood the value of money. And the job in the garden. I didn't always love working, but I loved getting my penny a minute. I'd always think "a minute went by, I got another penny."

The most important lesson that I can give to anybody is keep track of your money or have a budget early in life.

– Hüsnü Özyegin #BillionDollarGoldNuggets

Chip Wilson was earning substantial money as an employee starting at 18, but he didn't learn how to handle it properly until he was 20.

I got a job working on the Alaska oil pipeline, and I was the highest-paid laborer in the world. I was 18 when I went there, maybe even 17, and I made, I think in today's dollars, about $700,000 in about a year and a half. Unbelievable money. But I worked 18, 19 hours a day, and there was nowhere else to go. I took no time off. I had to leave because I was grinding my teeth.

No way to spend the money. But I sent my money back and I bought a house with three suites in it. I lived in one after I came back, and then I rented the other two out, which got me into thinking about cash flow and property.

The big mistakes there were I put a down payment on my house, but at that time, interest rates were 19%. So I had all this money in my bank account making me 2% interest, and I'm paying 19% on my mortgage. I didn't understand to shift my money from the bank into my mortgage so I wouldn't have to pay the interest rates. Cash flow is king.

As soon as he solved the problem, the money started to accumulate. This made him wealthy before the age of 25.

Limit Your Spending

Realize that whatever amount you cut your cost, it goes 100% toward your profit, and you would need a multiple of it in revenue in order to earn it otherwise.

Frank Hasenfratz is for me the world champion in cutting cost in business. After his daughter stepped in as CEO, he focused on his Cost Attack Team (CAT), which he created to do nothing other than finding opportunities to save money within the organization.

You've got to keep in mind, you make let's say 10% profit—if I can save $160,000 here, that took me 1 hour. I've got to make $1.6 million worth of work on the floor to make $160,000 profit.

Practice cost control and don't spend more than necessary.

Frank gets millions in savings for his Linamar company each and every year.

It's amazing what you'll find. In Europe, in two weeks, we identified $2.7 million, or maybe even more. It's not just a one-time saving; it's an annualized. If the job lasts for five years, it will go on for five years. Well, look at it this way: the average auto parts company makes, right now, from 3.5%–5% profit after tax. And Linamar makes after tax 8.5%. Only one other company does that. It's BorgWarner. So ask yourself, how can that happen? This is what we implemented this year already.

I looked at the table that Frank showed me and said, "Wow! It's $37 million! Is this per year?"

Yes. You always find something different. But you also have to give money back to the customer, 2% a year. So we have to find more than that in order to be profitable.

I asked Frank to give me an example of a cost-cutting measure.

A silly thing, yesterday. Each machine has a conveyor to take the chips out. We look at the first operation, the conveyor goes, but there's no chips. Very little chips. My assistant Alex said, "Wow, all the conveyors are running, but they're taking small cuts. A conveyor has 5 horsepower. That's roughly 4-kilowatt hour electricity use. A kilowatt hour is 11 cents, so that's 44 cents, times 24 hours, it's roughly $10 a day. Why not program it? You can program a computer to run the conveyor every

30 minutes for 5 minutes." I said, "You notice anything else? Okay, that's a good one." We have 400 machines there, and $10 a day times 400, you've got $4,000 a day. "What else did you notice?" The conveyor also brings out the cooling water, because when the conveyor runs, obviously some water stays on it. That goes out. Now we've got to take that away, and that is 9.5 cents a liter. So Alex was a smart ass; he said, "Why don't we give everybody a 1-liter bottle and take it home?" [laughs] I said, "Alex, you're so young, and you already try to make jokes?"

As you noticed above, frugality can easily turn into stinginess, and it sometimes does. There is this anecdote about Frank sitting with a dozen of his lawyers and accountants. One of them told a joke. Frank looked at his clock; it took three minutes to tell the joke. As the professionals are paid per hour, Frank quickly calculated how much he pays for three minutes to all the participants together. He said, "That joke just cost me $150. From now on, when we make jokes, we clock out, okay?" Cost cutting is a serious matter for Frank.

Jack Cowin told me another story about Frank visiting him on his yacht.

I said, "Frank, can I get you another drink?" It was the first time I met him. He says, "What's the cash equivalent if I don't have one?" [laughs] I said, "Frank, I now understand why you're so successful and why you've built such a great business."

Don't Spend More than You Have. Avoid Debt.

One of the most obvious and at the same time most disregarded rules in business is, "Don't spend more than you have." Although basic, it's one of the most important rules. And billionaires don't get tired of stressing it.

For Petter Stordalen, the Scandinavian Hotel King, it's so important he engraved it in stone. "Income before spending" is one of the Stone Rules of Gothenburg.

Income before spending.

– Petter Stordalen #BillionDollarGoldNuggets

Peter Hargreaves is a saver. Even in his youth, whenever he got some money, he saved it.

To become a chartered accountant, you had to have a contract, which meant you earned very little money. So the amount you earned was not a living wage. But even so, I never was without money because I was always very careful with it, and even though I never earned very much, when I was 21, I did have enough money to buy a car. And I bought a new car, which was quite unusual, because the amount of money I was earning would never have afforded it. I was just always very, very good at saving money. But I did, I was a saver. I've only had one very small mortgage in my life, and shortly after I had that, I could've paid it off. I've never had any fascination with spending money. I spend a minute proportion of my income.

Peter warns against borrowing and debt.

I think people borrow more than they need to borrow, and sometimes borrow when they don't need to. A guy that I know in Bristol had a successful business, and for some reason he got a venture capitalist to put some money in the business, and he never needed the money. I think a lot of people borrow money when actually, if they thought about it, they probably didn't need to. We never borrowed anything. We never borrowed any money at all.

Indeed, his Hargreaves Lansdown became one of the largest and most successful companies in the United Kingdom with this strategy.

I don't think anyone has ever created an FTSE 100 company in their lifetime without borrowing or acquisition. It's not been done before. I mean, people have created FTSE companies, but in general by buying lots of other companies and borrowing a lot of money, and of course, it means that their stake in the business is minute. But of course, we never parted with equity until we floated. So that's why I'm so wealthy; it's because I own so much of the stock. But we never borrowed and we never had any acquisitions, and I don't think anyone's created an FTSE company before without borrowing or acquisition.

People borrow more than they need to borrow, and sometimes borrow when they don't need to.

— Peter Hargreaves #BillionDollarGoldNuggets

Naveen Jain got the basic lesson in finance from his illiterate mother.

When I was going to college, first thing my mother told me was, "Look, you're leaving home. Hope you're going to be very successful. Just remember one simple thing: It doesn't matter how much money you make, as long as you spend less than what you make. Never take a debt and never spend more than what you have."

This was the most valuable piece of advice Naveen got in his life.

And I didn't realize that she was probably one of the best CFOs out there. Don't spend what you don't have. But she taught me the basic definition of profit that you should spend less than what you earned.

And I have never taken a debt. Never. And that is one of the things that stuck with me. I don't buy a house on debt. If I can't afford a house, I don't buy it. And I told all my employees always, you see every accountant will tell you it is the best thing, all the tax reasons why you should never pay for your house. You get a tax break, you get everything, and I say, what is most important? Peace of mind. Buy a house, pay off your house, and you know you will always have a roof over your head.

At the end of the day, debt and loss are the two things Naveen avoids in business. "Because that ultimately will kill you."

It doesn't matter how much money you make, as long as you spend less than what you make. Never take a debt and never spend more than what you have.

– Naveen Jain #BillionDollarGoldNuggets

Frank Hasenfratz got a basic financial education in childhood when together with his siblings he helped his parents at the farm.

We got paid for doing little chores, and we had chores. Everybody had chores. Even my sister, she had to cook or whatever. As a 12-year-old, she cooked dinner when everybody was working somewhere. But we always got a little money. And my dad used to say, "You want to get rich? There's one way to do it: spend less than you make. If you spend less and you accumulate, you get rich." And of course it was a dream to be better off.

Do You Enjoy Making Money or Spending It?

Ask yourself: What do you enjoy more, making money or spending it? Do you see your work and business as the "necessary evil" to make money you need to sustain your lifestyle or realize your dreams? Or it's your business what you actually enjoy doing, and spending money doesn't matter for you?

The following conclusion is one of the central claims in this book. If you had to only take away one sentence, this one would be a hot favorite:

The difference between financially successful people (millionaires) and financially super successful people (billionaires) boils down to the fact that the latter get pleasure MAKING money, but don't enjoy SPENDING it.

> ## You want to get rich? There's one way to do it: spend less than you make. If you spend less and you accumulate, you get rich.
>
> — Frank Hasenfratz #BillionDollarGoldNuggets

Michał Sołowow, the wealthiest person in Poland, doesn't like spending money. When I interviewed him in his office, he said, "I have always spent little and do not throw money around to this day. So spending is not something from my significant memories. I am not the best in spending." He added mockingly, "In some way I try to improve myself."

> ## The difference between financially successful people (millionaires) and financially super successful people (billionaires) boils down to the fact that the latter get pleasure MAKING money, but don't enjoy SPENDING it.
>
> — Rafael Badziag @BillionairePal #BillionDollarGoldNuggets

If you like money, don't spend it, keep it!

This is something Lirio Parisotto wanted to make sure I understand clearly.

People spend before they receive the money. So they are slaves of money.

Do you like money? If you like it, what do you do? The thing you like, you keep with you. But people nowadays don't like money. People don't like money because they spend it even before they receive it.

Lirio himself started learning to value money at the age of six when doing outwork, extracting and selling the corn straw used for wrapping tobacco and wrapping straw cigars.

We did it every night for two hours after dinner. And so my father and mother gave this money to me saying, "This is yours."

It was small money. I don't think it was possible to buy a pair of shoes or a shirt with it. But when you received the money, you put it in a hidden compartment. And I liked to sometimes go to see the money, open, turn the money. I loved to see the money and feel the good paper. I was in love with money. Because this was my money. This is what's important. It was my money.

Lirio learned also to save money instead of spending it.

We needed to save the money because at that time, we didn't have much. When we went to the doctor, to the hospital, we needed to pay the bill somehow.

Today, Lirio is a billionaire and one of the wealthiest people in South America.

If you like money, don't spend it, keep it!

– Lirio Parisotto #BillionDollarGoldNuggets

Be Money Smart in Business

Managing your spending in your private life is one thing, but watching your bottom line in business is a completely different ball game. Billionaires have developed an array of methods and tools to effectively support them in this area. I will share with you several conclusions that I have extracted from the interviews with them.

Realize that it's not about the revenue, it's about the profit. Optimize your margins and bottom line!

This is advice that guided Dilip Shanghvi throughout his life.

My father once told me that a cashier at the bank counts a lot of money, but it's important for you to keep in mind how much money he takes home. So you can earn a lot of revenue, but it's important for you to stay focused on the profit.

No wonder Dilip's Sun Pharma's revenue profitability was 25% when I interviewed him and its market cap was as high as four times its sales, a fabulous number for an Indian company.

You can earn a lot of revenue, but it's important for you to stay focused on the profit.

– Dilip Shanghvi #BillionDollarGoldNuggets

Chip Wilson was well aware of this relationship when he was building Lululemon, a legendary Canadian sportswear brand, in a way that allowed him to take advantage of it.

If you ask anybody, people would say Under Armour is a much, much bigger company, but because it's wholesale, actually Lululemon makes more money. That's the difference. Would you rather be in a company that makes more money, or in one that has more work?

Under Armour is in the wholesale business, so in other words, they make something for $10, they sell it to a wholesaler for $20, and then it's $40 in the shop. Lululemon makes a better-quality product at $12, and then can sell it for $38 through its own system. So the margins are much bigger. Plus it's like you can see that Apple and Tesla followed up into the same model, taking a technical product, making it beautiful, and going direct to the customer. This is a far better business model.

Chip had to leave the company he has created, but "by the end of Lululemon, it was the highest sales per square foot of a store in the world and highest margins of any vertical retailer outside of jewelry and Apple. The winning formulas I set up at Lululemon were just the best in the world, and I don't think anyone's done anything better yet."

Would you rather be in a company that makes more money, or in one that has more work?

— Chip Wilson #BillionDollarGoldNuggets

Are you smart with money, dear reader? What are your spending habits? Have you learned to handle money properly? Do you have debt or spend more than you make? Do you enjoy spending money more than making it? How is the financial performance of your business?

- Drifters like spending money; they spend everything they earn or more.

- Millionaires like making money in order to spend it.

- Billionaires don't see money as something to be spent privately; they like making money and dislike spending it; they build financially efficient businesses.

For more stories on this topic, go to:
http://TheBillionDollarSecret.com/resources

CHAPTER 17

Never Stop Improving

*One must still have chaos in oneself to be able
to give birth to a dancing star.*

—Friedrich Nietzsche

You need to prepare thoroughly in order to be able to perform.

For Sergey Galitskiy, certain things need to happen if you want to be successful. One of them is, first "you have to be ready and prepared intellectually, and second you have to believe in yourself."

Also, Lirio Parisotto believes that in order to build wealth, you need to be prepared for it.

> ## You have to be ready and prepared intellectually.
>
> **— Sergey Galitskiy #BillionDollarGoldNuggets**

Educate Yourself

Education is important.

Lirio believes what determined his success was good education.

In the case of my family, we felt very strongly about education. I remember my father always said, "For me, it's impossible to leave an inheritance to my children. The only thing I can try is to make my children study." Because he said the people who study, they have an opportunity. He kept saying this all the time. Unfortunately, he didn't have money to pay for our higher education. So I supported all my sisters and brothers. I paid for everybody's university education. It demanded great effort, but I think a big stimulus was the responsibility for them. You need to take care.

> ## People who study, they have an opportunity.
>
> **— Lirio Parisotto #BillionDollarGoldNuggets**

But it's not the school knowledge that is decisive. There is a great difference between schooling and education. Many billionaires may not have schooling, but they excel in education.

As Cai Dongqing put it:

School knowledge is not the decisive factor. I dropped out of school early, and I was not good at learning from the textbook. In the commercial world, I feel that more important factors are the desire and capability in absorbing new knowledge and the personality and behavior such as integrity and the sense of responsibility.

One of Cai's principles is to always learn and improve. Learn from your business and improve with every step. When I asked him what advice would he give his 20-year-old self, he answered: "Learn more!"

School knowledge is not the decisive factor. More important factors are the desire and capability in absorbing new knowledge.

– Cai Dongqing #BillionDollarGoldNuggets

Cho Tak Wong (Cao Dewang), whom I described in chapter 1, is one of the wisest people I have ever met despite his having had only five years of schooling. He resembles a Chinese philosopher and could pass as a Buddhist monk. I didn't know him before, but it seems that with increasing age and experience he got this wisdom of an old man who has seen it all, drew conclusions from it, and now teaches his well-thought-out and well-formulated ideas about life and business.

He never graduated from any school. He never attended any university. His poor family couldn't even afford an elementary education for him. Everything he learned in his life, he learned by himself. He has absolutely no formal education. In spite of all that, he is now among the most respected and wealthiest people in China, a self-made billionaire and the World Entrepreneur of the Year 2009. I asked him about wealth advice for young people. His answer will surprise you:

My advice for young people is, they should start to build up wisdom, not just making money but wisdom.

Use Every Opportunity to Learn

Use every opportunity to learn. You never know what it's going to be good for. So learn whenever and wherever possible.

Lirio Parisotto learned a lot during seemingly accidental weekend courses. The skills he learned there proved extremely helpful in his later career and paid for his college education.

After he was expelled from the seminary, he worked two years for a small salary as janitor in his uncle's college in Brasilia.

At the end of the week, they rented the rooms for weekend courses. These were small courses with some special scientific methodology. I remember technical design, tax declaration. There were many small courses of this kind. And I remember one I did was legislation for workers in unions, good for work in the HR department in some companies. Most of the time, I went there. I took these courses for free. I just spent my weekends there. And it made my head more clear.

When I went back to Rio Grande do Sul, I found a job in a small meat processing plant with 23 employees. At the end of the month, I did the bills of the employees.

Also, in January, February, March, I did the special service for income tax. Because in Brasilia I learned what is possible to do in order to optimize it, especially for the drivers of the trucks. Because at that time they had a 3% discount on the income tax. They thought that what they had paid was the final tax. I realized this was only the anticipated tax. At the end of the year, you need to do the balance. Most of them could receive money back. But they didn't do anything. They didn't know, because they thought this was the final tax. And I went, "We need to do the figures, maybe you will get something back." "No! The government! Do you think you will receive money back from the government? Forget it!" The first year was, "OK. I don't charge you anything. Only when you receive the money back, you pay me 20%." The deadline was the end of March.

In September, October, the money started to come. They received their money, and so I became a saint in our city, the only guy capable of getting money back from the government. The money I made from the commission was about the price of a VW Beetle.

With this money and the money I had, I was able to study.

Learn more!

— Cai Dongqing #BillionDollarGoldNuggets

Tony Tan Caktiong learns from everybody and at every opportunity.

I think one best way to learn is to keep an open mind and listen and ask the right questions. And I think everybody is a teacher. Every moment is a learning opportunity. Even simply talking to your customers and talking to your employees. So if you keep an open mind, that's where you learn and people will give you good feedback.

Everybody is a teacher. Every moment is a learning opportunity.

— Tony Tan Caktiong #BillionDollarGoldNuggets

Learn How the World Works

One of the main differences between millionaires and billionaires is their knowledge. Billionaires learn how the world works and understand it on an entirely different level. How do you build a skyscraper? How do you finance a factory? How do you negotiate with a government about the purchase of a mine? Those are the questions billionaires learn and know the answers to.

Let me give you an example: I asked Ron Sim about the acquisition of Brookstone, which was a big financial effort for his company, and how he dealt with it.

Because I had to deal with a lot of bankers, I forced myself to understand every aspect of finance and accounting. You need to understand all the financial derivatives and all the implications. You need to understand the profit and loss statement, balance sheet, cash flow. You need to understand how the market works from both the operational and financial standpoint.

You need to be mindful of a broader spectrum of things. There's so much to explore in finance. Corporate bankers, investment bankers, private bankers—there are all different bankers. They are each a specialty in itself. And if you do not know how to deal with it, your leverage power weakens. And when it weakens, you make a wrong deal. You pay the price.

Three Steps to Learn to Do Business

You can't learn to do business at school or from theory books. It's like learning to swim by reading a manual. No, you need to get wet by jumping into the water and trying to swim. But before you do that, it's advisable to prepare a little, so you won't drown immediately.

1. Prepare

In order to do business, you need to understand as much as possible about its fundamentals. Also, learn as much as possible about your industry.

You can do it by working for somebody else, like Hüsnü Özyegin suggests.

I advise our students at Özyegin University to first work in a corporate entity when they graduate and not jump straight into starting a new business or become a new entrepreneur unless they have an idea like Facebook or Twitter.

[laughs] They have to work in a corporate entity first and see how a corporate entity operates, and also meet people and learn, build up a network, become exposed to different industries.

So first learn your trade, start at the bottom, and work your way up in order to understand your business from the bottom up.

This is exactly the approach that Frank Hasenfratz advocates:

I only know one job that you start at the top and you're successful: when you dig a hole. There, you have to start on top. [chuckles] The rest of it, it's much better to come from the bottom up.

Narayana Murthy became the World Entrepreneur of the Year 2003. But his first business failed. He then decided to first learn the nuts and bolts of his industry as an employee.

I started a company called Softronics in Pune, in 1976, and it failed because there was no market for software in India and computers were very expensive. The banks did not give any loans, and most corporations did not trust small enterprises.

I failed in my first business. And it was good because I learned a very important lesson, and that is the market must be ready for your entrepreneurial idea. If the market is not ready, no idea will take off.

So, I realized my mistake in less than a year, understood that I had to focus on the export market, closed Softronics, decided to learn the tricks of export and the lessons of running mid-size enterprises, and became the head of software at PCS in Mumbai.

And I knew that sooner or later I would return to entrepreneurship. I had a team of about 200 software engineers, and I traveled abroad a lot to meet clients. So, I learned a lot about opportunities in the software export market, and how to promote a company in the export market, and how to organize an export-oriented company. I am very grateful to PCS for such a wonderful opportunity.

I only know one job that you start at the top and you're successful: when you dig a hole.

– Frank Hasenfratz #BillionDollarGoldNuggets

Read books and magazines, and instead of traveling for shopping, go to conferences or industry fairs, as Lirio Parisotto advises.

If you want to understand one business, any kind of business, you have books, magazines, Google. And instead of traveling just for fun, why don't people go to conferences, congresses, industry fairs? If someone wants, he will find a way to understand each specific area, if he is interested.

Open your mind and see what happens. Travel. I think one important thing is travel. But people travel most of the time just for shopping. And they do nothing, nothing, nothing.

You will read later in this chapter how Lirio's travel to New York inseminated in his mind a winning business idea.

2. Learn from Other People

Take advice from the people you admire and trust.

The first address is always the family. Are your grandparents or your parents entrepreneurs? If yes, take advice from them.

The next address are the great people in your industry. Sometimes they are your competitors. Seek contact with them and learn from them.

Hüsnü Özyegin, now the wealthiest self-made man in Turkey, confessed to me he was mentored by the legendary Turkish entrepreneur and philanthropist Vehbi Koc:

When I was the general manager of Yapi Kredi, I lived in the same apartment building as Vehbi Koc. He was famously modest. I was 40 years younger than him, and whenever I visited him, he would listen very carefully to what I had to say. Now I wish that I had made him talk more and listened. He was one of the greatest visionaries of our time, and many count him as being the founder of modern philanthropy in Turkey. He established important institutions such as the Turkish Education Foundation, Koc University, as well as museums and schools.

Frank Hasenfratz was exceptionally active in this area, always trying to learn something from the proficient people in his industry whom he admired:

I started a group, 10 people in manufacturing. It was a general manufacturing group, not just in the car industry. The deal was, "Each one of you has to do a presentation, what you think you did good, something that others can learn from. And brag a little bit." There's nothing wrong with bragging. But you can't have many people. Ten is the best. And usually six or seven showed up.

You can learn, like Petter Stordalen, from those with more experience:

If you're open-minded, you can learn from a lot of people. I've learned a lot from people working on different levels in the companies. But particularly in the beginning of my career, I was very lucky to work with people who had much more experience than I had, and so I learned a lot from people who had years and years of experience, and they taught me about it. So I didn't have to do all the mistakes myself.

Some billionaires, like Cai Dongqing, learn most from people with a different perspective.

The most useful advice is always by those who can give me a different opinion on my idea and point out its problems. Such advice is helpful and influential.

3. Learn Business by Practicing It

I asked Jack Cowin about the best way to learn to do business.

What is the best way to learn to do business? Obviously by experiencing it. You don't learn it in a classroom. It's by getting in and jumping off the dock into the water and learning how to tread water as you learn how to swim. Baptism by fire, not classroom theory. Getting practical experience. That's how you learn.

Naveen Jain confirms it:

There is no better way of learning to do business than doing it. I don't care how many books you read, I don't care how many professors you talked to; the only way to learn to do the business is to do the business and have great mentors.

> ### What is the best way to learn to do business? Obviously by experiencing it. You don't learn it in a classroom. It's by getting in and jumping off the dock into the water and learning how to tread water as you learn how to swim.
>
> **— Jack Cowin #BillionDollarGoldNuggets**

Whatever your journey, remember that experience is the most precious jewel you gain in your life. Cai Dongqing explains it as follows:

Experience is the most meaningful content in our life, but only when it comes with a goal will it be enriched with inspiration and fulfillment. The goal needs to be in line with what we really want to do, so that we could enjoy the experience all the time no matter if it is suffering or comfort.

There is no better way of learning to do business than doing it.

— Naveen Jain #BillionDollarGoldNuggets

Stay Curious

For your development in business and in private life, it is essential to stay young in mind. Be curious. Be open to new ideas. Explore new opportunities.

Petter Stordalen considers being open-minded the most important character trait for a businessperson, next to honesty. It's important "that you're open. That you listen to people around you, rather than to insist you have the right answers."

Openness to new ideas and asking the right questions are some of the qualities Narayana Murthy considers the most important for a businessperson.

It's curiosity that helped Lirio Parisotto find a perfect marketing model for his business.

I always was curious so I took some money and I went to New York. This was the first time I saw a videocassette and the camera with my own eyes. The cassette was 10 kilos probably, an old model. And they had also a possibility to connect TV to the camera. And so in the Broadway area a salesman recorded outside, and it appeared immediately in the TV.

But for me it was clear: you didn't need to go to the stores anymore. Because before the film was like a photo. You needed to develop it. And this one: do you need to develop? No! And also it was possible to re-record it, to use it over and over again.

They sold equipment, cameras, and also movies and some Broadway shows. So I took two suitcases full of movies and went back to Brazil to open a Video Club.

It was initially a retail store. They call it Video Club because people paid some monthly payment to become an associate of the club. They had the right to borrow the videos, but they have to pay monthly.

The secret was they needed the device. So, I started to sell the device as well, the device and also the TV. And this kind of client is a client with good purchasing power. And those are more open-minded people. They spend money to have a better TV, better sound, so the store started to grow.

But the most important part was not the Video Club. The Video Club was important to get the foot in. I put the Video Club in the end of the store. So the people needed to [laughs] walk in the middle of the equipment.

This way, Lirio was able to attract many customers and convert them into sales. Soon, he dominated the local electronic equipment market.

Engage in the Process of Constant Improvement

Being successful is one thing, but sustaining that success is another thing entirely. Keep on learning and improving in order to stay in the race. It's not the state of being educated, it's the process of learning that makes you successful.

Cho Tak Wong is somebody who learned everything he knows by himself. He went from a 14-year-old illiterate rascal to a billionaire and the World Entrepreneur of the Year 2009. He is a living example of what outrageous success is possible for you if you work on yourself, no matter where you start. I listened attentively to what he told me about learning: "If you do not keep learning, then this will become your boundary."

I heard similar words from another Chinese billionaire, Cai Dongqing:

You need to keep learning and self-transforming at all times, which I think is the key to continuous success. Keep learning and keep thinking. Learn everywhere and all the time.

Billionaires never stop improving. You would think you are perfect enough when you are the best entrepreneur in the world. Mohed Altrad became the World Entrepreneur of the Year 2015, and I asked him what he wanted to change about himself. His answer astonished me: "I want to be better at what I'm doing. Improve."

Michał Sołowow doesn't need inspiration to improve.

It's rather my inner energy, that internal pressure that whispers to me "go forward," "be better still."

When I asked him about his success secret, he told me:

One important thing is the ability to draw conclusions from defeats. To continuously learn and after all self-improve. Or the ability to accept that you manage people smarter than yourself and take for yourself what is best in those people. And a continuous search for such people from whom you can keep learning

Michał's advice is above all "to fight with your weaknesses and limitations."

Tony Tan Caktiong is an excellent example of never-ending improvement. He went to the university after starting a successful business; and even now, as the World Entrepreneur of the Year 2004, he still goes to Harvard Business School for a week each year.

I wanted to study further, more for self-development, so I went to AIM (Asian Institute of Management). They were the most popular at that time in Asia, and they are based here in Manila. So I attended the top management program. Then I also went to Harvard for some programs. I believe in self-development. I have passion and interest in trying to understand more or to learn more, so I started doing these management programs. I think in the business side there is still a lot to learn. So I still keep on going back to Harvard on a yearly basis for a one-week program. And then from time to time I read some business books, so it's still mostly on the business side. But also general knowledge.

Chip Wilson is an advocate of lifelong development. He took advantage of numerous courses, but the Landmark course turned out to be the breakthrough in his business career. It was at Westbeach, his first business.

I had two partners and we weren't getting along. The company wasn't making any money. I had one partner that was 10 years older and had kids and wanted a mortgage and a house, and I wanted to invest money in the company. And then my other partner was trying to be a middleman, but he hated conflict. So nothing was working about it.

We went to the Landmark course together, and really we came out of it to leave the past in the past. We were going to create our present for our future, so we decided we wanted to sell the company, but in order to do that we had to do a bunch of things. So we got together and forgave the past, so to speak, and moved forward. I think that that was a turning point in my life: realizing I had choice in life to operate a lot differently than I had operated before, and I had multiple choices of ways to operate, as both a businessperson and a leader and as a father, and not any one way is correct. There's multiple ways.

You don't need to know it all, but be the best in one thing and focus on it.

Of course, growing requires self-reflection. First know yourself, know your talents and deficiencies. Only this way can you know where to improve and what to develop.

Ron Sim recommends to "keep focused on your strong sides and perfect it." Everything else you should delegate or find business partners that take it from you.

Dilip Shanghvi, like many billionaires, improves constantly and competes with his own past performance.

I want to do what I am doing well, and I want to be better than what I was in the past. I generally don't compete with anybody else, but I compete with my own performance of the past.

Keep focused on your strong sides and perfect it.

— Ron Sim #BillionDollarGoldNuggets

For Petter Stordalen, this perpetual improvement is the main source of motivation:

To do things better today than yesterday, but not as good as tomorrow.

And keep in mind: There is always something you can improve.

Sergey Galitskiy confessed this to me:

I don't believe that there is anything ideal that exists for me. There is not an ideal of things. I always want to improve. It is not obsessive, but I am an improver. My wife even sometimes gets angry at me because I always want to improve something, change something, relocate something.

You never know everything. You always can learn something.

I asked Mohed Altrad, the World Entrepreneur of the Year 2015, if there was a moment when he finally realized he knew how it all worked.

I consider that I've never reached this point. Just really learn and carry on learning. The point is, are you justified to say, "I know everything"? Not really. I don't subscribe to this logic.

Frank Hasenfratz started with very little knowledge about doing business and has been improving his company for decades and decades, step-by-step; and the compound effect of this constant improvement is astonishing.

It's like day and night. The change is enormous, and it's changing every day today. We don't do things today like we did 10 years ago, and we didn't do things 10 years ago like we did them 20 years ago. Our industry is changing rapidly. Almost everything is automated. You walk through our plants, there's robots everywhere. When I got into business, I knew very little about business. You learn every day.

It's advisable to write down your lessons learned, like Frank does.

Whatever I learn from, I write down every year, "Lessons Learned." For 50 years. "Lessons Learned" is things we did wrong. That's what the lesson is. And we made some big mistakes. I mean, I made some big mistakes. So every year, I write it down.

As your company grows, your learning and your challenges change.

To get to the next level, you often need to change your perspective and look at things from somebody else's point of view.

I asked Kim Beom-Su about the changes he needed to make about himself in order to achieve what he has achieved.

I think the biggest thing that made an impact was having an open mind, or having a different perspective on things or relating to people with different perspectives. Ultimately, being aware that there is a limit to what you can achieve by looking at the world through my own framework, and realizing there is a different way. I think this was what was very important and played a big role in my success.

The most important thing that I mention is to not be caught in your own mind frame. Having a new perspective, you have to be open to a new world and approach it with a new perspective in order to see a new solution and form a new relationship.

Let's sum it all up with the wisdom Manny Stul revealed to me:

I think we're on this planet to learn and to grow and to evolve, and as much as we all have aspirations and desires, it's not the destination that's important; it's what you do along the way that's important. That journey that you have to whatever goals you're trying to achieve, that's your life. Not the goals and the achievement and the money and the wealth and the power. That's nonsense. It's what you do along the way that's important. That process ultimately determines your soul state of evolution. It's just wonderful to keep aspiring to higher realms. I don't do it consciously anymore. It's sort of part of me just like the winning thing.

We're on this planet to learn and to grow and to evolve.

— Manny Stul #BillionDollarGoldNuggets

It's not the destination that's important; it's what you do along the way that's important. That journey that you have to whatever goals you're trying to achieve, that's your life.

— Manny Stul #BillionDollarGoldNuggets

- Drifters stop improving after they finish school. Their education quickly expires.

- Millionaires stop improving when they achieve personal wealth. After that, their education decreases with time.

- Billionaires never stop improving. They may not have schooling, but their education never stops growing.

For more stories on this topic, go to:
http://TheBillionDollarSecret.com/resources

CHAPTER 18

Live with Integrity

If it is not right do not do it;
if it is not true do not say it.

—Marcus Aurelius

It is possible to become a billionaire while maintaining personal integrity. In fact, it is necessary to uphold those values in order to have sustainable success in business. The billionaires in this book are excellent examples for that.

Narayana Murthy's life motto is "The softest pillow is a clear conscience."

Do Not Lie. Do Not Cheat. Do Not Steal.

In some areas of our world, there is a conviction that you have to steal your first million. In fact, many people believe that the rich are immoral individuals who take advantage of others by lying and cheating. Nothing is further from the truth.

While it is possible to become a millionaire by scamming people, such wealth is short-lived. Cheaters are caught by society, which eventually takes away their short-lived fortunes and punishes them. Don't take shortcuts while compromising your integrity. You will never become a billionaire with this strategy.

Compete fiercely and fairly, but don't "cut in line."

Manny Stul, the World Entrepreneur of the Year 2016, found perfect words for it.

I think people can be successful in the short term without integrity, but not in the long term. It ends up catching up with you, and you'll pay a price for the lack of integrity, for doing wrong things. It may not be financial, but you'll pay a price with family, health. Something will happen. It's just karma. I'm a very firm believer that things equal out—if not immediately, sometime in the future. You see these people that do all these crooked things. I know that they'll pay a price for it. How, I don't know how, but there'll be a price to be paid.

Integrity is an important component in many billionaires' company cultures.

Honesty is one of the most important qualities of a businessperson. It's the number one quality named by many billionaires.

Manny Stul told me never to fool your customer:

When I started my first business, I learned very early on that it's imperative not to lie to maintain relationships and trust from people you're dealing with. It's very hard to win somebody's trust, but once you've got it, you probably have it for life, and you can lose it instantly by lying. I believe that once you've lost somebody's trust, you've lost it forever. Sure, they can forgive, sure, the relationship can be maintained, but it's not the same as it was before when they believed you always tell the truth. Life's so much easier when you're telling the truth.

I learned, more importantly than ever, never to lie, ever. Because if they catch you lying once, you can forget about it. Very important.

And indeed, honesty is extremely important for long-term business success.

I learned, more importantly than ever, never to lie, ever. Because if they catch you lying once, you can forget about it.

— Manny Stul #BillionDollarGoldNuggets

Don't take anything that belongs to others. And don't get involved in corruption even if it is expected from you and not complying hinders your business.

India has deep bribing traditions. Its economy and social system are based on bribes. Naveen Jain had very humble beginnings in India.

My father was an overseer. And we didn't have to be poor actually because he was responsible for building the buildings for the government. It's a good job. Except that in India they expect you to take a bribe. It is common culture that you will take a bribe. My dad decided that he wanted to be an honest man. He wasn't going to take a bribe.

This meant hunger, as his official salary wasn't enough to support the family.

The system works like that: He tells the contractor, "Hey, don't put the cement, put half cement and half sand, the money that you save give us a piece of it." He will take a small piece of it, pass it on to his boss, his boss will take his piece and pass it to his boss, and that's why everybody in the food chain will get paid. But he didn't.

Every now and then, his boss will call the contractor and say, "Hey, I'm not seeing any money. Is he keeping it all?" And contractor will say, "Do you know what he's asking me to do?" "What?" "He's asking me to build the building to the spec. Have you ever heard of it? When I bid on the building, I knew I don't have to use cement, so I bid low. Now, I have to use cement, I'm losing my shirt and you're telling me why am I not giving money?"

In government you don't get fired, so every year he got transferred. "That son of a bitch needs to go. Send him out. He's taking my money." We moved from village to village to village until the most remote villages where there is no building to be built. So he's not taking anybody's bribe now. We grew up in villages where there was hardly any electricity, no schools, no tables, no chairs. You sit on the floor, you write on the floor.

I remember very vividly, when I was 8 to 10 years old, I went to him and I said, "You know, you want to be honest, that's your problem. You still have to be responsible and feed the family." And I was very angry. And he looked at me and he said, "You know, I don't know what to tell you. One day you will grow up and you will realize I have given you more than most parents have which would be the value of integrity. And you may not appreciate it today but someday you will." And I still remember. . . .

Narayana Murthy built Infosys in corrupt India. He didn't accept bribing traditions either.

We demonstrated that it is possible to run a large and successful business legally and ethically in India. I have never paid a bribe. And when there were demands in the beginning in the early 1990s, we resisted. That led to some delays in approvals from the government. But once they realized that we were not going to give in, they actually supported us because they wanted to see a few good people around them. That is a very important lesson for us in India and for people in other countries with corruption.

Have Strong Values

Success is a by-product of living strong values.

Billionaires make sure they base their business on values.

I asked Cai Dongqing what he avoids in business. He said: "We cannot do business just for doing business. We do business with principles."

Petter Stordalen's formula for a good business consists of four values: "Integrity, honesty, openness, trustworthiness."

> ## We cannot do business just for doing business. We do business with principles.
>
> **— Cai Dongqing #BillionDollarGoldNuggets**

Be Humble

One of the most important things Naveen Jain made me realize is this:

Humility is a sign of success. So the only way you know you have been successful is when you become humble. If you still have an iota of arrogance in you, that means you're still trying to prove something to someone or yourself. Actually, if you meet people who are not humble, they tell you that they are still on the path to success, but they have not been successful yet.

Humility is a sign of success.

– Naveen Jain #BillionDollarGoldNuggets

I was indeed surprised by the humility of the billionaires I interviewed. See it yourself in some of their statements.

Dilip Shanghvi is a multibillionaire. He built Sun Pharma, the largest pharmaceutical company in India, and is the world's wealthiest person in pharmaceuticals. I asked him what he was most proud about in his life.

Personally, I don't think we've done anything remarkable that I need to be proud of.

Tony Tan Caktiong built Jollibee Foods, which, with an array of brands and thousands of restaurants, is Asia's largest food service company. He became the World Entrepreneur of the Year 2004. But when I asked him what success is for him, he answered:

I guess success, probably is . . . I think we are still going day by day. We don't think we are overly successful.

Cho Tak Wong started as an illiterate cowhand taking care of just one cow, in a poor, war-torn village in China. He built Fuyao Glass, and became the world's largest auto glass manufacturer and the World Entrepreneur of the Year 2009. You read his stunning story in chapter 1. His life is full of inspiring experiences. Nevertheless, he told me:

The reality is, I'm an ordinary person doing ordinary things every day, so no amazing story.

Be Good Rather than Rich

Dilip Shanghvi's father used to say, "Money will make you a richer person, but you need to try and become a better person." Dilip told me to not start measuring everything in terms of money.

Similarly, when I asked Hüsnü Özyegin how he wanted to be remembered, he answered:

I would like people to say, "He was a good man." That's all. That says a lot. Do you know what I mean? Not that "he was a rich man," but "he was a good man."

The same answer I've heard in various forms from other billionaires.

Money will make you a richer person, but you need to try and become a better person.

— Dilip Shanghvi #BillionDollarGoldNuggets

Wisely Choose Your Environment

Surround yourself with people with high business ethics and morals.

I asked Frank Stronach how he chooses his business partners.

I choose people that I think have great character.

Do business only with people you like and trust.

Petter Stordalen told me, "I only do business with people I like. I do business with people I trust. If I don't like them, I don't do business with them."

Don't spend time with cynical people who don't have personal integrity.

Stay Grounded

Keep both feet on earth. Don't let money influence your values, lifestyle, or relationships.

Dilip Shanghvi stayed humble despite the great financial success he has experienced.

I try not to allow that money to influence my value system, my lifestyle, my relationship with people. I of course know people who are very successful, but my closest friends are friends from school.

Similarly, Peter Hargreaves kept his friends from his youth. He still regularly goes with them to the local pub for a beer. He doesn't let his wealth interfere with his lifestyle.

You wouldn't be able to tell their wealth when you see many of the self-made billionaires on the street. A striking example of this is Cai Dongqing. If I had to use just one word to describe him, it would be humility. Cai certainly stayed the simple, unpretentious person he was. He kept both feet on earth, didn't lose contact with his roots. There is nothing luxurious about his appearance. He gives an impression of physical slightness, but there is a diamond inside, a strong, perseverant personality who never gives up until he achieves what he set out to do.

Do Good

Cho Tak Wong cautions to do good as it is beneficial for yourself.

> *Every day, every little thing you are facing, you have to make a decision if what you do is good for your life, good for society, if it's good for the state, if it is good for the human race. If it's good, then you do it. But if it's not, you will not do it. If you make sure to do things that benefit other people, then in the end it will be coming back to you and will benefit yourself.*

Manny Stul is a spiritual person. I asked him for one message he would like to share with the world audience. Here it is:

> *Do good, and if you can't, won't, or are unable to, don't do bad.*

Reliability Breeds Trust

Reliability breeds trust and trust is a driver for business. Be trustworthy. Trust makes a lot of things easier in business.

> ## Do good, and if you can't, won't, or are unable to, don't do bad.
>
> **— Manny Stul #BillionDollarGoldNuggets**

Cai Dongqing identified reliability as the main reason for the success of his company.

> *I think it was reliability and charm that helped us win much support and enduring cooperation from our partners. In the commercial world, many decisions and transactions are not just about business. It encompasses a lot of good faith or intangible things, such as reliability, integrity, sincerity, and the personality.*

If you are not trusted, you can't even open a bank account, so prove you are trustworthy.

For Mohed Altrad, banks were a great challenge at the beginning of his career in the scaffolding industry. He obtained a PhD in France, he had a great job in Abu Dhabi that earned him a lot of money, and then he doubled his money by founding and selling a computer company. But for the French banks he still wasn't trustworthy enough.

> *Banks didn't trust me. They were saying, "This is a Bedouin guy, Syrian, Arab, coming from computers and buying bankrupted companies." Really, I had the*

greatest problem to open a bank account when I took over Mefran. I wasn't asking for money, just a bank account. You can't work without it.

And then I succeeded in opening an account, because they took my house as collateral. And the first year there was some small profit, and the bank didn't believe it. They scrutinized the balance sheet many times to understand what's wrong. [chuckles] It's not possible. That was a great obstacle, really.

How to build your reliability?

Start with simple things: Be on time.

Such a simple thing as punctuality is among the basic success tools named by many billionaires.

Cho Tak Wong stresses to "always be on time, and if you promise somebody, always be there."

Keep your word. Your word is your honor.

Frank Stronach describes his approach as follows: "If you say something, you must keep it. Number one is do what you say."

It is easy to respect a contract favorable to you. But it is important to respect your contracts even and especially when they turn out to be a bad deal.

If you say something, you must keep it. Number one is do what you say.

— Frank Stronach #BillionDollarGoldNuggets

Don't make empty statements. Be credible.

Naveen Jain is known in the industry for making one-time offers and never renegotiating on them.

The rule in life is never say something that you're not willing to follow. If you say, "The price is 50 million," you can't then ask, "Would you take 40?" If you have broken the rule once, then the word in the industry goes out that you will make a counteroffer. It's about your credibility.

And always remember that it takes generations to build credibility and it only takes one action to kill it.

My conversation with Naveen about trust was an eye-opener.

Let me give you just one more thought about how business gets done in life. Most people tell you it's all about who you know. And that is just so wrong,

I think it is the people who have never really been successful in life [who say this]. It is never about who you know. It's not even about who likes you. There are three levels before a deep, long-term, sustainable business relationship is formed. They have to know you, they have to like you, but most importantly they have to trust you. So it's not about who you know, it's not about who likes you, it's about who trusts you. And if you can't develop that third level, you can have short-term deals with people, but you can never have a long-term business relationship.

Let's quote this golden rule of integrity: Trust is a greater compliment than affection.

It's not about who you know, it's not about who likes you, it's about who trusts you.

— Naveen Jain #BillionDollarGoldNuggets

Treat People with Integrity

Wish people well and be kind to them.

I asked Narayana Murthy what was success for him.

Success is about lighting up the eyes and bringing a smile to the face of people when you enter a room. You do not have to be rich, famous, beautiful, or powerful to bring a smile to the faces of people. They smile because they know that you are a decent person, you care for them, and that you wish them well.

Trust is a greater compliment than affection.

— Rafael Badziag @BillionairePal #BillionDollarGoldNuggets

Be Fair

Be straight and fair in your dealings with other people. Being fair has to do with ethics, but also it's beneficial in business. Fairly treated employees are more motivated, fairly treated business partners more loyal. But it also has an economic dimension. An unfair deal is a short-lived deal. So strive for WIN-WIN situations.

Success is about lighting up the eyes and bringing a smile to the face of people when you enter a room.

– Narayana Murthy #BillionDollarGoldNuggets

Tony Tan Caktiong thinks from the perspective of the other party to understand their needs.

My belief is always a shared reward; it cannot be one-sided. It's nice to let people think that they get more out of it instead of you getting more out of it. In any deal or in any problem, it is always a question of how do I make that person better. Can he get a better deal? Can he get a better future? And I think that works always, up to the point where people in my company will say in any negotiation, "Don't let Tony join, 'cause he will give away everything." But that's my belief. Once you let the other party feel that he also gets a lot, the deal becomes smoother.

This fairness is deeply rooted in Tony's life philosophy.

For Petter Stordalen, "A good deal is when both parties feel like they have come out on top."

Don't Wrong Other People

Billionaires follow the Golden Rule: Do unto others what you want others to do unto you. This is also Tony Tan Caktiong's life motto and the most valuable piece of wisdom for Jack Cowin.

Do not hurt people. I asked Cho Tak Wong what he avoided in business.

Anything which would hurt the customer's interest. Anything hurting other people I will not do.

A good deal is when both parties feel like they have come out on top.

– Petter Stordalen #BillionDollarGoldNuggets

Respect People

Billionaires treat people with respect.

Petter Stordalen explained to me why:

My father said that people will look at you. If you treat people good, they will be loyal and they will be good to you. And treat everybody equal. Every guest is important to me in the hotel. Doesn't matter if you come in jeans or in a new suit. Everybody's important.

You should treat a waitress as well as your business partner, says Naveen Jain.

Allowing people to treat other people who serve them with disrespect makes me cry. I have seen people who are extremely kind to you when you are doing business with them because they need something from you, and then they are mean to the waitress. And to me, that's the number one rule, I never do business with them because if they treat people like that, I know someday they're going to treat me like that.

You should not only respect people, but also recognize them when they do something good for you.

Trust People

Chip Wilson, like most billionaires I interviewed, is trustful of people. When we met in his house in Vancouver, Canada, he explained his approach.

I think in essence, my genius in life is I trust people implicitly, and my downfall in life is I trust people implicitly. Because I'm a trusting person, the legal system doesn't hold a lot of love for me. But there's this line that I have here. "I wish people were the dream I want them to be, but that's not how they show up. My love of possibility in people wants me to believe."

I've come to learn that I love to leave my car unlocked, and if people want to steal from it, fine. In business, I've had many people steal from me when I've left my car open, my business open. But I wouldn't want to change myself. I have an inherent love for people; I think it attracts really good people, but it also attracts sociopaths.

Yes, you will run into people who don't deserve trust. Frank Stronach explains why you should be trustful despite it.

Sometimes people say to me I'm too trusting. But look, I've done very well; sometimes I think you go further to trust people, and occasionally you run into people that are not trustworthy, or that maybe don't have the greatest character. But it's worth the risk.

Be Loyal

Loyalty is important in business for both sides.

Petter Stordalen explained to me why:

Be loyal. You meet a lot of people; be nice to everybody. Because there will always be times when you need help. If you have been treating people very good, they will help you, even if it's very tough times. Be nice to everybody on your way up. Doesn't matter if they work in cleaning, doesn't matter if they are out there washing dishes. Because you might need them when you are on your way down. And most people forget where they are coming from and forget the people who helped them.

Petter speaks out of experience. After the wondrous turnaround of Steen & Strøm that I wrote about in chapter 15, Petter started to buy shopping centers.

I started with the ambition to build the biggest shopping center company in Scandinavia, and we did. From 1992 to 1996, we had huge expansion. In 1996, we listed the company, earned tons of money, had a lot of cash in the bank; I was feeling this is my time, this is my company. Even though I owned a small portion, 3%, 4%, it was my idea. I had done the job, I was the CEO. All the guys were handpicked by me. We had the best people. We were the fastest-growing company.

At the peak of my shopping center career, I got fired.

Petter got into a conflict with a major shareholder who simultaneously was a tenant and wanted to see the rental contracts of his competitors. It was against business ethics. Petter didn't want to cave in and got fired.

Some people will agree that Mike Tyson hasn't said very many smart things, but he said this one smart thing, "Everybody has a plan until they get knocked out." I was knocked out. I was unprepared. I was humiliated. There was only one thing in my mind: revenge. "I will be back faster than last time. I will build a new company."

That's when Petter gave the famous press conference announcing he would now build the largest hotel chain in Scandinavia, which you read about in chapter 11. Fortunately, Petter made many friends on the way up. With their support, he was able to make it happen.

Recently, Petter returned to the shopping center business. He put a strong group together to buy a company, even bigger than Steen & Strøm.

With €1 billion it was one of the largest real estate transactions in Norway. One of Petter's backers was the same guy whose contract Petter didn't want to compromise, when he got fired.

And he said, "Petter, you have done so much good for us; I will support you." So they came up with a lot of money, and we bought back the shopping center company. Now, I'm back in the shopping center business as well. It's full circle.

Petter's loyalty paid off big-time.

Build a Reputation on Integrity and Win Respect

Reputation is the most valuable currency. It's better to increase your reputation than your wealth. As Frank Stronach says, "You can always make money, but once you lose the reputation, you can never repair it."

Ron Sim considers reputation the most important entrepreneurial asset and advises to start building it from the very beginning of your career.

Starting from Day 1, when you are small, your character is the basis of your reputation. Your mindset is the basis of your reputation. Your attitude is the basis of your reputation. And if you don't get it right, who's going to support you? Who's going to give you that credit? Who's going to help you? Who's going to believe in you?

You can always make money, but once you lose the reputation, you can never repair it.

– Frank Stronach #BillionDollarGoldNuggets

Cho Tak Wong was following Mao's words, "To do one good thing is very easy, to do it for a lifetime is very difficult."

And he did a lot of good things in his career. Believe it or not, he was probably the only entrepreneur in China to give back state subsidies. His company Fuyao got 10 million yuan from the local government to keep an unprofitable factory operating in a crisis and save jobs. Cho Tak Wong managed to make the factory profitable again and then gave the money back to the state, saying the company didn't need it.

As Naveen Jain told me, "Do everything with the highest integrity, and remember it takes decades to build a reputation and it takes one action to destroy it."

To do one good thing is very easy, to do it for a lifetime is very difficult.

— Cho Tak Wong #BillionDollarGoldNuggets

If you have a good reputation, people approach you with business opportunities. As with all the billionaires, this was also the case with Hüsnü Özyegin.

Since everyone knows I am a serial entrepreneur, they often offer me a slice of their new start-ups or companies. Some of these were incredible opportunities.

It takes decades to build a reputation and it takes one action to destroy it.

— Naveen Jain #BillionDollarGoldNuggets

Don't Lose Your Integrity

Jack Cowin warns not to lose your integrity. In his 13 life lessons, integrity is the second point. He read it for me:

If you lose your integrity, no amount of success will be meaningful, and it will produce a hollow feeling when you look in the mirror.

So don't stray from the path of good.

Cho Tak Wong made it more tangible for me.

Did you see the Indian film The Slumdog Millionaire? The film talks about a young man who used to just be a normal guy. Then luck made him a millionaire, and a lot of people tried to treat him bad and asked him to give in, but he had always stayed the good one, managed to keep his integrity, and then he became a millionaire. There is no magic about it.

If you lose your integrity, no amount of success will be meaningful, and it will produce a hollow feeling when you look in the mirror.

— Jack Cowin #BillionDollarGoldNuggets

Be Respected

Respect comes with integrity.

When Narayana Murthy founded Infosys, he proposed that their vision should be to become the most respected company, not the largest or the most profitable, as suggested by others.

I have always believed that seeking respect from every one of the stakeholders in every one of our business transactions will bring us revenues, profits, and market capitalization. This is my formula for good business.

If you deliver on every promise that you make to a customer, over a period of time, they will realize that you are an honest and dependable company. Similarly, if you follow the finest principles with corporate governance in dealing with investors, they will realize that they can trust their money with you. If you treat your employees with fairness, courtesy, and dignity, they will realize that you are a respected corporation. If you live in harmony with society, they will realize that you seek respect. Therefore, respect is the most important attribute that any corporation must seek.

Let us remember that respect from society is the most important attribute because society contributes customers, society contributes employees, society contributes investors, society contributes bureaucrats, and society elects politicians. So if society is happy with you, then customers will come, employees will join you, investors will invest in your company, and politicians and bureaucrats will create favorable policies for your industry. If you want to seek respect from society, you will have to conduct yourself as a model corporate citizen.

Narayana avoids "anything that will not enhance respect" for him.

For Cho Tak Wong, "Success is being respected by others." He is probably the most universally respected and liked businessman in China.

My biggest success is that I have been recognized by all levels of government officials and admired by all the people.

Success is being respected by others.

– Cho Tak Wong #BillionDollarGoldNuggets

What about your integrity, my dear reader? Do you have strong values, or are you cutting corners when necessary? Are you humble, grounded, and committed to do good? Are you reliable and trustworthy? How do you treat people? Are you fair, respectful, honest, and loyal to them? What is your reputation? Are you respected?

- Drifters don't have strong values; they sacrifice their integrity by taking shortcuts and drown in the chaos they create.

- You can become a millionaire by lying and cheating, but that won't last for long. In the long run, you get caught and punished. Most millionaires have strong values, but they don't focus on building a reputation and trust in the market. This sets a limit to what they can achieve in business.

- Billionaires focus on building trust and a great reputation based on integrity and reliability; they win deep respect among the people they deal with.

For more stories on this topic, go to:
http://TheBillionDollarSecret.com/resources

CHAPTER 19

Gratefully Give Back

Service to others is the rent you pay
for your room here on earth.

—Muhammad Ali

Acknowledge that whatever you have achieved, it is society that made it possible for you. You have been schooled by it; you have received your employees, customers, and investors from it. Be grateful and "give back."

You can't really give back to all the people that have helped you on your way, but you can and should pay it forward to others. What do I mean by that?

The following story from Naveen Jain will explain it to you.

After my first company was very successful, I got a call from a woman saying, "My husband is in ICU and he wants to speak to you." My first reaction as you can imagine was oh my god, she had lots of medical bills and she wants me to pay them. And I said, "Ma'am, I completely understand. We have a foundation; please send me an email. I will make sure whatever help you need, we'll take care of that."

And she said, "No. Would you be kind enough to just spend a minute with my husband? He really wants to speak to you." And I'm a little annoyed, but I'm just thinking, "It's probably easiest for me to spend a minute and just be done with it." So I take the call. And my first thing was, "Sir, what is it that I can do for you?"

And this is what changed my life. His answer was, "Nothing, Naveen. You don't remember. When you wanted to leave the country, I asked you to stay. And I have been watching your success, and I am just so proud of you, and I just want you to know it."

It was the guy who asked Naveen to stay in the United States when he wanted to leave after his bad experiences in New Jersey, and helped him get a great job in Silicon Valley.

It took me a deep breath, and it occurred to me, "Oh my god, what have I become? The people who helped me not only I don't remember, worse yet, they don't need my help." And I said, "I will never let that happen." Now I can't pay back so I'm going to pay forward. And I'm going to help every single person I meet, if I can help them, I'm going to help their dreams come true because that will be my way of giving back to the gentleman. There are many more people like this guy who may have helped me that I don't remember.

Be Grateful

The first step is to be grateful for what you have.

I asked Lirio Parisotto about his dreams. What does a billionaire dream about?

No, I don't have dreams. I just thank God every day for all the things I have. If it's possible to do more, I will, but I need also to look back and thank God for that. I had enough.

The second step is to appreciate your life and the people around you.

Chip Wilson was struggling in his first company until he made a certain discovery.

I was living my life in the past, in angst about things that I'd done in the past, or I was living my life in the future. But I was never appreciative of right now and the people that I'm with or what I've accomplished. It seemed to me I was always in survival mode, so it was like learning from the past, and "what am I going to do in the future?"

I recognized that I spent probably 40 years of my life not saying, "Oh, isn't life great?" So I started to think, "Oh, I live a great life. How can I be a better person within that life? Maybe it's not all about me. Maybe it's about the world and making the world a better place, making a difference in the world."

Life as an onion. Have fun peeling layers of it.

I asked Dilip Shanghvi what he wished he had known when he was 20.

The fun for me has been the kind of life I have had. It's a kind of onion, I keep on peeling layers as time goes by and learning new things. So the question is that if I knew everything on Day 1, then maybe I wouldn't have had the happiness that I got along the way.

Hardships help you really appreciate what you have and let you look at life and people differently.

When Frank Hasenfratz arrived in Canada, he didn't have any money.

In order to get to his uncle in Montreal, he first needed to earn some money, but meanwhile he was literally living at the railway station.

The railroad station has wooden benches, but it's warm. It was late May, and it was still cold outside in Quebec City. So I stayed there for a few days. I couldn't shower anywhere, so I just washed my torso. I shaved. I had a little bag. I must've smelled terrible. The bench gets very hard, but it was okay. People were very nice.

I asked about work. "There's a few car dealers down here. They're always looking for people to wash their cars." So I go down there. "Have you ever washed cars before?" "No, but I can learn."

Frank didn't speak any English.

But you can make yourself understand. If you have to, you can. Twenty-five cents per car wash.

I made let's say five dollars a day. I bought one loaf of bread for 18 cents and one liter of milk for 19 cents. That's all I ate. Half a loaf of bread in the morning, half a loaf in the evening. It was that sliced bread, and it tasted like cake. I thought it was great. And I saved money. I could live on 50 cents a day. So eventually I saved up for the train to Montreal.

But I must've smelled. I wasn't aware of it, but in Montreal somebody said to me, "Why don't you wash?" "What's wash? I do wash." "You do wash?" "Yeah, I wash cars." "But you wash." [laughs heartily] It was funny, you know? In Montreal too, I stayed at the railroad station. And then I went to Toronto.

I was homeless for almost four weeks. It wasn't bad.

Can you imagine that? Somebody who was homeless, living at the railway station, sleeping on a bench there, and later becoming a billionaire?

This experience taught Frank to survive on the bare minimum and appreciate every bit of comfort in life.

Do Good for Society

And the third step is to do good.

Many people are busy taking care of themselves and claim not to have time for taking care of others. But, as Naveen Jain points out, doing good and doing well are not mutually exclusive. In fact, in order to do well in life, you have to do tremendous good.

If you want to create a billion-dollar company, you solve a $10 billion problem. If you can help a billion people, you can make a lot of money.

As Frank Stronach told me, "The more things you have, the more good you can do. The better example you can be."

It's Not about You

It's not about you, it's about making the world a better place.

For Naveen Jain, "Success is measured by the impact you're making on society."

Billionaires want to improve our world.

I asked Manny Stul how he wanted to be remembered.

Obviously I'd like to be remembered as a very successful businessman, but also for the good that hopefully I'll be able to do, more good, between now and when I pass away. Leaving the earth a much better place than when I arrived, than if I had not been here.

Success is measured by the impact you're making on society.

— Naveen Jain #BillionDollarGoldNuggets

I asked Narayana Murthy for the message he would like to share with the world.

Every one of us should try, in every one of our actions, to make this world more equitable, inclusive, harmonious, peaceful, and sustainable.

Abundance and Generosity

Have the mindset of abundance rather than scarcity.

Tony Tan Caktiong, the World Entrepreneur of the Year 2004, complains about the scarcity mentality predominant in business.

In Jollibee's early days, the founder and owner of one fast-food chain in the Philippines actually told me I should not compensate my people that much. And that company does not exist anymore. So I think that abundance mentality is underestimated.

I asked Tony about the message he would like to give to the world audience.

Let's try to share because things are abundant. Things are in abundance. We can share, and the more we share, the more we get back in other things.

Let's try to share because things are abundant.

— Tony Tan Caktiong #BillionDollarGoldNuggets

Be generous. Whether it is your employees, your followers, or people you don't know, it will come back to you.

Chip Wilson's life motto is to "Give without expectation of return."

I love people. I love when I can sense that I've made a difference in someone's life, and that they've taken a big leap in who they are because of something that I've done for them.

The more we share, the more we get back in other things.

— Tony Tan Caktiong #BillionDollarGoldNuggets

One of the most generous people I know in the world is Jack Cowin. He was incredibly generous with his time and his effort to me and also to some other billionaires I interviewed. He has two yachts. Really big billionaire yachts with a crew of a dozen people including a chef. I stayed in Monaco on his yacht and talked to the captain, who told me one of apparently many stories about Jack's generosity:

Once there was a gentleman on the yacht with his wife. He used to work for Jack for something like 35 years. When he retired, Jack said, "Retirement present. Take the boat for a week, free of charge." And he wasn't a CEO or in any high position. He was just an ordinary guy on the ground. It's amazing.

You need to realize the upkeep of a yacht goes into tens of thousands of dollars per week.

Give without expectation of return.

— Chip Wilson #BillionDollarGoldNuggets

Use Your Power for Good

Use your power for the good of society, of the less fortunate. Contribute to the lives of other people.

Cai's objective is to "bring benefit to society. Not just thinking about ourselves, but think more about others."

Mohed Altrad is happy "whenever I do something, even small, that contributes to you, to my neighbors, to my family, to my employees."

Also, Petter Stordalen looks behind his company.

I feel a lot more responsible not only for the people in the company, but for society, for the future of the planet, for my kids, for the next generation.

Instead of making money, make a difference.

Petter sees his mission in contributing to the transition to a more sustainable business.

For me—Nordic Choice has never been about making money. It's about making a difference. For the people who work for us, our guests, and for the community. I see Nordic Choice as a vehicle for changing the world for the better. This is the heart of the business. This is the reason I want guests to choose our hotels.

Narayana Murthy's family's focus was on learning universal values. And the most valuable for him was: "Put the interest of the institution and the community ahead of your personal interest."

That's where he derived his adage from, when dealing with the government and society: "No corporation can succeed over a long time unless it builds goodwill with society."

Put the interest of the institution and the community ahead of your personal interest.

— Narayana Murthy #BillionDollarGoldNuggets

Help

I asked Naveen Jain about the message he would like to share with the world.

Help someone who needs help. And help as many people as you possibly can. Nothing will give you more happiness and more fulfillment than truly doing something for someone without expecting anything back. And the amount of joy you get from that, there's nothing in life you could own that will give you that much joy.

No corporation can succeed over a long time unless it builds goodwill with society.

— Narayana Murthy #BillionDollarGoldNuggets

For Frank Hasenfratz, helping others is the way to success.

You want to be successful, you'd better be a people person. The rest of it you can learn, but at an early age try to make friends, and try to help. Don't ask, "What can you do for me?" Just ask, "What can I do for you?" Just start up like that. If that person can help you, he will help you anyhow. But don't expect people are going to do things for you. It doesn't work like that.

**Help someone who needs help.
Nothing will give you more happiness
and more fulfillment than truly doing
something for someone without
expecting anything back.**

— Naveen Jain #BillionDollarGoldNuggets

How Self-Made Billionaires Give Back to Society

Drifters don't spend much thought on philanthropy; they demand it from others. It's always the others, the rich who should do more to help the world. Many millionaires and celebrities engage in charity. They give away money at balls and happenings mostly because it is considered fancy and good PR. But billionaires do it differently. They don't engage in charity; they engage in philanthropy. They don't just give money; they build powerful philanthropic organizations to effectively pursue the causes they care for. Some billionaires don't even talk about all the good they do for society.

Almost all my interviewees are big-scale philanthropists. Usually, they focus on business in their young years, and the older they are, the more they move from business to philanthropy.

Ron Sim is 50 and still heavily involved in business. This is how he learned to help others:

When I was in Primary 4, about nine years old, there was this very strict disciplinary master in the school who happened to be my class teacher. And we all hated him because he would punish us like hell. In the early days, they would make you squat. They would make you do silly things. They would put a shell on the floor and ask you to kneel. They would put a pen in your fingers and rub until it bruised. It was corporal punishment. [laughs] I mean, you hated them, you know?

But one day I learned he's a very good man, because I stayed back in the class, and I didn't have money to go to recess. I lost my five cents playing football, and because of that I didn't get to go, because no money.

So I stayed in the class, and he came in and he said, "Why are you in the class?" I said, "No money, I lost my money." He looked at me, he took out 20 cents, and gave me 20 cents.

I think that kind of made me turn around and see that, hey, this guy is a bad guy in terms of corporal punishment for the kids, but he has a good heart.

Today, Ron is the main donor to the Straits Times School Pocket Money Fund that gives pocket money to 9,000 children in Singapore, so they can buy food at school.

So far I probably gave $6 million.

Billionaires give back to society either through their products, their services, or through the philanthropic causes their commit to. It would take an entire book to describe their vast activities in this field. Let me give you this small and inevitably incomplete selection:

Hüsnü Özyegin is one of the greatest philanthropists in Turkey. Together with his wife, Ayşen, the scale of his activities in this area is mind-blowing. He has founded a university, built 65 schools and dormitories for underprivileged girls, set up parent education, women's empowerment, and rural development programs, and literally saved the lives of hundreds of addicts. Through his philanthropy, he has **helped over a million people.**

Petter Stordalen is one of the top philanthropists in Scandinavia. His Stordalen Foundation focuses on climate change, rain forest protection, renewable energy, and the development of ecological technology.

Narayana Murthy supports the underprivileged in Indian society through his Infosys Foundation.

We have built hospitals, schools, libraries, destitute homes, and lunch kitchens in rural India. We have instituted scholarships and improved education for the poor, and helped the needy at times of floods in India and the United States. We have supported several institutions of higher education in mathematics, physics, and computer sciences.

Infosys spends 2% of its annual profit on philanthropy, which amounts to $50 million each and every year.

Frank Stronach's Magna implemented the Fair Enterprise concept. It not only shares the profits with the management and the employees, it also gives 2% of its profits to social projects. We are talking about $40 million a year.

Dilip Shanghvi's philanthropy is about education for underprivileged and health. And he does it out of his own pocket.

The Filipino billionaire Tony Tan Caktiong's School Feeding Program has fed more than 180,000 students in over 1,800 schools on a daily basis.

Lirio Parisotto engages in social projects in the Amazonas. He protects the rain forest over an area the size of Portugal by supporting 40,000 Indians living there with education, medical assistance, and buying products from them coming from sustainable agriculture.

This way the people can sustain themselves without cutting the trees.

He also built a hospital and is involved in children's health care.

But probably the most preeminent philanthropist I have met is the Chinese billionaire Cho Tak Wong. **He has already spent over $1 billion on philanthropy** and is one of the greatest philanthropists in Asia. Cho Tak Wong gave away a big chunk of his Fuyao Glass to the Haren Foundation, which uses the dividends for various philanthropic causes.

For example, last year, we had in Haren a $30 million dividend on investment. We used this for the earthquake in Nepal.

Chip Wilson is deeply engaged in philanthropy through his Imagine1Day Foundation, which brings quality education to Ethiopia.

The Australian billionaire Manny Stul is involved in philanthropy on a personal and a company level. Moose Toys gives as much as 10% of its profits to philanthropic causes with a focus on children's health and welfare. Among other things, they support autism research and are a major sponsor of Clown Doctors, which makes sick children a little bit happier. Additionally, Manny personally donates 10% of his personal income to a variety of charitable causes.

Tim Draper started several philanthropic and social projects, including educational projects BizWorld and Draper University.

Mohed Altrad gives away to philanthropy much more than he takes for himself from the company.

Every year, I've given something like $10 million to poor people, to disabled people, to children, children who have no parents. That is important.

His causes are "work against sickness, against hunger. People who die because of hunger. And also Doctors Without Borders, who go to the fighting places to save lives."

Sergey Galitskiy spends a lot, mainly for his city Krasnodar. He made a park for the city, renovated sidewalks and revived public lawns and alleys, built a football stadium, one of the best in Russia. He is the greatest philanthropist in the region and the most respected citizen of his town. It is common in Eastern Europe to envy and vilify the rich. I did some field research asking people on the street what they think about Sergey. Not a single person had anything negative to say about him. The general opinion was: "If anybody deserves wealth in Russia, it's him." And this means something in Russia.

Business—The Best Philanthropy

For Tony Ton Caktiong, "the greatest form of philanthropy is to build a business because one employee is able to help his entire family. So, one employee is able to help five people, on the average, at least in the Philippines."

Also for Naveen Jain, "Business is about helping people."

Naveen wants to positively impact billions of people by solving the biggest problems of our world. For him the best business is philanthropic in nature, because it works to solve the great problems of humanity.

Any business that can solve a freshwater problem, energy problem, the food problem, any of these problems is a trillion-dollar problem. That means there is a trillion-dollar opportunity somewhere, and some entrepreneurs will solve it. So for me, business and philanthropy go hand in hand, doing good and doing well.

Billionaires employ social principles in their businesses and give their model of capitalism different names.

Business is about helping people.
– Naveen Jain #BillionDollarGoldNuggets

For Petter Stordalen, the ideal is sustainable capitalism.

I want the capitalism which is thinking in the long perspective. Because we can't save the world if we are not thinking long-term. I believe in climate change.

I want to do something because one day, my kids will ask me, "So Papa, why didn't you do anything?" Maybe I will say, "I had information. I see today I didn't do enough, but I tried." That's my life. I always try. I will be a part of the change.

Narayana Murthy calls his model compassionate capitalism.

We demonstrated by our large stock option plan that it is possible to combine the best ideas of capitalism and socialism and create what I call Compassionate Capitalism.

For him, "Business is about making this a more comfortable world." Infosys gives jobs to 200,000 well-paid employees, and Narayana wants to create a million jobs for people all over the world.

Frank Stronach is proud to have developed the Fair Enterprise system, which allowed him to create over 150,000 jobs in Magna.

And these are well-paid jobs, and people can participate in wealth creation.

Business is about making this a more comfortable world.

— Narayana Murthy #BillionDollarGoldNuggets

Kim Beom-Su set up a project called C Program, which he describes as venture philanthropy that invests in child-care education programs.

We saw how children in the Korean education system lose all their creativity and autonomy and the like because of how the system is structured to test well in the college entrance exams. We realized that this was a big problem and that children need to play.

Philanthropy should never be about giving money, it should be about solving a problem, says Naveen Jain.

Social problems are a great playing field for business.

Kim Beom-Su shared with me his thoughts on this.

Ultimately, social problems are also problems to solve. When you hear about a problem, you set a hypothesis and then contemplate how to solve it. That's why I argue that corporations are the most efficient organizations to solve problems. Especially with our company, I think we could help solve problems with technology, and so I want to try solving them with an entrepreneurial spirit.

Role Models

There are a number of role models in the field of philanthropy that billionaires follow.

Bill Gates is probably the one most often named by my interviewees.

Narayana Murthy explains why:

*We all admire **Bill Gates**, not just for his business leadership but also for what he did later—giving away so much of his money for fighting malaria, AIDS, and other diseases that afflict the poorer sections of our world. It is truly extraordinary. He is a great role model for all of us.*

There is an array of historic philanthropists that billionaires get inspiration from, among them:

- Henry Ford, who built hospitals and schools for the workers.

- John D. Rockefeller Sr., who, although very controversial, was one of the greatest philanthropists in history. He built schools for black people and two universities. His research institute developed many important vaccines.

- J. P. Morgan, who gave away over 80% of his wealth for philanthropy.

What is your attitude, dear reader? Are you grateful for what you have? Do you see abundance or scarcity around you? Do you help others or expect to be helped? How do you contribute to the people around you, to your society, to the world? Follow the example of billionaires and do good by paying it forward.

- Drifters have a receiving attitude toward society.

- Millionaires have the mindset of scarcity and sometimes give some of their hard-earned money to philanthropic organizations run by others.

- Billionaires have the mindset of abundance; they are givers aware of the social responsibility business has; they build philanthropic organizations for the causes they care for.

For more stories on this topic, go to:
http://TheBillionDollarSecret.com/resources

CHAPTER 20

Pay the Price

The price of success is much lower than the price of failure.

—Thomas Watson, the early chairman and CEO of IBM

Great results require great sacrifice.

Building a billion-dollar company is connected with long years of toil, a huge investment of time and energy, sleepless nights, and sacrifices in your private life. It means working 24/7 for long periods of time at the expense of your leisure, your family, and relationships with your friends. It is a lifelong uphill climb with countless obstacles in ceaseless uncertainty and constant suspense due to the danger of stumbling and slipping down. It also means enduring harsh criticism of less ambitious or less successful people. If you want to be successful on this path, you must be willing to pay that price.

You need to be able to sacrifice a big chunk of your life to reach that goal while having only a small chance of success.

Manny Stul, the World Entrepreneur of the Year 2016, puts it in simple terms:

I think it's very, very important, if you want to succeed, you've got to have faith in what you're doing, total commitment, and be aware that if you do succeed, you'll pay a price. No question. Might be lack of time with your family, might be relationships, but there is a price to be paid to be very successful. I'm not talking about being just successful.

He often repeats, "You can't be half-pregnant with it."

Be aware that if you do succeed, you'll pay a price.

— Manny Stul #BillionDollarGoldNuggets

Sacrifice

A huge investment of time, energy, and effort means sacrifices in your private life. Are you willing to make this sacrifice?

I asked Tim Draper about the most important qualities for a businessperson.

A willingness to sacrifice for the good of the company and the customer and the opportunity.

You can't be half-pregnant with it.

— Manny Stul #BillionDollarGoldNuggets

These great sacrifices are the reason why some billionaires discourage followers.

I asked Mohed Altrad about wealth-building advice to young people.

Don't follow my path. It's difficult, because the price you pay for it is 30 years' work and maybe 14–15 hours a day. This is the price to pay.

Also, Lirio Parisotto is cautionary.

I don't know if people need to go this way. Of course, the final result is worthwhile. But people need to understand what it takes: Before success, we have to work a lot.

It is 30 years' work and maybe 14-15 hours a day. This is the price to pay.

— Mohed Altrad #BillionDollarGoldNuggets

Your permanent absence is at the expense of your private and family life.

I asked Lirio about his advice to somebody who wants to be as successful as him.

I don't give suggestions for anyone to become me because it's very hard. I don't know whether certain people are prepared to not have a vacation, to stay at work on the weekend, especially when you start the business. So I don't know if people have this energy. Sometimes the price is so high. Especially with relationships with your friends, the relationships with your family. Only very few people are prepared to do that. But with me, I was born in a poor family. I didn't have another option, so what I wanted was to leave. I needed to find something better. Today, the more developed the country becomes, the more complacent people get.

Before success, we have to work a lot.

— Lirio Parisotto #BillionDollarGoldNuggets

Especially the first decades in business are tough.

Cho Tak Wong confessed to me:

The first 20 years, I worked seven days a week. Every day it's the same. No time for family. And I wasn't working just during the day, but also every night until 8–9 p.m.

On the way to billions, you don't have time to enjoy life.

Believe it or not, some billionaires are jealous of ordinary people for having leisure time. Contrary to the media image, they don't indulge in lavish parties and endless vacations.

Hüsnü Özyegin surprised me when he said that due to lack of time, he hadn't experienced many of the great flavors of life that many regular people do.

I see people around me who are basically traveling more and doing more enjoyable things. Like whoever I call during the New Year, they're either in Phuket or some nice place or other while I'll be working. [laughs] I blame myself for that. I'd love to go and see the fjords in Norway. I just got a very nice book from my friend, who was in Alaska traveling for three, four weeks, and he did a great book with pictures of fishing and doing all kinds of things. I'm jealous of them, but I guess I enjoy working too much.

I asked Cai Dongqing what he would like to change about himself.

More time for enjoying happiness. I would like to be more happy and joyful. Work time should be less. What I want to change is reaching a balance of life and work. Try my best to enjoy both life and work. I would like to have more time to enjoy life. Travel around.

Frank Stronach also surprised me when I asked him what he wished he had known when he was 20. His answer was: "That you're young only once."

For many billionaires, business consumes all their time, energy, and thoughts.

Jack Cowin considers himself unable to have a hobby.

If my wife was here, she'd say "You are a workaholic." I have two boats; the reason I have two boats is because my wife said I didn't have a hobby, so I had to have a hobby.

Jack then bought two boats to distract him from business. It didn't help.

I've turned those two boats into little businesses. We charter them out. So I've probably got some areas that I can improve on. But I guess one of the areas I probably should pay more heed to than I do is the fact that you are getting older, and you cannot continue to do what you're doing today forever. There is no immortality in life. Eventually you're going to run out of life.

Yes, it is a real danger. On the way to billions, you may run out of time to live your life. And in fact, most people do.

Responsibility and Stress

As a billionaire, you carry a huge burden of responsibility and stress. You are responsible for thousands or even hundreds of thousands of employees and their families. You can't drop the towel or quit your job just because it has become too stressful or it doesn't fulfill you anymore.

Sergey Galitskiy points out that big money limits you in your private life and means a lot of stress.

The more money you make, the more limitations you have to place on yourself, in everything. And many people don't want to be slaves to such a large number of limitations. You can't really have a family. You have a family, but you can't spend as much time with the family as those people that are simply rich. You have to work harder, and you have to also understand that the amount of money you have is in direct proportion to the level of stress. And many people are not prepared to endure this stress starting with a certain level.

The more money you make, the more limitations you have to place on yourself, in everything.

— Sergey Galitskiy #BillionDollarGoldNuggets

It may surprise you, but some billionaires would have preferred to be an employee.

I asked Cho Tak Wong what he would do if he had to start from zero again.

If I were at the beginning, I may want to go first to get a good education and then to have a good skill so that I can become a professional business management member. And then I would do the job for the company, but I don't need to do it myself because there is a lot of pressure, a lot of responsibilities. That way, as an employee, life can be much more comfortable. If I started from the beginning, I would not be an entrepreneur. I would like to be a professional, a manager.

I couldn't believe it and asked again if he would sacrifice all he has achieved just to have a more comfortable life.

Yeah, I'd like to be a professional. Not too much risk. Less risk, as other people take risks.

You can't really have a family.

— Sergey Galitskiy #BillionDollarGoldNuggets

Some billionaires go even further. They wouldn't have started their business at all if they had the opportunity to turn back the clock.

Frank Hasenfratz told me:

To start now, I probably wouldn't. [laughs] Because I know what I went through and the mistakes I made. It would probably be a lot harder to start again now.

The amount of money you have is in direct proportion to the level of stress.

— Sergey Galitskiy #BillionDollarGoldNuggets

Runner's Solitude

Hardly anybody understands the problems billionaires experience on their level and can help them with solutions. Billionaires often face disbelief, skepticism, even accusations. They suffer from "long-distance runner's solitude."

Michał Sołowow described to me this peculiar solitude he suffers from:

A majority of men like me suffer from "long-distance runner's solitude." You are in fact lonely, lonely in your life experiences. You are not able to share them with anyone. In other words, you suffer from a social misunderstanding and even a lack of acceptance for what you create. The surrounding environment always strongly oversimplifies your image and frowns upon you and looks from a perspective of "This is impossible, it must be about cheating because I could do it but didn't achieve it." That is the simplest viewpoint. And those attitudes that try to understand something do not have access to the knowledge.

I have a very limited number of people with whom I am able to talk about my work. Generally those are people from the inside of the organization rather than outside. This is the kind of loneliness of a long-distance runner, isn't it?

Please imagine yourself in such a situation. You run in an ultra marathon, of course in order to win, at least trying to win, because that is the sense of competition at the highest level. . . . You are at the 110th kilometer on a desert and a journalist approaches you and asks: "How is your running going and what is your strategy for the later part of the run?," while of course stopping you in that run. You are leading the race at that point. So what is your first thought? That is "What is this question about?" The second thought is that: "That chap knows nothing about ultra running, if he asks me about it in such a moment. . . ." He carries out his work, right? But in fact, he simply doesn't have a clue on the matter, and you are not able to tell him what happened to your pulse, how many crises you had in the meantime which you had to overcome, how much it had cost you, what happens with your water management. And you feel all that. You have thousands of sensations, which you feel and you know. And you talk with a guy who happens to have 10 seconds of time just now to ask you and didn't even bother to figure out what the score is, didn't read anything wise about the processes taking place in the body during a run because he assumes that he will learn everything from you. He didn't even carry out that minimum effort. And after such next, next, next event you run farther, you don't stop . . . because there is nothing to talk about.

For billionaires, there is nobody to call for help.

Ron Sim sees himself as a lone eagle.

I've got no one to call. It's the toughest thing in my life. I don't even want to talk to my wife about my problems, because I only talk to my wife when I feel certain things are clear, easy for her to choose. My problems, I never tell her. Because you give her more problems, you give her more worry. I have enough worries. I don't need another person to worry. So it's true that it's lonely at the top.

It's lonely at the top, but as you see for other reasons than most people think.

As an employee, life can be much more comfortable.

– Cho Tak Wong #BillionDollarGoldNuggets

If you want to be that successful in business, you need to be prepared and accept the "solitude of power."

Lirio Parisotto explained this concept to me.

One of the things that is common for billionaires is the solitude of power. It's difficult for normal people to understand.

It's difficult to discuss with people when you sometimes have investments of half a billion dollars, $1 billion, $100 million. No one advises you about that. You are alone. So, if you win, it's OK. But if you lose, you can complain to yourself. Most of the things are impossible to talk about with others. Not because others are not competent or something, but it's difficult for them to understand because they are not in this situation.

And the other reason is everybody has his goal, his objective. So people want a house, want a car, and some money in the bank, or "I'd like to have $1 million," another $10 million. And then they realize that I want more. So a lot of people ask me, "Why don't you stop work? Why? You have enough." I tell these guys, if I stop work I may die, because then I don't have a passion anymore. I need a passion. I need to do something I like. Passion, involvement, and feeling you are useful for society.

You also have some risks because if you do something wrong in a petrochemical company and you have an environment problem, you go to jail. But the passion is stronger than these kinds of problems.

Another challenge is the difficulty to trust people that many billionaires develop upon bad experiences from the past.

Naveen explained to me how it works:

Once you become successful, it becomes obvious to you, essentially by pattern matching, that 99% of the people who come talk to you and become your friend, they need something from you. So in life, the way I look at this stuff is when you are rich or when you are beautiful as a girl, it's in some sense god's curse to you because you attract the wrong type of people coming to you. People can rarely see through the facade of you being rich or you being beautiful. People don't get to know who you are as an individual because they see the outside of you. They never get to know the inner you, and that hollowness, loneliness is what makes people so unhappy even with the money. No one creates real relationships anymore because people are afraid to have that deep, real relationship because they think it opens them up to be vulnerable.

Are Billionaires Happy?

So, is it worth it? Are billionaires happy? This is probably the question I've been asked most while I was writing this book.

Let's dissect it a little bit.

For Mohed Altrad, like for many other people, "success is happiness."

Frank Stronach gave lots of lectures at universities.

The first thing I taught the students is: The success of life can only be measured by the degree of happiness you reach. But let me tell you from my experience, it's a lot easier to be happy if you've got some money. The smart students have asked, "How can you make money?" I said, "Look, when you are around 20, you don't really know yourself. You should experiment a bit."

The success of life can only be measured by the degree of happiness you reach.

– Frank Stronach #BillionDollarGoldNuggets

The general public tend to represent one of the two extreme opinions. The first one is "Money will make you happy"; the other extreme is "Those poor Billionaires, they are so rich but unhappy."

In reality, money doesn't change much about your ability to be happy. It just magnifies your personality. If you were a happy person before you got rich, money will increase your happiness. But if you were unhappy, money will make you miserable. Trying to become happy by amassing more money is a delusion.

Money doesn't give you happiness. It gives you choice. And a lot of money gives you a lot of choice. It's up to you to take advantage of the choices money offers.

It's a lot easier to be happy if you've got some money.

— Frank Stronach #BillionDollarGoldNuggets

So, are billionaires happy? The short answer is "Yes, but not for the reasons you may think."

Despite the price they pay as described above, consider the following:

Certain personality traits and habits from the ones described in this book are helpful both in making a lot of money and in making you happy. Let's have a closer look at them.

Billionaires are experts in human psychology and communication. This allows them to build harmonious long-term relationships, and those naturally increase their personal happiness.

In contrast to public opinion about the rich, the self-made billionaires I have met and interviewed have simple, even uneventful private lives. They choose a tolerant partner who covers their back and supports them in what they do. There are no personal dramas, no divorces. The wife and kids give them stability in their private lives, which allows them to excel in business but also provides for a high level of self-comfort.

Hüsnü Özyegin considers marrying his wife one of his most important accomplishments.

She has been the most supportive life partner I could have wished for. She has done an incredible job of raising our children. I was not able to be there for the birth of either of my children. When my son was born, I was in Baghdad, and when I landed in Istanbul, my driver told me that Murat had been born, and we drove straight to the hospital. When my daughter Aysecan was born, I was in Tripoli, Libya, and I got a telegram informing me that I had had a daughter. She never once complained about the fact that I was working so hard when our children were young. Whenever I travel, no matter what time of day or night, she would always get up and see me to the door and pour water behind my car. This is an old Turkish tradition that wishes the traveler well, for his travels to flow as easily as water and for the traveler to return home safely. Even today I always call her before I board a plane and as soon as I land, no matter where I travel.

For Frank Hasenfratz, a supportive partner is an essential condition to business success:

One thing I very strongly believe in is to have a good partner. I had a very supportive wife, both in business and social life.

Billionaires love what they do. They love their business and the industry they are in. Of course, this makes you happier than having to do what you don't like.

For Dilip Shanghvi it's as easy as "you solve a problem, it makes you happy."

I asked Cai Dongqing what makes him happy.

Doing what I want to do and enjoying the process.

The next aspect is freedom. Billionaires are free in the sense that they work not because they have to, but because they like doing it and find it important. As Sergey Galitskiy puts it, "Freedom in life is the ability to spend your time on things that are important to you and that you like."

More money means also more control over their lives and over their environment. As I pointed out in chapter 9, billionaires are not the flag in the wind, they are the wind. Their abilities and their money give them more options to react to negative situations in their lives and create positive outcomes.

I asked Jack Cowin what made him happy.

I think being able to control my own agenda. I don't mean that in a selfish sort of way, but you know, we all have moods, so being able to control what I want to do at the time, rather than having somebody tell me. One of the problems that I've found in life is as you get older, you become less and less tolerant of someone giving you direction. My wife will say, "Can you please do that?" "Do I have to?" "Yeah." [chuckles]

Freedom in life is the ability to spend your time on things that are important to you and that you like.

– Sergey Galitskiy #BillionDollarGoldNuggets

Billionaires are pretty happy with who they are. They are proud of what they have accomplished. They don't need to prove anything to anybody anymore. They can afford to be fully themselves.

Cai Dongqing confessed to me, he felt "fulfillment when our business is making remarkable progress."

Michał Sołowow made this feeling tangible for me:

I am also happy that I build homes in which others live, that I build and produce, that I make life easier. . . . Please remind yourself what I called my first company on the stock exchange: "Polish Life Improvement.". . . I have an impression that I improve other peoples' lives, not only my own . . . .

Achievements make you happy. And billionaires have a lot of them.

Billionaires are creators. They see how their thoughts materialize. This is a deeply fulfilling process.

I asked Sergey Galitskiy what made him happy.

When things happen according to how I planned. When I see that my thoughts, not necessarily quickly, but they do materialize. When my thoughts come to fruition, when there is some physical realization of my mental thoughts, I can stand and look at this for hours. If I wasn't getting tired, I could stay for days.

One of his thoughts that materialized was a magnificent soccer stadium he built for his home town, Krasnodar. It offers space for 34,000 fans.

Similarly, Cai Dongqing loves "the process of bringing our blueprint of the company into reality."

The recognition and respect billionaires get adds to their happiness.

Cho Tak Wong told me it made him happy "if everybody around you acknowledges that what you do is right and they respect you for it."

Also, their positive contribution to the lives of other people and seeing these people grow, succeed, and be happy makes them feel fulfilled.

I asked Petter Stordalen what made him happy.

Seeing people grow, seeing my wife succeed, seeing that my kids are happy. Seeing my dogs happy. Seeing the people in the company happy and proud of the company. Seeing that people go from one job, maybe in reception, to be a manager. Seeing people reaching and fulfilling their whole potential. Most people don't see the whole big potential they have, and when I see people really fulfilling everything, that makes me happy.

Michał Sołowow told me, "What makes me happy is when I see the people I've touched are happy. That makes me tremendously happy and emotional."

Let's not forget the gratitude and the stoic attitude of many billionaires. Those help their happiness.

Life itself makes Tim Draper happy. Dilip Shanghvi told me:

I think generally, I am happy. I don't need an external event to be happy. I try not to allow the key to my happiness or unhappiness to be an external event. Problems don't make me unhappy; in the same way, success also doesn't make me very happy. I have very little ability to rejoice. Also, I don't become unhappy. If something doesn't work, it also doesn't make me very unhappy.

Despite common belief, billionaires really appreciate the simple things of life, since they are the ones who have tasted it all.

I asked Peter Hargreaves what made him happy.

I think simple things in life. Certainly I have a nice garden, and one of my greatest enjoyments is digging vegetables for lunch on a Sunday morning. Just going out and digging up the vegetables, picking the sprouts and whatever.

And sometimes I walk round the fields and look for mushrooms. Of course, they're worthless. Sometimes I don't even eat all the ones I find. But the joy of finding a mushroom is brilliant.

And nature, I do love nature. That's why I enjoyed the fell running. I love October, when you get the autumn colors and the crisp mornings.

So the things that make me happy are very much the simple things in life. Just anything like that. And good company, good food and good wine, and heated discussions, mayhap. As long as I win. [laughs]

I also love to see other people's success. I'm very emotional when I see people's success. I'm always more emotional about happiness. When somebody achieves, and you see the elation. And when young children do something that's really rather nice, I think that makes me very, very happy. I am a very emotional person.

Let's not forget other billionaire traits and habits that support happiness: belief, optimism, trust, having a purpose and following your mission, taking care of your health, being proactive, being yourself and not bending yourself, personal integrity, and giving back.

Of course, all of the above doesn't protect billionaires from personal tragedies like illness or grief after the loss of loved ones. And, of course, not all billionaires are happy. But considering all the factors, I believe that on average, billionaires are happier than the rest of society for the above reasons.

Are you willing to pay the price and do what it takes to give yourself a chance to get to the billion-dollar league? Are you prepared to sacrifice a big chunk of your life to make it happen? It means a great investment of time of energy. Are you willing to accept the huge amount of stress and the burden of responsibility? Are you prepared for the runner's solitude?

- Drifters don't want to pay the price; they want to enjoy their life now and are not willing to make sacrifices in their private life.

- Millionaires are willing to pay the price, but they often don't realize how high the price is or don't convey it to their environment. In effect, they may get discouraged or burn out or their environment may force them to make concessions as to the amount of time they can invest or the amount of stress and responsibility they can take.

- Billionaires are willing and prepared to pay the price; they set up their mindset and their environment in such a way that allows them to make all sacrifices necessary to reach their goals.

For more stories on this topic, go to:
http://TheBillionDollarSecret.com/resources

EPILOGUE

So, my dear reader, we have reached the end of *The Billion Dollar Secret*. You have learned the secret principles of the most successful entrepreneurs in our world, the self-made billionaires. They have revealed their innermost wisdom to enable you to become as extremely successful in business as they are. It's now up to you to follow their steps.

Keep in mind, the external factors are not decisive about your success; you are the one responsible for your life. So leave the nest, and take off to conquer the skies. Let your insatiable hunger guide you on your way. Build a solid B.O.A.T. out of your belief, optimism, assertiveness, and trust that will carry you through the stormy oceans of your career. Avoid the gold digger's trap. Learn the Six Skills of Business Mastery, and develop the Six Habits of Wealth. Find your purpose and sharpen your vision. Take action! Don't be the flag, be the wind. Recognize and seize opportunities. Be bold. Don't let fear stop you from doing things. Take risks, but do it wisely. You will have to fail many times before you succeed. So be willing to fail, but don't give up; persevere and keep fighting! Don't be afraid to be different. Do not conform. Your passion will enable you to work hard for many years on the way to your dreams and overcome all the obstacles. But only if you are smart with money and F.A.S.T. will you have the chance to outcompete others. So never stop learning. Subscribe to the process of constant improvement. Don't compromise your integrity. Build a great reputation and don't forget to pay it forward. And always remember: to achieve great things, there is a price to be paid.

Never before have we been surrounded by so many opportunities that are up for grabs. The best time to act and take advantage of them was yesterday. Next best is today. So get on it, apply yourself to the 20 principles of *The Billion Dollar Secret*, spread your wings, and soar. Here is the road map I laid out for you. I'm here to help you and guide you on your way. Let me be the first to congratulate you and to celebrate with you when you reach your goals, whatever they might be. I am crossing my fingers for your success!

APPENDIX

The Billionaires

Mohed Altrad Badawi

Citizenship/Residence: France/Montpellier

A 71-year-old, French self-made billionaire and Syrian immigrant, founder and chairman of Altrad Group, a global company offering services and equipment for the construction industry in over 100 countries. The company, with its 200 subsidiaries, has become a world leader in its main market: scaffolding. Mr. Altrad is the owner of the Montpellier Hérault Rugby Club and an accomplished writer with three novels under his belt. He was awarded Knight and Officer of the French Legion of Honor and was named the World Entrepreneur of the Year 2015 by Ernst & Young. He is the first Frenchman to win this honor.

THE BUSINESS CARD

Made his first million with: scaffolding business

Business is . . . life

Success is . . . happiness

Would like to meet in person: Obama

Passion: literature

Skills he doesn't have: capacity to write books that will be read in a century

The best book on business: books by Max Weber

Still wants to achieve: "Change the world. Find something to change the world to be better. Because if we carry on, I think it will be worse."

Most admired thought leaders: Nelson Mandela, Helmut Schmidt, Giscard, Francois Mitterrand

Tony Tan Caktiong
The Genius of Sharing

Citizenship/Residence: Philippines/Manila

A 65-year-old, self-made billionaire, founder and chairman of Jollibee Foods, Asia's largest food service company operating 13 restaurant chains (Jollibee, Greenwich, Chowking, Red Ribbon, Mang Inasal, Smashburger, the Filipino Burger King franchise, Highlands Coffee, Yonghe King, Hong Zhuang Yuan, and others) with over 4,300 restaurant outlets in 18 countries throughout East Asia, North America, Europe, and the Middle East. Jollibee has been recognized as one of the most admired Asian companies and one of Asia's best employers. In 2013, Forbes included it on Asia's Fabulous 50 list. Jollibee Foods is the world's only local fast-food company to beat McDonald's in their country. Tony's philanthropy focuses on food for students. He was awarded the title World Entrepreneur of the Year 2004 by Ernst & Young.

THE BUSINESS CARD

Made his first million with: food service business

Business is . . . fun

Success is . . . the result of working with other people

Life motto: "Do unto others what you want others to do unto you."

Most valuable piece of advice for him: honesty and integrity

Passion: having good food

Skills he'd like to have: good command of English language

The best book on business: *How to Win Friends and Influence People* by Dale Carnegie

Still wants to achieve: "Our biggest goal now is to be able to be a big player in the U.S. fast-food market."

Avoids in business: "We avoid having partners that don't fit in the culture, especially on the integrity side."

Most admired thought leaders: Buddha and Hindus

Jack Cowin
Mission Impossible

Citizenship/Residence: Australia/Sydney

A 76-year-old, Canadian-born self-made billionaire. He is the owner, chairman, and managing director of Competitive Foods Australia, one of the country's largest food processors and the largest franchiser of restaurants in Australia, including Hungry Jack's, the Australian Burger King franchise, branded after his name. He was an early pioneer in introducing fast food to Australia, first chicken (KFC), then hamburgers (Burger King), then pizza (Domino's Pizza). He is a major shareholder in Domino's Pizza Australia with over 2.400 restaurants in Australia, New Zealand, Japan, France, Holland, Germany, and Belgium. Jack also engages in an array of other businesses in Australia and North America. He is an active member of the World Presidents Organization. His philanthropic activities are directed at higher education.

THE BUSINESS CARD

Made his first million with: fried chicken

Business is . . . fun

Success is . . . fulfillment of your goals in life

Life motto: "Never give up."

Would like to meet in person: Richard Branson

Most valuable piece of advice for him: "Do unto others as you hope they do unto you. Treat people fairly."

Passion: work

Skills he doesn't have: "Probably patience. As you get older, patience runs down, and you get less tolerant of people's mistakes."

The best book on business: *Driven to Succeed* by Rod McQueen, a biography of Frank Hasenfratz and *Little Black Stretchy Pants* by Chip Wilson

Still wants to achieve: "I think that we can have a New York Stock Exchange listed company eventually, if we continue to do the things we're doing. Which means big league."

Avoids in business: "Dumb ideas, I guess. Unnecessary risk. Risk is necessary, but don't do things which are superfluous to what the endgame is."

Most admired thought leaders: Nelson Mandela, Pierre Trudeau

Cai Dongqing
The Persistent Dream Catcher

Citizenship/Residence: China/Guangzhou

A 49-year-old, Chinese self-made billionaire, founder and chairman of Alpha Group, one of the most powerful and innovative animation corporations in China. It is the only Chinese group managing a complete industrial chain from animation production, brand licensing, media operation, to product design and marketing in toys, games, baby products, and cartoons. Alpha Group has also branched into movies, operas, theme parks, and other interactive activities involving entertainment, consumer products, Internet networks, culture, and education. With over 100 animation toy patents every year, it ranks No.1 in the industry. Cai has been dubbed the Walt Disney of China.

THE BUSINESS CARD

Made his first million with: selling little toy trumpets

Business is . . . cooperation

Success is . . . learning

Life motto: "Without experiencing the storm, how could you see the rainbow?"

Would like to meet in person: Masayoshi Son

Most valuable piece of advice for him: "from those who can give me a different opinion on my idea and point out its problems. Such advice is helpful and influential."

Passion: his business

Skills he doesn't have: swimming freely in the ocean, flying an airplane

The best book on business: *The Art of War* by Sun Tzu and biographies of Li Ka-Shing, Jack Ma, Bill Gates

Still wants to achieve: "We want to build the Chinese Disney."

Avoids in business: "We cannot do a business just for doing business. We do business with principles."

Most admired thought leaders: Laozi, Confucius

Tim Draper
Riskmaster

Citizenship/Residence: USA/Silicon Valley, California

A 60-year-old venture capitalist legend listed on Forbes Midas List and considered the number one most connected investor in Silicon Valley. He is the founder of the VC firms Draper Fisher Jurvetson and Draper Associates, as well as Draper University. Tim is largely credited as the inventor of viral marketing. As founding investor, he contributed significantly to the success of such tech giants as Hotmail, Skype, Tesla, SolarCity, and Baidu. He is also a major investor in SpaceX, Indiegogo, Tumblr, Foursquare, and over 1,000 other companies. In 2015, he received the Entrepreneur for the World Award from the World Entrepreneurship Forum. Tim is a vocal Bitcoin enthusiast.

THE BUSINESS CARD

Made his first million with: VC investment in Parametric

Business is . . . fun

Success is . . . continuing to be willing to fail

Life motto: "Anything is possible."

Would like to meet in person: Steve Jobs

Most valuable piece of advice for him: "It doesn't matter who's buying and who's selling. What matters is the personal connection."

Passion: "To spread entrepreneurship and venture capital around the world"

Skills he doesn't have: playing guitar

The best book on business: *The Startup Game* by William H. Draper

Still wants to achieve: transform real estate, health, insurance, banking, investment banking, and government

Avoids in business: "I avoid backing the trendy. I look for the trend, not the trendy."

Most admired thought leaders: George Washington, Deng Xiaoping, Gorbachev

Sergey Galitskiy
What the F--k Is Happening

Citizenship/Residence: Russia/Krasnodar

A 51-year-old self-made billionaire, founder and longtime CEO of Magnit, the largest food retailer in Russia with over 17,000 convenience stores, cosmetics stores, hypermarkets, and supermarkets. With 290,000 employees, Magnit is also Russia's largest non-state employer with the country's largest network of 6,000 trucks. The company grew to this size organically without acquisitions. Sergey is the owner and chairman of the soccer club FC Krasnodar. He is the internationally most respected Russian businessman, listed by *BRICs* magazine as the most admired Russian entrepreneur.

THE BUSINESS CARD

Made his first million with: distribution business

Business is . . . game of minds

Success is . . . enjoying every moment in life

Life motto: "Honesty is the best policy."

Would like to meet in person: "Albert Einstein. Not because he created the theory of relativity, because he never accepted anybody's authority."

Most valuable piece of advice for him: "That I have to give people a second chance. I got it from my partner."

Passion: competing

Skills he doesn't have: math and physics

The best book on business: *Steve Jobs* by Walter Isaacson

Still wants to achieve: "I would like to achieve in football what I have achieved in business. Not get the trophy, but create a properly working mechanism."

Avoids in business: "spending time with stupid and cynical people"

Most admired thought leaders: The German philosopher Hegel

Peter Hargreaves
Beyond Your Wildest Dreams

Citizenship/Residence: United Kingdom/Bristol

A 72-year-old self-made billionaire and industry leader in the United Kingdom's financial services sector. He is probably the only person who managed to build an FTSE 100 company from scratch without borrowing or acquisition. His Hargreaves Lansdown manages assets as high as $120 billion, which compares to a yearly budget of a medium-size country. In 2014, he was appointed Commander of the Most Excellent Order of the British Empire (CBE).

THE BUSINESS CARD

Made his first million with: financial services

Life motto: If anything seems too good to be true, it probably is.

Would like to meet in person: anyone that's successful

Most valuable piece of advice for him: "I suppose the guy that said to me 'make investment easy.'"

Passion: the business

Skills he doesn't have: another language

The best book on business: *Up the Organization* by Robert Townsend and *One Up on Wall Street* by Peter Lynch

Still wants to achieve: to give the people in the financial services industry the social recognition they deserve

Avoids in business: meetings

Most admired thought leaders: Margaret Thatcher

Frank Hasenfratz
I Did It My Way

Citizenship/Residence: Canada/Guelph, Ontario

An 85-year-old, Hungary-born self-made billionaire. He is founder and chairman of Linamar, specializing in production of automotive powertrain systems and wind turbines. Linamar's subsidiary Skyjack is the world's leading manufacturer of aerial work platforms. With 30,000 employees, Linamar operates over 90 fabrication facilities and other branches in 17 countries across North America, Europe, and Asia. Linamar is recognized as one of the most innovative, tech-savvy, and profitable enterprises in the industry, receiving awards for its superior quality on a regular basis, like the Canada Award for Business Excellence. Mr. Hasenfratz is a member of the Order of Canada, the Canadian Business Hall of Fame, as well as the Hungarian Knight's Cross of the Order of Merit.

THE BUSINESS CARD

Made his first million with: defense work

Business is . . . pleasure, challenging

Success is . . . when you are satisfied

Life motto: "Measure everything you do."

Would like to meet in person: "I can't think of anybody right now."

Most valuable piece of advice for him: "Work hard; my father gave me that advice."

Passion: work

Skills he doesn't have: more education

The best book on business: *Straight from the Gut* by Jack Welch

Still wants to achieve: "steady growth for the company. Not for myself. For myself, I am happy. But I'd like for the business to succeed."

Avoids in business: overextending

Most admired thought leaders: Ronald Reagan

Naveen Jain
Man Who Knew No Limits

Citizenship/Residence: USA/Bellevue, Washington

A 59-year-old, India-born founder of Infospace, Intelius, TalentWise, Moon Express, Bluedot, Viome, vice chairman of Singularity University, and trustee of the XPrize Foundation. He became a billionaire with his first enterprise, Infospace, providing content and tools for mobile Internet. With Moon Express he works on making the dream of private space exploration a reality. Among other accolades he was awarded the Ernst & Young Emerging Entrepreneur Award, the Albert Einstein Technology Medal, and was named the Most Admired Serial Entrepreneur by Silicon India. As a philanthropist and entrepreneur, he wants to touch as many lives as possible.

THE BUSINESS CARD

Made his first million with: working for Bill Gates

Business is ... about helping people

Success is ... about having a positive impact on society

Life motto: "Live with integrity and always remember that it takes generations to build credibility and it only takes one action to kill it."

Would like to meet in person: Albert Einstein

Most valuable piece of advice for him: from his mother: "Always spend less than what you earn."

Passion: his children and helping people

Skills he doesn't have: better command of the English language

The best book on business: *Games People Play* by Eric Berne and *I'm OK, You're OK* by Thomas Harris

Still wants to achieve: "I'm going after every one of the major industries. I started with space and I'm going into health care. Next thing I'll probably attack will be education. I'll probably attack food, and I'm going to continue to attack these biggest problems because I know the biggest problems are the biggest opportunity for an entrepreneur."

Avoids in business: "At the end of the day, debt and loss, because that ultimately will kill you."

Most admired thought leaders: Bill Gates

Kim Beom-Su
The Venture

Citizenship/Residence: South Korea / Seoul

A 52-year-old, Korean self-made billionaire, founder and chairman of Kakao, one of the largest companies on Kosdaq. Kakao operates KakaoTalk, a mobile messenger used by 95% of Korean smartphone owners and more than 220 million registered users worldwide. Kakao Taxi disrupted the taxi industry in Korea, winning almost 9 million users in the first 12 months. Kakao operates Daum, the second-largest search engine on the domestic market, and Melon, the country's largest music streaming service. Kim was named the Entrepreneur of the Year 2015 by Ernst & Young. With his K-CUBE Ventures, the 100 CEOs Project, and the C Program, he is deeply involved in fostering a risk-friendly start-up environment in Korea.

THE BUSINESS CARD

Made his first million with: Hangame (computer games)

Business is . . . setting a hypothesis and then proving it

Success is . . . "making the world a better place than when I was born and making at least one person happy"

Life motto: "Enjoy everyday adventures and maintain balance in your life."

Would like to meet in person: Bill Gates, Friedrich Nietzsche

Passion: "Giving a positive energy to Korean society, or making the quality of life better for the poor"

Skills he doesn't have: language skills, for example, in Chinese

The best book on business: *Profit from the Core* by Chris Zook and James Allen

Still wants to achieve: "The online-to-offline business is spreading throughout the world, and I want to make a successful business model for that in Korea."

Avoids in business: "A business that takes away somebody's livelihood"

Most admired thought leaders: Korean admiral Yi Sun-shin

N. R. Narayana Murthy
Act Like There Is No Tomorrow

Citizenship/Residence: India/Bangalore

A 72-year-old cofounder and longtime CEO of Infosys, the first Indian company to be listed on the NASDAQ and one of the world's software giants with 200,000 employees. Narayana is a self-made billionaire. With Infosys he has created six other billionaires and over 4,000 millionaires. He has been listed among the 12 greatest entrepreneurs of our time by *Fortune* magazine. In 2013, he was named Philanthropist of the Year in The Asian Awards. *The Economist* ranked him among the most admired global leaders, and the *Financial Times* as one of the most respected business leaders. He has been awarded the Padma Vibhushan by the Government of India, Officer of the Legion of Honor by the Government of France, and Officer of the Order of the British Empire by the Government of the United Kingdom. An important philanthropist, in 2003 he was chosen the World Entrepreneur of the Year by Ernst & Young.

THE BUSINESS CARD

Made his first million with: software

Business is . . . "about making this a more comfortable world"

Life motto: "The softest pillow is a clear conscience."

Would like to meet in person: Richard Feynman, the physicist

Most valuable piece of advice for him: "Put the interest of the institution and the community ahead of your personal interest."

Passion: speed of action

Skills he doesn't have: "I would like to be more intelligent than I am."

The best book on business: *Winners Never Cheat* by Jon M. Huntsman and Glenn Beck

Still wants to achieve: Create a million jobs for people all over the world.

Avoids in business: "Doing anything that will not enhance respect for me"

Most admired thought leaders: Mahatma Gandhi

Hüsnü Özyegin
Just a Good Man

Citizenship/Residence: Turkey/Istanbul

A 74-year-old self-made billionaire, the third wealthiest man in Turkey, and one of the biggest Turkish philanthropists. He created 75 companies in 12 countries and is founder of the Özyegin University in Istanbul. He started in the banking sector by founding Finansbank and then spread his business activities to a broader range of finance, retail, real estate, energy, health, hotels, and ports in his Fiba and Fina Holding. His vast philanthropic activities focus on different stages of education. In 2011, he was awarded the Harvard Business School Alumni Achievement Award.

THE BUSINESS CARD

Made his first million: working as bank president for 13 years.

Life motto: hard work

Would like to meet in person: Warren Buffett, or historical persons: Fatih the Conqueror, Michelangelo, architect Sinan

Most valuable piece of advice for him: "My father always said, 'I know you have good grades, but make sure you have good friends.' That was my father's advice. I think it's really important who you make friends with. That's also very important in business."

Passion: his work and his family

Skills he doesn't have: "I would like to use technology better. I would love to have played a musical instrument."

The best book on business: *Titan* by Ron Chernow about John D. Rockefeller Sr. and *Steve Jobs* by Walter Isaacson

Still wants to achieve: "To grow our university, and make it one of the best research and teaching universities in Turkey, where students, with their professors, invent things that add value to Turkish exports. This is what my goal is from now on."

Avoids in business: "To be overconfident. To be too sure that something will happen without really assessing the pitfalls and the probabilities that it may not."

Lirio Albino Parisotto
Curiosity Is His Best Company

Citizenship/Residence: Brazil/Manaus

A 65-year-old self-made billionaire and the largest individual investor on the Brazilian stock market. He is the founder, president, and main shareholder of Videolar (today Videolar-Innova S.A.), earlier manufacturer of audio and videotapes, floppy disks, CDs, DVDs, and Blu-rays, now a petrochemical company, a major manufacturer of plastic materials in Brazil. With his Geração L Par Fund, Lirio invests in banking, electricity, mining, and steel companies, as well as in real estate. In 2002, he was awarded the title Entrepreneur of the Year by Ernst & Young. He is deeply engaged in the protection of the Amazon rainforest.

THE BUSINESS CARD

Made his first million with: electronic retail

Business is . . . a challenge

Success is . . . to do what you like

Life motto: "Never accept a no."

Would like to meet in person: Warren Buffett, Mahatma Gandhi

Most valuable piece of advice for him: "You won't go anywhere with an angry face."

Passion: "My passion is to do something well."

The best book on business: *Made in America* by Sam Walton and *Made in Japan* by Akio Morita

Still wants to achieve: "I need now to [be thankful] for everything."

Avoids in business: "staying in businesses that completed their cycles and are no longer useful or desired. In business, you've got to know the timing."

Most admired thought leaders: Winston Churchill, Henry Ford, Akio Morita, and Steve Jobs

Dilip Shanghvi
The Art of Effectiveness

Citizenship/Residence: India/Mumbai

A 63-year-old self-made billionaire, founder and managing director of Sun Pharmaceuticals, India's largest drug maker and among Asia's Top 10 most valuable companies. He is currently the world's wealthiest person in the pharmaceutical industry. He was named Entrepreneur of the Year by Ernst & Young in 2010 and by Forbes in 2014, Indian of the Year by CNN, IBN and Businessman of the Year by Business India. In 2013, his Sun Pharma was awarded Company of the Year by the *Business Standard* and *Economic Times*. Forbes counts Sun Pharma among the World's 100 Most Innovative Companies.

THE BUSINESS CARD

Made his first million with: psychiatric medicines.

Business is . . . fun

Success is . . . when you achieve your objective.

Life motto: "My father once told me that a cashier at the bank counts a lot of money. But it's important to keep in mind how much money he takes home. You can do business and count a lot of turnover, but it's important to stay focused on the profit."

Would like to meet in person: Mahatma Gandhi

Most valuable piece of advice for him: by his father: "Money will make you a richer person, but you need to try and become a better person."

Passion: to build the business, grow the business

Skills he doesn't have: "I don't understand technology at a technical level. I try and simplify technology for myself in logical fashion, but I can't understand it for its real complexity."

Best books on business: *Loyalty Factor* by Carol Kinsey Goman and *Good to Great* and *Built to Last* by Jim Collins

Avoids in business: "Disputes, disagreements. I don't like fighting with people. If I can live with it, then if you and I can't get along, then I will stop our relationship and forget, even if we are to take a loss."

The most admired leaders: Steve Jobs, Bill Gates, Warren Buffett

Ron Sim
Resourcefulness without Resources

Citizenship/Residence: Singapore

A 60-year-old self-made billionaire, founder, chairman, and CEO of OSIM International, the number one Healthy Lifestyle products brand in Asia with over 400 outlets in 21 countries. Main product: He is also a stakeholder in malls in Singapore and China. He is also the owner of TWG Tee, Brookstone, Richlife, and GNC. In 2004, he was the recipient of the Entrepreneur of the Year award by Ernst & Young and the Businessman of the Year award by the *Business Times*. He is a dedicated philanthropist and enthusiastic triathlete pushing his employees to tackle this challenge as well.

THE BUSINESS CARD

Made his first million with: selling household products

Business is . . . about people. You build people to build business.

Success is when . . . you achieve what you believe that you can do. If you are happy with what you are doing, it's success.

Life motto: "challenging my spirit to do my best"

Would like to meet in person: the first Emperor of China

Most valuable piece of advice for him: by his grandmother and mother: "Live the life for a very well purpose."

Passion: "to create a successful legacy which I can be proud of, and satisfied with"

Skills he doesn't have: "I always admire people doing some of the sports that I think I can't do, like skateboard jumping or base jumping."

The best book on business: *Good to Great* and *Built to Last* by Jim Collins

Still wants to achieve: to build a stronger team, stronger structure, stronger entities

Avoids in business: poor partnership

Most admired thought leaders: the first Emperor of China and Lee Kuan Yew

Michał Sołowow
Once-in-a-Lifetime Opportunity

Citizenship/Residence: Poland/Kielce

A 56-year-old self-made billionaire. He is the only person who floated five companies onto the Polish Stock Market (GPW). Michał has started up and sold several companies in the construction, real estate development, retail, and production sectors. His main assets are Barlinek (floorboards), Cersanit (sanitary ceramics and tiles), and Synthos (chemical industry). He also invests in technology and start-ups. At the same time, he was for many years one of the finest rally drivers in Europe. In 2014, he was chosen "the best entrepreneur of the post-communist Poland." Currently, he is the wealthiest person in Poland.

THE BUSINESS CARD

Made his first million with: construction works

Life motto: "Don't give up."

Would like to meet in person: Warren Buffett, Mark Zuckerberg, Robin Li (Baidu).

Passion: "My passion for 11 years has definitely been rallies. Generally my passion is sport, competition."

Skills he doesn't have: "I would like to be decidedly more consistent. Be systematic."

The best book on business: *It's Not the Big That Eat the Small . . . It's the Fast That Eat the Slow* by Jason Jennings

Still wants to achieve: to be financially the most effective organization in the world

Most admired thought leaders: Lech Wałęsa

Petter Stordalen
The Strawberry Seller

Citizenship/Residence: Norway/Oslo

A 56-year-old self-made billionaire, nicknamed the King of Hotels, with nearly 200 hotels in his Nordic Choice hotel chain. He has built one of Norway's greatest commercial real estate firms. His Strawberry group operates in real estate, finance, hotels, and the arts. He recently invested in a PR company and shook the Scandinavian publishing business with his new publishing company Strawberry Publishing. Petter is often described as the most flamboyant Scandinavian alive. He was chosen Entrepreneur of the Year 2010. He is an environmentalist and one of the greatest private philanthropists in Norway.

THE BUSINESS CARD

Made his first million with "a project in Trondheim to connect three shopping centers into one, where nobody believed, and I believed, and the bonus was one million."

Life motto: the strawberry philosophy: "Sell the berries you have, because these are the only ones you can sell."

Would like to meet in person: Jesus

Most valuable piece of advice for him: Believe in your dreams.

Passion: "Hotels. Because it's about people. I love people's business."

Skills he doesn't have: to sing and play guitar

The best book on business: "I have not read any books on business, to be honest. . . . no. That's not true. I have read one. *Moments of Truth* by Jan Carlzon."

Still wants to achieve: "to have a true triple bottom line company. That means that you have one area for profit, you have one area for sustainability, and you have one area for social responsibility, and all are equally important, and you release figures and targets on every one of these. We do this today, but we have a long way to go to be a true triple bottom line company."

Avoids in business: "to work with people I don't like"

Frank Stronach
The Road to Economic Freedom

Citizenship/Residence: Canada/Aurora, Ontario

An 86-year-old, self-made billionaire, an Austrian immigrant in Canada who founded Magna International, now one of the world's greatest auto parts suppliers, with 170,000 employees in over 400 factories and other business centers spread across 27 countries and around $40 billion in revenues. In 2000, he was awarded the Entrepreneur of the Year Lifetime Achievement Award by Ernst & Young. His Stronach Group is America's leading racetrack owner and operator. On top of that, he is one of the most successful horse breeders and owners in the world. He has also pursued a political career in Canada and Austria, which included founding a political party signed with his name and succeeding with it in the Austrian national election. Today, Frank produces beef on his nearly 100,000 acres in Florida.

THE BUSINESS CARD

Made his first million with: selling automobile components

Business is . . . "economy. If the economy doesn't function, nothing else will function."

Success is . . . to be happy, healthy, and economically free.

Life motto: "I developed my own—to be free. Free, and also economically free."

Would like to meet in person: Henry Ford

Most valuable piece of advice for him: "I grew up alone. Life taught me how to live."

Passion: "I do like horses. I've been maybe the number one horse breeder in the world, in America, for many years."

Skills he doesn't have: "I constantly try to evaluate myself. I'm always trying to correct myself to be a better person."

The best book on business: Henry Ford's autobiography and *Money, Gold and God Players* by Roland Baader

Still wants to achieve: "to balance out the political management with the socioeconomic management by citizen representatives. You can't let politicians make all the decisions for the country."

Avoids in business: "I do avoid losses."

Most admired thought leaders: Mao Zedong

Manny Stul
From Refugee to World Entrepreneur of the Year

Citizenship/Residence: Australia/Melbourne

A 70-year-old Australian self-made billionaire, chairman of Moose Toys, a global toy manufacturer considered one of the most innovative and fastest-growing companies in the industry. Its Shopkins toys were named the Girl Toy of the Year by the Toy Industry Association for two consecutive years, beating by numbers sold any other item in the industry, including Barbie, My Little Pony, and Lego. The company has received over 40 consumer and industry awards worldwide. Manny's philanthropic commitment is directed at children and health care. Ernst & Young named him the World Entrepreneur of the Year 2016. He is the first Australian to receive that title.

THE BUSINESS CARD

Made his first million with: wholesaling innovative giftware

Business is . . . fun

Success is . . . health and happiness

Life motto: "Treat others exactly how you would like to be treated. And never give up."

Would like to meet in person: Yogananda, Warren Buffett

Most valuable piece of advice for him: "Surround yourself with great people with integrity."

Passion: business and sport

Skills he'd like to have: athletics, public speaking

The best book on business: *Good to Great* by Jim Collins

Still wants to achieve: "Sustain and grow the company to be bigger and more successful; keep growing spiritually."

Avoids in business: "dealing with people who I'm very uncomfortable with."

Most admired thought leaders: Buddha

Chip Wilson
40,000 Days, Then You're Dead

Citizenship/Residence: Canada/Vancouver, British Columbia

A 63-year-old Canadian self-made billionaire, founder of Lululemon Athletica, a publicly traded technical sportswear retailer with the highest sales per square foot of all stores in the world and the highest margins of any retailer outside of jewelry and Apple. He also founded Westbeach, specializing in surf, skate, and snowboarding apparel, and is currently involved with Kit and Ace, specializing in technical casual wear. In 2004, Ernst & Young named him the Canadian Entrepreneur of the Year for Innovation and Marketing. His vast philanthropic activities include higher education in Canada (The Wilson School of Design), elementary education in Ethiopia (Imagine1Day), and local community projects in Vancouver.

THE BUSINESS CARD

Made his first million with: sports apparel

Business is . . . loving people

Success is . . . a healthy, loving family

Life motto: "Give without expectation of return."

Would like to meet in person: Ayn Rand, Muhammad Ali, Jimi Hendrix

Most valuable piece of advice for him: "That I have two more big things in me after Lululemon."

Passion: athletics

Skills he doesn't have: "Being able to put my thoughts and ideas into a structural form."

The best book on business: *Good to Great* by Jim Collins

Avoids in business: negotiations

Most admired thought leaders: Ayn Rand, Marcus Aurelius

Cho Tak Wong (Cao Dewang)
Heart of Amber

Citizenship/Residence: Hong Kong/Fuqing, China

The 72-year-old founder and chairman of Fuyao Group, the world's largest manufacturer of automotive glass. In 2014, Fuyao Group was listed on BCG Global Challengers Top 100 and on Fortune China's Most Admired Companies five times consecutively. With donations going into the billions of dollars, he was awarded the China Charity Award for several years consecutively and named No.1 Philanthropist of the Year 2012 in China. Despite being an elementary school dropout, Wong became a self-made billionaire and the Ernst & Young World Entrepreneur of the Year 2009, the only Chinese person who has ever won this accolade. He is the most respected entrepreneur in China, both by people and the government.

THE BUSINESS CARD

Made his first million with: production of water meter glass

Business is . . . a hobby

Success is . . . be respected by others

Life motto: "Continuously developing and making people around you improve together."

Would like to meet in person: Wang Yung-ching, the Formosa Plastics founder, and Zeng Guofan, a historic Chinese leader

Passion: success

The best book on business: "the book about Zeng Goufan"

Still wants to achieve: "I have not finished yet. It's only partially success. I keep working. I want Fuyao Glass all over the world, so everybody uses it."

Avoids in business: "Anything which would hurt customer's interest. Anything hurting other people I will not do."

Most admired thought leaders: Confucius and Laozi

ACKNOWLEDGMENTS

Today, as I am writing this, I am amazed at how many people are needed to make such a project happen. This is to give them their deserved recognition.

There are three people who inspired this book and without whom the idea to write it would never have crossed my mind. There is Jack Canfield, whose "Cliff Young Story" brought me on the path of self-development. Then T. Harv Eker, whose book *The Secrets of the Millionaire Mind* made me realize that our wealth was the result of our mindset. And finally, there is Napoleon Hill, whose book *Think and Grow Rich* made me want to research the minds of the very best entrepreneurs, like he did, but on a global scale. I want to express my gratitude to these outstanding thinkers. Without you, I wouldn't be where I am today.

I want to thank all the people who believed in my vision for this book from its very inception and trusted it could be accomplished against all odds. Thank you to all those people who supported me in this long process that sometimes resembled an uphill battle against skeptics in the publishing industry. Forgive me for using their first names only; this is for data protection reasons. But you guys know who you are.

This book would have stayed only a crazy idea if not for the persuasive Marco, who was the first person I revealed this idea to and who made me believe it could be done and provoked me to actually take the first step.

Let me express my gratitude to my assistants Mario, Mine, and Archie, who took up the challenge to work with me on setting up billionaire interviews at a time when this project was in an embryonic state and seemed so unreal and scary. Thank you, guys, you are my heroes!

Let me thank all those wonderful people who believed in the book's vision to the degree that they put me in contact with the entrepreneurs interviewed in this book and supported all my requests throughout the project: Andrzej, Ayla, Magnus, Pandu, Rainer, Carolin, Frederick, Ronnie, Mary, Thomas, Markus, Mari, Uta, Julia, Anna, Sabrina, Don, Carlo, Elizabeth, Tim, Dana, Sergei, Selmo, Jonathan, Andrew, Rebecca, Xiaojing, Xiaozhi, Jessie, Esther, Alice, Connie, Kathryn, Samantha, Andrea, Buster, Desley, Simon, and Karen. Without you I wouldn't have been able to convince such extraordinary entrepreneurs to share their wisdom with us.

My thanks go to the protagonists of this book, the remarkable personalities who opened their hearts, souls, and minds to me so that you can benefit from their secrets. They are the modern-day business heroes who make the lives of millions easier through the products and services they provide. They belong to the greatest entrepreneurs of our times, the role models for every entrepreneur around the world. You will find their bios in the appendix and their stories on every page of this book. I can't tell you how grateful I am to you for giving me this once-in-a-life-time opportunity. I am thankful for your hospitality, your openness, and the insights you've shared with my readers. I would like to give a special thanks to Jack Cowin, who opened many doors for me. Late in the project, he was for me what Andrew Carnegie was for Napoleon Hill—a connector, confidant, guide, and mentor, whose generosity I can't stress enough. Thank you, Jack!

I would like to thank Melody and Mindy of Book Midwife, who helped me organize the material, crystallize my thoughts, and apply a massive amount of work to put all that on paper. Your great help can't be underestimated.

Let's not forget the industry veterans Gary, Grace, and Rick, who helped me find the way in the maze of the publishing industry. And Jack Canfield not only provided a great foreword but also shared his experience and gave me some decisive pieces of advice on how publishing works in the United States. Thank you!

Thank you to Nick, Greg, Angie, Christine, Brittany, Lindsey, and Mandy of DNA, who worked relentlessly on making my message heard in the world.

I want to thank Adi and Zoe for the best cappuccino in the world. It was the fuel that drove me for the long hours when I was working on this book. Your cafe is my second home.

My dear friends Albert, Andrea, Artur, Ingrid, Mike, and Monica found time in their busy lives to read through my imperfect manuscript and give me valuable feedback. Thank you for improving it considerably.

I want to thank my YouTube audience, all those kind people who were cheering me throughout this process for voicing their support and words of encouragement. Thank you! And I also want to express my gratitude to all the naysayers, who gave me many reasons to prove it could be done.

Let me use this opportunity to thank my dear employees, assistants, and freelancers Olaf, Silas, David, Greg, Kamil, Martin, Sebastian, and Tom for managing my companies and projects. Thank you, guys, for taking so much off my shoulders.

My greatest thanks go to my family and friends who had to endure without me through years of my travels and my work in solitude. Without your understanding and massive support, this project wouldn't have been possible. Thank you for holding my back free, for your unshakable faith, for investing yourself in me.

At the end, I want to thank you, my dear reader, for taking your time to read this book. I did my best to make sure it's worth it.

ABOUT THE AUTHOR

Rafael Badziag is a global entrepreneur, top TED speaker, and an award-winning author. As an expert in the psychology of entrepreneurship specializing in self-made billionaires, he has been featured on NBC, ABC, CBS, and FOX, as well as in *USA Today, Wall Street Journal,* and other national newspapers and TV networks in several countries.

In the 1990s, he built his first multimillion-dollar business, pioneering e-commerce in Europe. Rafael has given some of the most successful TED talks in history. The book *Ready, Set, Go!* that he has co-authored with Brian Tracy became an Amazon bestseller and received the Quilly Award.

In recent years, Rafael has been working with over two dozen self-made billionaires around the world to find out what made them so extremely successful in business. He is the first person ever to win that many billionaires for a book project on a global scale and is called the Billionaire Magnet.

Find out more:
http://TheBillionDollarSecret.com

Support us in our mission to raise the global level of excellence in entrepreneurship. Give us input for the next book:

- Which business-related questions would you like to see answered?

- Which billionaire-related questions would you like to see answered?

- Which other billionaire would you like to see interviewed?

- Which aspects of this book would you like to see explored in more detail?

- Tell us how this book helped you in your life or business.

- Tell us the story of the billionaire you work for.

Email us your input to:
feedback@nolimits.co